SPITFIRE SUMMER

THIS IS A CARLTON BOOK

Design copyright © 2000 Carlton Books Limited
Text copyright © 2000 Malcolm Brown
Images copyright © Imperial War Museum

This edition published by Carlton Books Limited 2000
20 Mortimer Street
London
W1N 7RD

A CIP catalogue for this book is available from the British Library.

ISBN 1 84222 043 8

Executive Editor: Sarah Larter
Senior Art Editor: Diane Spender
Design: Simon and Zoe Mercer
Maps: Simon Mercer
Picture Research: Lorna Ainger
Production: Garry Lewis

Printed and bound in Great Britain

IMPERIAL WAR
MUSEUM

SPITFIRE SUMMER

When Britain Stood Alone

MALCOLM BROWN

FOREWORD BY SIR CHRISTOPHER FOXLEY-NORRIS,
CHAIRMAN OF THE BATTLE OF BRITAIN FIGHTER ASSOCIATION

CARLTON
BOOKS

Spitfire

1. A person of fiery temper.

2. A British monoplane fighter, descended from the Supermarine racing seaplanes of the 1920s and 1930s. The Royal Air Force's most modern warplane at the start of the Second World War and the only British aircraft to remain in production throughout the war.

Summer

The warmest season of the year with the longest days.

Spitfire Summer

Phrase of uncertain origin, betokening a period of historic importance in the history of Great Britain; lived through with defiance and looked back on with pride.

CONTENTS

FOREWORD

T HE YEAR 1940 MUST FOR MANY REASONS be regarded as one of the most momentous in our history. During it disaster struck down a number of major powers narrowly evaded by others. The author does not attempt to cover the major potential political and military issues, rather he concentrates on the background with a number of illustrative, vivid individual experiences recorded.

The narrative is divided into three major stories, Dunkirk, The Battle of Britain and the Blitz. With regard to Dunkirk we should never forget Churchill's dictum that wars are not won by withdrawals, there remains also a number of mysteries which are still unexplained but were vital at the time. For example, just why did Hitler call his armour to a halt when victory lay within its grasp?

The mystery of the Battle of Britain was one. Applying traditional staff college criteria to the battle, the Germans must win. If they did not the reason can only be given that all elements of British society, mostly of course the fighter pilots but everybody else involved performed at an almost superhuman level far higher than could have been expected from past performance. As far as the Blitz was concerned the victory lay in our refusal to surrender to mass bombing, a victory repeated by the Germans in their own turn later in the war. In 1940 the accepted wisdom after bombing of Guernica, Warsaw, Amsterdam and so forth was that the morale would inevitably collapse. After Coventry and the London docks it did not.

But perhaps the deepest and most lasting effect of 1940 was on the German armed forces, particularly the Luftwaffe; as a very senior officer of the Wehrmacht said to me after the war: "we realized for the first time that we were not invincible."

Perhaps of 1940 it can be said, as Churchill said of Alamein, later in the war, "it may not be the beginning of the end, but perhaps the end of the beginning."

Sir Christopher Foxley-Norris,
CHAIRMAN, BATTLE OF BRITAIN FIGHTER ASSOCIATION

A Small Churchyard in Sussex

I OPENED THE GATE AND WALKED THROUGH into the churchyard. It was a winter morning but it was sunny, almost warm, and the grass was firm and dry, so instead of going straight towards what I had come to see I left the path and circled slowly past the ancient graves, noting the ages of some of the village's more long-lived inhabitants: people who had died in their 60s, their 70s, even their 80s. Then I turned towards the far corner where I knew I would be struck, as I was the first time I had come here almost forty years before, by the stunning whiteness, the neat military regularity, the unavoidable pathos of the war graves. There were far more than I had remembered. I had expected to see a dozen or so British headstones, plus a handful of German. I counted over fifty, men of two nations who had braced themselves for war and now lay buried here alongside each other and the civilian dead of this ancient parish. And almost all of them so very young.

I paused by one typical grave, noting the date of death, the age of the airman there buried and the inscription added at the request of his family:

745631 SERGEANT C J HOLLAND
OBSERVER
ROYAL AIR FORCE
23RD JULY 1940 AGE 19
HE WROTE:-
WHAT GREATER CAUSE IS THERE
THAN THAT OF RIGHT,
FREEDOM AND GOD

Curiously, even in this sedate English setting, I found what I had often seen during numerous visits to military cemeteries in France and Belgium: the grave of an unknown. "An Airman of the 1939–1945 War" ran the standard formula with, at the base of the headstone the moving phrase devised after the 1914–1918 War by Rudyard Kipling, "Known Unto God".

The line of German headstones, all with the same date "13.8.1940", suggested a bomber shot down, possibly by a fighter pilot who himself lay buried here. One of the German graves arrested my attention: that of Karl-Wilhelm Brinkbaumer, birthdate given as "25.10.16": born during the Battle of the Somme, died during the Battle of Britain. A brief, tragic twentieth-century life, book-ended by two famous, if quite different battles. Born in Germany during the terrible, hard-fought slog of the four-month marathon in Picardy; killed in the summer skies over England a little under twenty four years later.

I had first come to Tangmere back in the early 1960s as a national serviceman of a very different conflict: a Cold War, which happily never became a hot one, and had consisted of bluster and shadow-boxing rather than battles. Like many others of my generation I had been there as part of my training as an interpreter in the language of the most likely opponent, should that war have turned into a shooting one. We lived and studied in the officers' mess of the former front-line RAF station that had had its heyday during the Battle of Britain; the old control-tower, all but derelict, still stood far out on the airfield, a haunting reminder of times past. It seemed odd, indeed almost pathetic, that where young men of a previous vintage had waited to dash to their aircraft to repel a real enemy we should be droning away none too seriously at our Russian preparing for encounters with a merely notional one. When on my first visit there I had slipped away to visit Tangmere church and its enclave of war graves, I had found myself overwhelmed by a sense of good fortune that my contemporaries and I had not been called upon to meet the life or death challenges which the young men lying there had had to face. And by a sense of profound gratitude. For these men had done much to ensure that my generation would have a decent, free, if still a potentially dangerous world to grow up in.

I had returned to that small Sussex churchyard because I knew that I would shortly be asked to compile a book about the summer in which so many of these airmen had perished, and I had taken advantage of being in the area to make a kind of personal pilgrimage. It seemed a necessary act, if only to remind myself, and perhaps through myself the reader, that the people whose stories are told in these pages are, or in so many instances were, as real and as human as the men whose names surrounded me that winter morning.

I had one other motive for concentrating my mind by such a visit. I had been very much alive when the events of 1940 unfolded, but only a child and, again by sheer good fortune, living well away from any epicentre of danger. The fighting war, even the bombing war, had been something far off; evacuees came to, rather than went from, the town where I lived and no bombs fell within its boundaries. Being so far removed from the realities of conflict, when some of the airmen buried at Tangmere were fighting their actual battles, machine against machine, man against man, I – like many others – was responding to the figures of aircraft shot down (as announced nightly on the BBC News) as to the scores of a test match.

But this was no test match and so to some extent my visit there was a kind of apology for my childish unawareness and an indication of a commitment to tell their story, and that of all those celebrated in this book, so that their contribution might be honoured and understood.

Spitfire Summer is the striking title assigned to this book, but there is another more famous phrase linked to that vital period of 1940; that used by Winston Churchill in the memorable speech in which he prophesied that it would become known as Britain's "finest hour". That now distant summer was, as the following pages will show, by no means a period without spot or blemish, but it is heartening to state that the general verdict is that by and large Churchill's claim still holds good. It was a high point in the nation's life and it is a signal honour to be offered the opportunity to re-evaluate it.

At the same time it is important to stress that this dramatic summer is only worth revisiting if it is now seen as history, to be recalled without hatred or rancour. In the church at Tangmere a framed scroll lists the deaths by date throughout the year of all the servicemen buried there, without distinction of nationality, so that they might be remembered and prayed for. In the graveyard itself the text of a recently unveiled memorial significantly commemorates "those airmen of the British Commonwealth and German Air Force who fell from the skies either by combat or by accident and whose grave is the restless and eternal earth", concluding with the simple prayer: "May they rest in peace".

This is surely the right note to strike when looking back after so many years at events which still have power to move and fascinate but of which we can now surely say with confidence and thankfulness that we will not see their like again.

Malcolm Brown,
April 2000

CHAPTER ONE

The Hour, the Man, the Weapon

I T WAS AN EXTRAORDINARY SUMMER. There were high points that were solemn, and some – or so they could seem at the time – that were almost sublime. There were moments of amazing heroism and courage, sometimes on the part of a few, sometimes on the part of the many, which had the rest of the nation agog with admiration. There were moments of a curious nonchalance, with a dash of the debonair, which almost made people think that Britain could win the war by cheerfully ignoring it. There were moments of sheer comedy, if not farce, when the only possible response was at the least a raised eyebrow, at best a peal of incredulous laughter. There were moments of serious endeavour, with people desperately eager to do their bit, however minor or meaningless it might be in the overall scale of things. There were also, here and there, chilling portents of fearsome realities to come.

One such occurred in a cartoon published in *The Daily Telegraph* on May 11. The name of the artist, Louis Raemaekers, who had honed the cutting edge of his wit in powerful visual onslaughts on the enemy in the First World War, was an omen in itself. The subject, which might easily have been passed over at the time as not being central to the nation's preoccupations, has a far more potent resonance when looked back at from the vantage-point of today. A bent and stumbling Jesus carrying a Swastika-headed cross is being lashed forward to his Calvary by an angry Hitler. And the caption? "I'll replace him by an Aryan". That even the Jewishness of Christ should be an offence to the mad dictator in Berlin! It needs little imagination to see Raemaekers' grim vision as an inspired prediction of the Holocaust. If ever a horrific coming event cast its shadow before it, it was surely in that cartoon.

There was another heavy portent, and one of greater immediate impact, in the same edition. The reader who turned the page with Raemaekers' cartoon would be confronted by a map entitled "The Western Front". The day before, May 10, Hitler's invasion forces had crossed into Holland and Belgium while air attacks on France had showed that she would surely be the next victim. To those who had lived through the long ordeal of the First World War those three words must have carried a terrible sense of "We have been here before". Was the war of the trenches going to have a repeat showing? Was the Western Front to start claiming new victims like some terrible reawakened monster?

There had been significant flurries of action in the weeks before the German attack of May 10. The Germans had occupied Denmark and mounted an airborne invasion of Norway. A British and French Expeditionary Force sent to Norway had been ousted after some initial success by early May, though fighting would continue to the north at Narvik until June. Some blows had been struck, particularly by the Royal Navy; the Germans had lost one heavy cruiser, two light cruisers and ten destroyers sunk, while two battleships were damaged and a pocket-battleship put out of commission for a year. The campaign had also produced the war's first Victoria Cross, a posthumous award to Captain Bernard Warburton-Lee of HMS *Hardy*, who died of wounds after leading his destroyer flotilla in a Nelson-like seek out and destroy mission during the first battle of Narvik; the King's presentation of the award to his widow would make a modest headline in early July. There had been German naval successes too: the aircraft-carrier HMS *Glorious*, hurrying back to Scapa Flow for reasons that have never been fully established, was dispatched by the *Scharnhorst* along with her two attendant destroyers, *Acasta* and *Ardent*. In the final count, however, the Allied initiative failed; it neither achieved its first purpose – to halt the transport of iron ore from Norway to Germany – nor its second one, that of sustaining Norway's efforts to hold out against the German invader. Norway succumbed, though her people continued their resistance, helping to hold German soldiers thus far north who might have been used to greater effect elsewhere.

A confusing imbroglio which few people understood, Norway's prime effect for Britain was to bring about one of the key parliamentary occasions of the century. The dramatic Norway debate helped to topple a Prime Minister, Neville Chamberlain, who did not lack determination but who could not command the ruthlessness and the flair required of a wartime leader. He was also tarnished by his earlier dealings with Hitler to the disadvantage of Czechoslovakia, which had been hailed by many as a triumph but were now being denounced as a betrayal. Out of the ruck had emerged the controversial, much distrusted figure of the man who, by a curious irony, had been more responsible than most for the Norway débâcle, the then First Lord of the Admiralty, Winston Churchill. Chamberlain, if he had to yield the premiership at all (and he was most reluctant to do so), would have preferred to be succeeded by his Foreign Secretary, Lord Halifax. Clever, cold, aloof, no natural leader and physically remote from the give and take of politics by being a member of Parliament's Upper Chamber, Halifax had far greater support in the dominant political party, the Conservatives, than the maverick Churchill. The latter had been too harsh a critic of Conservative governments in recent years for their liking. King George VI was no Churchill supporter either; he was even prepared, should it come to it, to sanction an emergency constitutional fix that would allow Halifax to speak in the House of Commons.

Fortunately, that never became necessary. Halifax himself conceded that a Peer was not the most appropriate leader in wartime. Add to that the fact that the Labour Party would not support Chamberlain's bid to retain power and there could only be one outcome. So the one figure in British politics of Shakespearean dimensions strode on to the stage and the great duel of Churchill versus Hitler began. A British bulldog, a British lion in human form: there are numerous ways in which one might describe Winston Leonard Spencer Churchill, descendant of the famous soldier-aristocrat the Duke of Marlborough, but the plain fact was that Britain needed a strong champion to fight her corner, and the occasion had called forth the best possible candidate. No one would claim that Churchill was a man for all seasons, but he was certainly the man for this one.

The war had been largely "phoney" to that point; it had even been nicknamed "the Bore War". Having failed Czechoslovakia, Britain and France had announced that they would stand by Hitler's presumed next victim, Poland. When an unde-terred Hitler invaded Poland on September 1, 1939, the two western Allies had duly declared war two days later, but had then been unable to do more than watch the appalling spectacle of Poland being bombed and beaten into submission. Unable to intervene in the east, they had prepared to defy the enemy in the west. The French had mobilized their forces and the British had sent an expeditionary force to support them. But thereafter the situation had settled into a kind of queasy stalemate. The French had put their faith in their recently constructed defence system, known as the Maginot Line, which stretched in a great arc east-ward from the Ardennes – an area of hills and forest deemed unfit for serious fight-ing – along the Franco-German border to the Swiss frontier. There was to be no mad-dash battle of the frontiers, no war *à outrance*, which had failed so dismally in 1914 and had produced such a mass of casualties. Meanwhile, perhaps the most aggressive thing the British did at this time was to sing of their intention to "hang out the washing on the Siegfried Line", Germany's riposte to the Maginot – a concept that would not become a practicality for five years, by which time that most fatuous of songs was long forgotten. Indeed, the situation had gone so quiet that in December 1939 Chamberlain had said to a rising general whom the war would make into a national hero, Bernard Law Montgomery: "I don't think the Germans have any intention of attacking us". Montgomery demurred, but the sentiment remained. In the words of the eminent soldier-historian Sir David Fraser: "It was convenient...for the government to suppose that because the Western Front was inactive it was somehow stable".

The German onslaught of May 10 had rapidly put paid to that theory. The "Bore War" ended and boredom would not be an option in the weeks that followed, as the Germans rapidly disposed of Holland and Belgium and, with a stunning *Blitzkrieg* attack on France which at a stroke destroyed any notion that there would be a return to the stalemate war of the trenches, produced the sequence of events which ended with Britain fighting on alone. The tension would continue for many weeks, weeks that included an air war so touch-and-go that it was rightly called "The Battle of Britain". This would produce numerous heroes, but in a curious way the best hero of the summer to come was a small elegantly-designed aeroplane, just 36 feet long by 30 feet wide, that flew in the skies over England like a graceful bird: it was called a Spitfire and for those who lived through that time it was a name they would never forget. The mention of it could bring tears to their eyes for years to come. There was a wide range of planes competing for air space over Britain that summer. On the German side there were their three principal bombers: the Dornier Do 17, nicknamed the "Flying Pencil" from its elongated shape, the Heinkel He 111, to be relegated to night-bombing only by September for lack of power and speed and, their best and most versatile aircraft in the pack, the Junkers Ju 88. These would often arrive accompanied by the Messerschmitt Bf 109, an outstanding fighter, though on maximum fuel supply only good for ten minutes over inland Britain, or the two-engined Messerschmitt Bf 110, no match for the Spitfire in terms of speed but faster than most Hurricanes and formidably armed. A valiant defender on the British side was the Hawker Hurricane – in fact, in 1940 the Hurricane made up two thirds of the defending force – but it was the Supermarine Spitfire that brought the catch at the heart and claimed the headlines.

One of its most famous pilots, Richard Hillary (author of the classic work of the 1940 air war, *The Last Enemy*) wrote of the moment when he saw them in close-up for the first time: "The dull grey-brown of the camouflage could not conceal the clear-cut beauty, the wicked simplicity of their lines". Thus they seemed on the ground; in the air they were magnificent – though it should not be forgotten that they were also the tombs of many fine young men. Hillary was himself shot down in one, and was pulled from the sea with his face and body badly burned. He never flew one again, and his almost inevitable death came when, desperate to return to the air after months of plastic surgery, he crashed flying a trainer aircraft, tragically taking another airman with him. But it was the Spitfire with which he and others like him would always be associated, adding to the legend of the superlative aircraft that did so much to reassure and give hope to a people in peril.

But this is to anticipate. The Spitfire came into its own only after the disastrous campaign across the Channel, which took Britain's continental allies out of the action and brought Britain herself to the brink of defeat.

CHAPTER TWO

Operation "Sicklecut": Defeat in France

I N ITS ORIGINAL FORM, the German plan for their attack in the west bore some similarities to that which had launched the first offensive of the previous war, in that its principal element was a thrust through Belgium. There was a major difference in that there was no provision for any southward hook to encircle Paris; rather the aim was to brush aside all forces opposed to their advance and aim for the Channel coast. Indeed, at first there was no thought of a decisive victory, merely of an occupation of territory that would push the Allies out of the Low Countries and secure the industrial area so important to Germany, the Ruhr. But Hitler was not satisfied with so modest a plan with such predictable objectives. He singled out the Ardennes, deemed a virtual no-go area by most professional soldiers, asking "Can I get through here?". His generals were discouraging, but the idea was noted and developed by the soldier now widely regarded as Germany's best military strategist, Major General (future Field Marshal) Erich von Manstein. He devised a scheme whereby, while one army group, Group B, concentrated on the northern attack already agreed, the main thrust would be mounted by another army group, Group A, which would force its way through the Ardennes and southern Belgium with the aim of splitting Franco-British forces in a drive to the coast. Tanks and armoured cars would be the hammerhead of this group. Rather than make for the coast by the shortest and most obvious route, it would thrust far to the west then turn up in a great hooking movement that would take Étaples, Boulogne and then Calais from the south, while seizing – literally *en passant* – such notable names from the Great War as St Quentin, Abbeville and Amiens. Effectively, this would achieve what the Germans under Ludendorff had repeatedly but vainly striven for in 1918, despite repeated attempts: split the Allied forces arrayed against them down the middle. In this way they would divide to conquer. All those to the north of the line of attack would be forced either to a surrender or be sent packing across the English Channel.

The obvious advantage of an Ardennes attack was that it would be entirely unexpected. Manstein was at first criticised by the German General Staff for what was seen as an over-ambitious scheme, and ordered to a posting in the east, but he knew its unconventionality would appeal to Hitler. So, on his way through Berlin, he contrived to see the Führer and disclose his concept in person. The ruse worked. Hitler was captivated and the General Staff had no option but to yield and to work out the details. The scheme was given the code-name *Sichelschnitt*: "The Cut of the

Sickle", or "Sicklecut". It would be described by the historian Alastair Horne as "one of the most inspired blueprints for victory that the military mind has ever conceived", while the subsequent campaign, in which Manstein served as number two to the brilliant General Gerd von Runstedt, would be praised by that doyen of military thinkers Basil Liddell Hart as "one of history's most striking examples of the decisive effects of a new idea, carried out by a dynamic executant".

To add another twist to an already ingenious scenario, Group B would now attack on a more northerly axis through Holland (an uninvolved neutral in the First World War), doing so ahead of the Ardennes offensive. This would act, to use another Liddell Hart phrase, like "a matador's cloak", drawing the French into a counter movement out on their left flank, while the lethal blow was to be delivered to their right.

In view of this it is small wonder that the Allied efforts to rebuff the advancing Germans were never to have the greatest chance of success. The Germans would not have things entirely their own way. On May 21 a small-scale British armoured attack near Arras would surprise Group A at the height of its charge from the Ardennes towards the sea. The attack could not be sustained, but it made the German commander whose 7th Panzer division took the brunt of the attack, Lieutenant General Erwin Rommel, think there was a major counter-move in prospect. It has been speculated that this might have contributed to German doubts and hesitations later on. Meanwhile north-east of Laon the future General de Gaulle, still at that time a Colonel, led an improvised French armoured division in an attempt to destabilize the Germans' advance by two hard jabs at their left flank, one at Moncornet and a second at Crécy-sur-Serre. With, however, no radio, hardly any artillery, almost no infantry, and no defence against the German Stuka dive-bombers, all he could achieve was of nuisance value only. But it gave him a name, an item in his CV, as it were, for which he could later claim considerable credit, and it gave some lustre to the French cause at a desperate time. At least he had tried when most of his military superiors were only too ready to lay down their arms.

The headlines of the following weeks charted a series of dramatic events which produced shock-waves across Britain and much anxiety, at that stage merely impotent anxiety, elsewhere; except, that is, in Fascist Italy, where Mussolini saw the opportunity to join Hitler in collecting the spoils. "Germans take Arras and Amiens"; "Mussolini Declares War on the Allies"; "French Government Falls"; and finally "French Sign Surrender at Compiègne" – in the very railway carriage where they had exacted the German surrender in 1918: all this was bad news indeed.

Before France fell, however, out of the burning there came a major miracle, the extraction from the troubled continent of enough men to make it possible to continue with a war which might otherwise have been lost.

For the British in this curious campaign there was no escaping the memories of the previous conflict. While retreating towards the coast through Belgium, an NCO of a troop carrying company, F.A.G. Harding, found himself at Ypres, focus of the much fought over Ypres Salient of immortal, or alternatively fearful, memory. He visited one of the most famous shrines commemorating the Great War and was much moved by the experience:

> The Menin Gate seen at full dawn on a fine day caused me to think. I wonder have we kept faith with those who came this way before, that we should have to come again. Here I must put in an opinion. There was not a man I have met who was unworthy of those who went before... I have seen men of twenty-one and two – the average age in this army is about twenty-three – do things any man would be satisfied to do. I have taken them into action and brought the remainder back and I am firmly convinced that given the tank and air assistance which will allow them to breathe, Jerry can no more win this war than he can grow wings and fly.

Courage and confidence in ultimate victory might assuage the rigours of defeat, but a defeat it clearly was. Harding was writing not from the fields of Flanders but from the West of England, that very fact an indication that for the time being at least the odds were more on "Jerry" winning than on losing – while there was a real possibility that, in the form of the Luftwaffe, he might indeed grow wings and fly. More, Harding was back home after a campaign in which the British had been humiliatingly thrown back in a way that had no parallel in the first war. The diary of a private of the Royal Corps of Signals, Sidney Leach, cool and laconic in style, nevertheless tells a grim, even at times shocking story; again with reference to places well known to the previous generation.

His unit had been just eight days in Belgium when they were forced to retreat – a retreat in which, he wrote, "we saw hundreds of Belgian refugees mown down by machine gun fire and blown to pieces by bombs, most of them women and children". Their first destination in France was the town famous for its Mademoiselle, who allegedly had not been kissed for forty years; many a Tommy of the earlier war had kept his spirits up by singing of her dubious attractions while footslogging along the roads behind the then Western Front. There was small cause for such singing now:

> We moved down to Armentières, where we were inadequately billeted in a factory with a glass roof. Nothing happened that first night and we slept till about 8 a.m. Just after dinner a large formation of Heinkels came over. The first bomb landed about a hundred yards from us, and the roof started to come in. We made a hurried dive for shelter and the planes bombed the main part of Armentières.
>
> The officers made no attempt to move us till next day, when we moved to a small wood at Houplines just on the outskirts of Armentières. At dawn, a strong

patrol of enemy bombers came over and machine-gunned the wood, but nobody was killed. At dinnertime, my detachment was called out to extricate some bodies from wrecked houses.

With planes continually diving on us we managed to rescue two girls and a six-month-old baby. The baby died on the way to hospital, being badly crushed. I shall never forget the courage of one girl. Her legs, from the waist downward, were trapped, but she kept conscious all the time and directed the operations. She never flinched until a couple of us lifted her up. Then she fainted and afterwards went off into hysterics. She was about 18 and the mother of the dead baby.

Amid much confusion they were moved away from the area, only to be ordered back to Armentières to pick up stores that had been left behind:

Hardly had we drawn up in the main street, when a reconnaissance plane spotted us. I just dived under the trailer, and then they came. Howling down, two at a time, they came straight at us. It was a terrible ordeal. The houses were falling on us, and the bombs were being dropped three and four at a time.

The first bomb hit our ration lorry and blew three others off the road. Then they tore up and down the street machine-gunning all the time. During the first lull, a number of us dashed across the road to a cellar. I was stumbling over dead chaps, and the cobblestones and slates were falling down in all directions. We had not been there long when we got orders to make a dash for the remaining lorries.

It was boiling hot, as most of the houses were burning fiercely, and we had some trouble turning the lorries and trailers round. The trailers, which were full of useless stores, were nothing more than death traps, for they hindered us at every turn.

At last we got on the move, and what a mess Armentières was in. During the raid, I was hit by a piece of glass, from the church in the Grande Place, which I still have in my possession. The houses were, for the most part, burning, and there were dead bodies everywhere.

Withdrawing in the general direction of the Channel coast they reached Cassel, the one-time headquarters of the former Royal Flying Corps and where a mounted statue of Marshal Foch, Allied generalissimo in 1918, looks out over the Flanders plain. A number of the unit went off on some mission of which Leach knew nothing while he and the rest looked after the lorries:

Suddenly, an infantry officer dashed up, and asked us what the hell we were standing there for and if we were attempting suicide. We regarded him as a little mad, until he informed us that the guns on the hill about a mile away were German, and that nine divisions of German armoured car units numbering 20,000 men were advancing and were about 2 miles away. Needless to say, we made a hurried move.

One senior officer who saw the new 1940 version of the Western Front collapsing about him and was dismayed by what he saw was Lieutenant-General E. A. Osborne, a veteran of the First World War and now a divisional commander. His brief yet forthright diary is basically an account of one disaster piled on another. His 44th Division had also been treading ground much fought over in the previous war; such places as Merville, the Forêt de Nieppe, Estaires, Bailleul, all briefly referred to as the campaign developed, had featured in the fighting of 1915 and more significantly in that of 1918. In that year the pressures had been enormous, Haig's "Backs to the Wall" message had convinced many soldiers that the game was up; at one time there had even been the serious prospect that Britain might have to pull her forces back across the Channel. But the line had held and, miraculously, the tide had turned. It was not going to turn this time. In fact, on the evening of May 26, the British Cabinet authorized Lord Gort, Commander-in-Chief of the British Expeditionary Force, to evacuate his troops to Britain. On May 27 he began to withdraw his force into a perimeter around the French port of Dunkirk. Adding to the unhappy mix of events, Belgium capitulated on the following day. When Holland had succumbed a fortnight earlier, Queen Wilhelmina had sought sanctuary in Britain to continue the fight. By contrast, Belgium's monarch, King Leopold, surrendered unconditionally, and was held under house arrest, or more strictly palace arrest, at Laeken, never to play any effective part in the war or politics again. Belgium's sudden exit felt like a body blow, especially to the French, who now felt totally exposed.

On the day of Belgium's surrender, May 28, General Osborne – his headquarters now virtually on the Franco-Belgian border – visited General Aisne, the commander of the French IV Corps, to which his division was attached. Osborne himself was still in defiant mood but it was clear that General Aisne had already given up hope:

> He asked me if I had heard the news and then told me that the Belgians had given in. He said that this meant that the German Eastern Divisions would close in from Ypres and that next day we would have to surrender. I told him I thought this was nonsense and that if we put his Cavalry Corps in front we could go out via Dunkirk. He agreed but said that General Prioux, commanding the First Army, would not hear of it. I went at once to see General Prioux at Steenwerck, about two and a half miles away. I went into a long room where he was in conference with his staff. He was gloomy beyond words and said there was nothing to do but surrender. I said that I was prepared to fight and that we could fight out all right. It was a gloomy party, but there were one or two who showed by their faces they thought I was right.

For 20 minutes we argued. My French was abnormally fluent. General Prioux urged in turn that:

(a) it was not an operation of war
(b) that an embarkation at Dunkirk was impossible
(c) that if anyone got off it would be the British and they would leave the French.
I replied that:
(a) if we broke out it would be acclaimed a great feat of arms
(b) that it was enough for me to know that General Adam and others were arranging the embarkation
(c) I was certain that once in the perimeter every Frenchman would have an equal chance with an Englishman.

In the event, great feats of arms were simply not possible. It became virtually a matter of *sauve qui peut* – every man for himself. But Osborne was determined this should be done in an organized fashion; this was to be a retreat, but no rout. His diary records a brief echo of the old-fashioned attitude of "death or glory" on the part of one of his senior officers: "Johnny Kelso wanted to wait till morning, form square and die fighting. I vetoed this". By contrast, Osborne ordered his battalions to disengage, instructing them to make for the well-known vantage-point of the Mont des Cats, one of the few hills to rise above the Flanders plain. Topped by a small monastery which had been used as a hospital in the previous war, it was rather like a smaller Monte Cassino. The attraction for Osborne was that he believed the hill to be effectively tank-proof:

> If we could stay there for the day we could go by small parties to Dunkirk next night. Ivor Hughes (6th Queens) asked to be allowed to go direct. He did and Kelso went with him. They got through, but they were lucky; more than a battalion couldn't have done it. There was an officer present from the Buffs. He was sent with orders to Hamilton, who was on the left with two companies. He never got through and a warrant officer sent later never tried. Next morning the RWKs (Royal West Kents) turned up at Mont des Cats and said Hamilton had stayed on, not having orders. Hamilton and his crowd were captured. Orders having been issued, I told all the Div. H.Q. present the story of General Prioux so that all should know it and sent off John Stewart on a motor-bike to get through to Dunkirk to tell Third Corps what we were doing. We've never heard of him since. We then destroyed motors, left all our kit and started the six-mile walk to Mont des Cats.

That night there was a major gathering of forces on the hill – three battalions of infantry, a field regiment with its guns but unfortunately no ammunition, a Royal Horse Artillery regiment with four guns, which were immediately got into action.

The hours of darkness were spent in preparations for a speedy withdrawal at first light next day:

> By dawn we were fairly ready and I didn't expect the Boche before about 10–11 a.m. as that was their ordinary hour to start. But as soon as it was light we could see lorried infantry and tanks, etc. coming over the plain and in an extraordinarily short time they were plugging us with trench mortars. The RHA (Royal Horse Artillery) shot up some of the lorries but had two guns knocked out quick. A good few wounded were being brought into the passages. Then about 6.30 a.m. we got what we knew was coming: the dive bombing attack. It was noisy and unpleasant and all the monastery windows went in. Then Paddy Beard suggested that to wait till night would mean a lot of casualties and why not try and dodge them by going now. I had a conference and decided to do so and orders were got out to go in two columns to Poperinghe.

Thanks to the efforts of a determined rearguard the break-out was remarkably successful:

> Evidently the enemy didn't spot us, for they kept on at the monastery for some hours and eventually set it on fire.

Poperinghe, across in Belgium and to the west of Ypres, was the immediate goal but Dunkirk the real one. By this time innumerable groups of men, in greater or lesser concentrations, were heading for that now vital destination.

Second Lieutenant Norman Strother Smith, a young officer of the Royal Horse Artillery, had arrived in France on May 14. Now, under a fortnight later, he was one of many thousands heading back as best they could the other way:

> We were forever running into the ditches for shelter from aircraft, not for fear of being bombed so much as for being spotted and attacked. Hour after hour seemed to go by but in the heat and dust no track of time could be kept. We passed roadblocks manned and covered by anti-tank rifles, anti-aircraft guns and all sorts of minor defence positions.
>
> It was the hell of a march; the heat was terrific and most of us were dressed to the full, wearing greatcoats to save them and carrying blankets for the night. I had mine slung round my neck and made great use of it as a ground sheet in the ditches I jumped into and so saved my stuff from a lot of dirt.

Finally we reached the main canal at Bergues. Here we collected all the strag-
glers together and formed up afresh. By now my feet were quite raw and I could
only hobble. The road was right on the edge of the canal bordered by trees and
this gave us some protection from observation, but I am afraid it was too late then.
However, we had no direct raids for some time, though we saw plenty of bombers
in the vicinity.

Our orders were to continue on the main road until we reached the houses on
the outskirts of the town of Dunkirk. Here we were to rendezvous for further orders.
As we approached the houses the air became hot with bombers and we had little
peace from then on. I suppose it was 2.00 p.m. then, though I could not be sure and
I reckon we had three raids in every hour. We never met anyone to rendezvous and
so a large body of us kept on down the sound into Dunkirk. All the way we were
continually bombed and had to take shelter.

Dunkirk was a terrible sight. The road was covered with debris and all along
one side were lorries, cars and motorbikes jettisoned, some were in the canal. Some
had been blown up. In the road were two cars burnt out and still smouldering and
in places were bodies of men covered with blankets. There was equipment, petrol
and all sorts of stores destroyed. Houses were blazing furiously from recent
bombs and the others were all shattered. All the time the sky was full of black
smoke from oil tanks that had been blazing for some five or six days.

One element curiously missing from most accounts of Dunkirk is the fear of being
overwhelmed by tank attack. Tanks were the cutting edge of *Sichelschnitt*, and had
been the prime cause of the present crisis, but the thought of these mechanical
monsters thundering to deadly effect on to the evacuation beaches to spread
destruction and mayhem does not seem to have been part of the general expectation. As it happened – though this could not have been known at the time – the
Panzer divisions had been expressly held back from so doing on the personal inter-
vention of the Führer. Hitler's order of May 24 will always remain a matter of
controversy. Was it that he wished to reserve his strike divisions for the next step,
a major thrust towards Paris? Was he allowing England – an enemy he respected
and with whom he would really have preferred to reach an accommodation
rather than be forced into attempting a conquest – a breathing space to recognize
the apparently inevitable and come to terms? Or was it that his companion and
collaborator of many years Hermann Goering, ace fighter pilot of the earlier war
and now head of the Luftwaffe, was eager for his own specially favoured bomber
force to deliver the knockout blow? In the end, air power was not to claim the day,
but its attempts to do so certainly spread fear, even terror, among those gathering
into the Dunkirk perimeter. Second Lieutenant Strother Smith was in no doubt
as to their impact:

The air raids were something I shall never forget. The noise was something incredible. The bombers came over in waves of three generally, at least a dozen strong, and the Dornier had a peculiar engine noise of its own. It had a low-pitched throb which could be heard for miles so that a dozen of these made a roar something terrific. As they approached the AA guns would open fire. The air would be full of the cracking of heavy guns, light guns and quick-firing Bofors and each one made the same noise on bursting. The sky was full of puffs of smoke. And then the bombers would start their machine-guns firing on the battery positions. It was a deafening noise; the guns and automatics and all the time the throbbing of engines. All of a sudden could be heard a screaming noise. At first one wouldn't know what it was, but after the first raid we all knew the sound well. It was bombs.

They took some 10 to 18 seconds to fall and all the time we could hear this screaming getting louder and louder. It always sounded as if we were sure to be hit, but each one seemed to pass right overhead and the sound died away and almost as soon the ground shook as the bombs hit it and the air was full of the roar of explosions or, if they didn't burst, the thudding of each bomb could be heard. Very frequently there was no burst.

Each wave of three planes loosed off the same attack and the noise would start again. All the time we would have our faces buried in the ground and our muscles taut and ready for any nearby explosion. The raid would last about five or ten minutes, but it seemed like one hour from the moment that the planes could first be heard.

But more often than not the raids were far less effective than might have been deduced from their din and psychological pressure:

Afterwards, we would get up to see what damages had been done, all expecting to see hundreds of dead and all the place shattered and blazing. But the bombs did little damage. I never saw one man hit and at the worst I saw a few cattle killed and perhaps one house shattered and smoking.

At last the goal of the Dunkirk shore was reached, though next would be the small matter of getting across the slim stretch of water that now lay in front of them. Meanwhile, the experience of retreat, in which there was at least the possibility of positive action, would now give way to the culture of waiting, in which the initiative would largely be in the hands of others. Strother Smith's narrative continues:

At about 6.00 p.m., after my body of men had got as far as Dunkirk itself and been turned back by the colonel, we were collected and taken to a field where we were to shelter. No boats were to leave that night and we were to be safer in the fields outside the town than in it or on the beach. Many of our men had got away from

us and were in the town. I saw one café open in the middle of the main road and
I managed to get a glass of beer and my bottle filled with Vittel. It was like an oasis
in the wilderness. There were many numbers of French soldiers who had lost their
units and were just waiting for the Germans to come. They would spend their day
wandering about collecting food and drink, and the nights they slept in the fields.

   We were taken to a field where the men had buried themselves in the hedges
so that not a sign could be seen of them. There we stayed. Planes came over and
bombed us and went away. Back they came, wave after wave, hour by hour, until
it was dark and then we hoped for some peace.

The withdrawal to Dunkirk was far from being a straightforward affair, with or
without the attentions of Goering's bombers. The roads to the coast were already
jammed by refugees pouring out of Belgium and the threatened parts of France.
They inevitably offered a huge problem to those notionally there to defend them,
even as the majority of these latter were, effectively, planning to leave them in the
lurch. Second Lieutenant Strother Smith was vehement about the hazard this
massive displacement of "ordinary people" constituted, especially when, as was
widely assumed at the time, they must have been infiltrated by innumerable traitors:

> The refugees were of course the biggest reason for the success of the German
> onslaught. Their vast numbers blocked the roads to our transports and columns
> moving up and down the main roads. They must have had a million German agents
> in their midst and there was little chance of checking the identification of each and
> everyone. Papers could easily be obtained or forged and, anyway, Belgian citizens
> themselves had many Nazi Agents in their midst for years. Finally, and worst of all,
> the Germans were using the refugee hordes as a shield for their advancing troops. It
> was not possible for our bombers or artillery to aim at a German convoy when it was
> surrounded by Belgians and French and equally so we could not easily bomb or shell
> villages known to contain both German troops and Belgian and French refugees.

For most people today the concept of the "human shield" might seem like an invention of the Gulf War of the 1990s, yet here it was, alive and well in 1940.

One other soldier much concerned about the refugee problem was Patrick Mace,
a gunner of D Battery, 52nd Heavy Regiment, Royal Artillery. Before the crisis began
he and his comrades had been comfortably billeted at Bois-Grenier to the south
of Armentières, at a farm kept by a brother and sister who owned, as he put in his
account, the "resounding name" of Seneschal-Duburgrave. "It was," he recalled, "a
clean place [where] we slept in a great loft on sacks of straw encased in palliases,

and slept very comfortably." Then the Germans attacked.

They recognized at once that "the pleasant days of the last six weeks were over". But they were still optimistic and did not worry much over the action that they thought would soon come. The major went up into Belgium – it was thought to find new positions – and meanwhile they did what they could to reassure their host and hostess and to care for the first trickle of refugees. The trickle all too soon became a flood. The gunners were not impressed by what they saw, as Mace put it, writing in some heat:

> The French government acted with great foolishness with regard to the evacuation of the natives. They were, I think, forbidden to move – at any rate no arrangements were made for them – until the last minute. Individual families and parties were coming from Lille and Tourcoing, mingled with the Belgians, but the exit of all the villagers round us was sudden and unorganized. The farms emptied themselves in a few hours – the people had hardly any time to pack their belongings. I came down to find the Seneschals gone. They had harnessed their two horses to a cart and left everything – all their livestock, all their little possessions, taking only a certain amount of food. We were left – seven of us – with the farm on our hands. There was myself, Cullen, Peter Pod, Trefewy, Harry Nolton and two reservists – the rest of our crowd were engaged elsewhere or living in their lorries. We broke into the farm and enjoyed ourselves immensely for 24 hours, but it was pathetic to see it left as though by enchantment – all the little, few household possessions in their places, a bed still unmade, everything left with the strict tidiness characteristic of all these farms. M. Seneschal had been at work that morning.

By this time the refugees were coming by in a great continuous stream from dawn until dark. The richer ones, in their cars, had passed first:

> Now came great crowds on foot, pushing carts and bicycles, strange horse-carts from Belgium, women in slippers with small parcels, all that was left of their homes – every kind of bag, cart or receptacle in which they had been able to throw a few things. They slept and rested by the roadside and then pushed on again. Now they were beginning to grow thirsty and hungry. We had milk – and this we gave to the babies – water, but little food. They were, on the whole, amazingly brave. One party, some women and children and a young boy with a bad foot, we took into the farm, meaning to give them a night's rest. They spoke English well and set about preparing a meal – one woman was very anxious to make us a salad. We had some bread, butter, eggs and jam and coffee, which Pod had made. These people told us something of the hell which was now in Belgium and was sweeping down on us, how fast we did not know. Then at nine o'clock that night an order came through that no one was to take refugees into any of the farms. Ours had by then settled in for the night. It was a beastly thing to have to do, to turn them out then,

they not understanding the necessity and the babies crying. Afterwards, we wished we had disobeyed the order as they did on some farms.

The next day we were fleeing ourselves. This upset our nerves and made all of us irritable. It was impossible to do anything to help these people. We had to stop them to see their identity cards, but we let many through without – it did not matter. Another thing which upset us was Jackie, the Seneschals' little dog, which they had left behind – strangely, for they had been very fond of him. He was old and a little lame, bewildered and angry to see us in the house and we had to leave him there when we left. One dog in such a disaster is an atom, but it is the small sufferings which one saw that one remembers.

At first they saw their withdrawal as routine rather than serious, having no idea of the sheer scale of what was taking place:

We were told, and believed, that only a comparatively few tanks and motor bicycle combinations had broken through, and these, we thought, were isolated. That is, when we thought at all. A man in the ranks, during any sort of action, has neither time or scope for thought; he sees only a tiny piece of what must be a whole and in a great disaster, when all is lost or broken, no-one, perhaps hardly the enemy, can have any clear idea of movement.

"Movement", however, there now was, and with increasing urgency. They had no choice but to join what had now become a mass exodus making for the Channel coast:

The roads were a hopeless mass of convoys and marching men, moving in both directions and stoppages were frequent, so that it was something to have kept the convoy together at all. The blessed darkness fell and we went on – now racing along, now crawling and many times stopping altogether. Bands of men passed singing and we exchanged shouts with them. We went through empty villages and towns, passed farmhouses and along avenues of trees, through a country which must, not so long ago, have been a very pleasant land. Then we stopped in a town, the lorries lined up along the road and we were ordered out – quickly – all save the drivers. We fell in on the road and then set off, marching, with the major at our head and that was the last we saw of our lorries. Guns, lorries and kit had now all gone, but nevertheless we half enjoyed that march. All was quiet, no guns nor planes, no one moving in the houses we passed and every step, we hoped, taking us nearer the coast and home.

It was on that march that we first saw the immense blaze which was burning, day and night at Dunkirk. It was on our left, still some distance away. We marched all night and soon before dawn halted by a small country house. "Take cover here", the Major said, "and stay in cover all day. Don't show yourselves," and we set about hiding ourselves. I found Cullen and Macneil in a very good place between a wood pile and a tree and joined them there. We had a couple of groundsheets, rather they had, and, lying on one and pulling another over us, we all three went to sleep.

When I awoke the sun was up. It was a beautiful day and the dew hung heavy on the early summer bushes and grass. All was peaceful and still, and I leaned smoking on the fence enjoying the quietest moment for many days. Captain Williams came out and smiled, but there was no sign of the others. They were all hidden like woodland creatures in the thick undergrowth and in ditches. Behind us, stretching from Dunkirk as far as could be seen, was an immense bank of smoke, as huge and impenetrable as a bank of clouds.

Inevitably, they too became the target of the omnipresent Luftwaffe:

The sun had not been up very long when the first bombers arrived and they continued, without half an hour between waves, until eight o'clock that evening. Our own fighters met and fought them, fight after fight, all through the day and it seemed to us planes fell like rain out of the skies. The noise of AA fire and the cruel rap of the planes' machine-guns, the distant crash of bombs into and around Dunkirk were in our ears all day. From time to time a white parachute floated down the blue skies. We lay there, flattening ourselves down when they passed near, dozing off in the short lulls, smoking and talking.

At the first attack some of the reservists incontinently broke cover and ran about. Half a dozen dropped down by us, thinking we were in good cover, and were told angrily to go elsewhere. It was a strange thing to see how these men were incapable of remaining in cover, even when their own lives and the lives of all the battery were involved. Were there no planes near they walked about with a swearing assumption of carelessness. When a plane swooped near they ran about, lost and half in panic. Luck was with us for we were not seen, but it was a dismal display of intelligence. From time to time an officer came out and shouted, "Keep in cover, keep down, you bloody fools, keep down".

For myself, I could not help a fit of shivering, half fear half excitement, as each fresh wave of planes came over. We lay as flat as possible, pulling our tin hats over our heads though no bombs fell very close. Once a Spitfire, shot down, roared clean over our heads not a hundred feet up, with a German on his tail. We thought he was going to crash on us. Macneil went headlong behind the wood pile and Duncan flattened himself into a filthy ditch he had, till then, avoided.

But our position was well chosen and we were not in much danger of actual attack and were outside the furious onslaught upon Dunkirk. I cannot remember what we talked about, but obviously we must have argued as Mac was there. Once we discussed what we most liked doing in civilian life and what we wished to be doing then. Cullen spoke of Bedford and motor tour and tennis parties in the evening, I of walks round Winchester, or winter evenings with a book before a fire, Macneil of his school. Such matter of fact details of life seemed to us then paradise enough and I doubt if any of us had much hope – or hope only of seeing England again. And we prayed also for nightfall.

One question occurred to many as they made their way under frequent air attack towards Dunkirk: where was the RAF? Mace's account is unusual in that it records air battles as opposed merely to air strikes. It also includes two notable Spitfire sightings: an earlier successful contest with an enemy bomber when they were still based at their farm; and the one as referred to above, in apparent distress and about to be shot down. But he also refers to "the usual jokes on the scarcity of our air force" whenever German bombers appeared. Strother Smith's diary, referring to the period of his unit's long wait at Dunkirk, contains the acid comment "sometimes the planes would come over and this morning at an odd time we saw some Spitfires –most of us had forgotten what they looked like". To the men of the retreating army, it would seem, the Spitfire summer was not preceded by a Spitfire spring. But what was the reality of the situation, and were there reasons why British air cover seemed so patchy to the men on the roads to Dunkirk?

The RAF was certainly present, but it was faced with numerous problems. This was its first major test in battle; its pilots were flying from constantly shifting bases over unfamiliar ground and against a well-trained, confident and resourceful enemy. In the six weeks of the campaign, British air losses, including aircraft of the Fleet Air Arm, amounted to 900. Of these 453 were fighters: 386 Hurricanes – of which only 75 were victims of combat; the rest were either destroyed on the ground or had to be abandoned while under repair – and 67 Spitfires. The remaining losses were sustained either by Bomber or Coastal Command. The RAF's losses in personnel amounted to 1,382, of whom 915 were aircrew, 534 of them pilots. Had the request of the French been acceded to, and more aircraft, particularly fighters, been sent across the Channel, the ensuing Battle of Britain might well have been lost. As it turned out, that conflict was won only by a very narrow margin. In the cruel logic of war, it is perhaps arguable that men died on the way to, or on, the beaches of Dunkirk who might have been saved by a greater commitment of aircraft to the Battle of France. But against that it has to be said that in the end it was the Battle of Britain which stemmed the Nazi tide, and therefore made possible the ultimate victory.

The evacuation from Dunkirk – or at least certain aspects of it – was memorably recorded on film and in photographs. Some of the images thus created could be said to have achieved almost iconic status. Especially powerful are the scenes showing the long lines of troops waiting on the beaches, the queues down to the water's edge, infantrymen taking furious pot-shots at enemy aircraft like sportsmen on a grouse moor, men wading out to the boats with the sea almost up to their necks, Dunkirk itself burning, ships large and small, naval and civilian, under immense clouds of smoke. Above all it is the lines of men that remain longest in the mind, distant black dots so merged in the lens of the camera that they seem to lose identity, becoming mere strips of anonymous crowd, yet each dot a human being desperately hoping to survive.

Signaller Sidney Leach of the Royal Signals was one such dot. He had an exhausting time getting to Dunkirk and spent several wretched days there waiting for rescue. His unit had not made much distance from Cassel, from which they had beaten a hurried retreat on hearing that the Germans were little more than a mile away, when their vehicles ran out of petrol. As the men scattered on foot, Leach found himself making his way alone:

> I walked on until I came to a scotch regiment. I saw a little action with them and then an officer told me to try and find my brigade. I searched all over the country, dodging German infantry and tanks occasionally, until I found an RASC officer, who told me to make for Dunkirk. Luckily, I had a map, so off I set. At Wormhout I met up with Lt Beaumont, who was OC of my section; he had a couple of chaps with him. We fell in with some more chaps and walked along with them.
>
> Most of the land was under flood, and wrecked lorries were scattered about everywhere. We halted at a point, about six miles from Dunkirk, and rested, or tried to rest, for a couple of hours, then on again. The ditches were lined with dead and wounded and, to add to our discomfort, it started to rain, a very fine drizzle which drenched us in no time.

Eventually, after more hard walking, they got within sight of the sea, to find at that moment a strangely empty scene:

> Not a ship was in sight, and we could see no planes. A thick black cloud hung like a pall over us, tinged with red from the burning buildings. About seven miles to our left a number of buildings were on fire, and we could hear the whine of shells and the explosions as they found a mark.

It was not long, however, before the absence of enemy aircraft he had noted was abruptly remedied:

> Suddenly, a plane dived out of the clouds and dropped a few bombs. The first landed about 10–15 yards away from me. I flattened out in the sand and was lifted about two feet in the air. Small pebbles and sand covered me, and there was a rotten smell of cordite.

Whether from fear or sheer fatigue, or both, Leach crashed out, or as he put it:

> After a brief look round I fainted, and it was a few hours before I woke again. I
> found a chap out of my section, Jock Stewart, and we crawled along the beach for
> a while. Then down came a plane and dropped hundreds of flares, then followed
> the worst bombardment I had experienced. The planes came down in hundreds,
> whining and screaming, and I buried down in a bit of a dip and waited for one to
> get me. But luck was with me, and apart from some shrapnel splinters in my feet
> and a scratch on my cheek, I was unscathed. One of the chaps with me had some
> shrapnel in his thigh and I helped him to take it out.
>
> During the lull we moved about two miles to our right, crawling all the way on
> all fours, stumbling into bomb craters and over dead bodies. We had not eaten for
> so long that we were practically immune from hunger. Eventually, we reached a
> flat part of the beach where there was a large hospital. It was dawn by then, and
> I was very thirsty. Taking my water bottle, I tried to get some water, but I was
> unlucky; all I got was a stray machine-gun bullet, which nicked a little piece out
> of my right leg. It was damn painful after a bit, too.

Again Leach seems to have found himself alone, eventually attaching himself to a
Royal Army Service Corps unit. Earlier, parched with thirst, he had met a
Frenchman who had replenished his bottle with *vin rouge* and water. Now two or
three of his new RASC comrades offered to share their food – one tin of peas, one
tin of bully beef and some hard biscuits – after which modest meal it was judged
time to make a serious attempt to get away, though it was obvious from the sheer
mass of waiting men that this would be no easy matter:

> We went and joined one of the queues, about four or five hundred yards long and
> about ten deep. For ten hours I waited, and just when it came my turn, the boats
> started on another queue and I was sent to the end of it. It was getting dark then,
> and a naval officer came up and asked us if we would care to go to the pier
> (about 11 miles to our left) and catch a liner, which was docked there. I volun-
> teered, and about 250 of us started out. The beach was being shelled then, and
> these kept falling all around us. Delayed action bombs were going off all over the
> place. Dead-beat, we went on and on. The chaps were dropping out continually,
> most of them driven frantic by thirst, others exhausted.

By now Mace and his comrades had also got to the beaches, greeted by a fierce strike
from the air. They would be there for three days and nights which, as he put it, would
"run into one another in a manner I had never before experienced – literally, we did
not know what day of the week it was and I still find it difficult to disentangle the
days". There would be numerous moments of hope and as many disappointments:

The night after the air attack we spent in a long file of men waiting to be embarked and actually, after long hours of waiting, reached the edge of the sea. Then for some reason, we were sent back: someone said the small boats could not come in until the tide changed. After more waiting we went back to the sand dunes to sleep. It was a dark night; the wet beach glistened in the flames of Dunkirk and lights winked from the destroyers and ships at sea. Once a depth charge exploded far out to sea, but mostly everything was quiet. My final waking was once more in daylight.

The next day there were more destroyers – long lines of them came in and went out over the horizon – and many other large boats. The small craft crept to and fro and the multitudes of men swelled. Long files of men stretched down to the sea, and boatloads were taken from the head of the file, which never seemed to diminish.

Cars and motor bicycles ran up and down the beach, which was beginning to be piled with debris – kit, water bottles, coats and clothes of all sorts. Soldiers appeared in amazing dress – officers' coats, French hats and so on. The day was fine and there were many attacks – planes dancing in and out of the smoke from Dunkirk and attacking the ships. A large vessel was sunk opposite us and the water became more and more littered with wrecks. Yachts, cargo ships, large passenger ships, lovely white hospital ships, came in. Each destroyer, rushing off, was so many more men saved, and one nearer our own time. Some were hit, but quietly and slowly the work went on. English planes appeared, but one could never be sure, as the Germans were using captured planes against us. We were still bitter at the scarcity of our air force – it was only after we got home that we came, slowly, to realize what the RAF did in the business.

Next day there were attempts to marshal troops into some sort of order, serial numbers being given to regiments and units. There was much starting and stopping, with one officer, as Mace put it, "shouting and frenziedly active, supplying the comic relief". They ended up once again resting among the dunes. Thirst was a constant anxiety: 'Someone found water but it was too brackish to swallow – most of us rinsed our mouths out with it only, for the taste made one want to retch". Then the next day came and went, also with little progress:

I only remember irrelevant incidents – an unexploded air torpedo washed up, picking and choosing a water bottle from the sand, a man relieving himself with great deliberation in the middle of the beach, amid laughter and applause, tired horses going by, a plan Harry Nolton and I made of getting a rowing boat and pushing out on our own. Sometimes one wandered down to the sea's edge to look longingly at the ships and the men wading out. A fair sea was running, which made embarking difficult. A hospital ship was attacked but passed out of sight before the result of the fight could be seen. From time to time parts of the beach were machine-gunned, but mostly the planes attacked the ships.

All this time they had been some way from Dunkirk itself. Their CO presented them with a choice:

> We could stay and take our chance of getting into a small boat, or follow him into Dunkirk and leave from the harbour. Most decided to follow him and, once more in a mile-long file, we set off. At a French AA post (where a pretty woman was spotting) there was water and I scrambled up the dunes to fill my water bottle. The post was attacked while I was there, and after the attack I refilled my bottle, after a long drink, and rejoined the others. I meant to keep water with me but in a very short time the bottle was empty again.
>
> That night we reached the front of Dunkirk, a long line of once fine hotels which merged into the Mole.* The sunny day ended, and a dark, quiet night fell. All that night we moved forward, perhaps a hundred yards at a time, then an hour's stoppage, a little sleep and forward again. The fire of Dunkirk burned in front of us, we could see the dark shapes of wrecks in the sea and the noise of guns was nearer. From time to time a shell whistled into the town from somewhere. Up the beach a ship was a blazing mass. I thought, unless we are off before dawn we are done for.

Second Lieutenant Strother Smith's RHA party reached Dunkirk on May 28:

> During the night we had one bad stir. The French from the west of the canal withdrew to the east and passing by us frightened the sentry by telling him that the Germans were in Dunkirk. This got the men up and dressed trying to move. They got the officers up with the story that we were moving and it was some job to get them back into the hedges again. By morning they were in an awful state of nerves. However, we had news that we were to move and that cooled them down.
>
> The bombers left us alone this time and I think a quick firing AA gun had a lot to do with this. We had tea and biscuits at about 8.30, but I never learnt where they came from. At 9.15 we started our last march. We set off in the direction of Malo-les-Bains. Through side streets outside the town and so right into the middle. It was a pitiful sight. One time a fashionable seaside resort – residential houses, private hotels, boarding houses, shops and cinemas – now all shattered. Dead bodies, bad smells and general filth. We trudged on in silence.
>
> We passed ambulances jettisoned. One was a gift of the British residents of Brazil or so it said on the car itself. Everyone was dying of thirst and my bottle was the only one full. In one shelter we found a bucket of water and were promised it was good. There were here and there a few civilians.
>
> And so on to the beach. Troops were wandering everywhere and the planes were

---

* The "Mole" in Mace's account is the "pier" referred to by Leach in his. Officially known as the Eastern Mole, it is the great jetty or breakwater forming the eastern flank of Dunkirk harbour from which the majority of troops were evacuated. Malo-les-Bains is the resort to the immediate east of Dunkirk.

forever flying over but for some strange reason they didn't bomb us. On the beach we found the Navy. It was a strange sight to see a party of them there amidst all that we had seen. They were listening to jazz on a portable radio they had. It was a very strange contrast. There were boats out to sea lying abandoned, one with a great rent in her side. The sea was almost as horrible a sight as the town.

For Lieutenant-General Osborne, having given up all thought of further resistance following the successful withdrawal from Mont des Cats, there was one thought uppermost in his mind: to live to fight another day. After numerous difficulties and delays, he and his party arrived in the vicinity of Dunkirk, like Strother Smith, on May 28, having managed the last six miles by hitching a lift on a lorry of 42nd Division. Eventually, "by much enquiry", he made his way to the casino, where he found some members of 3rd Corps HQ. It was not the most joyous of welcomes:

> They were dead beat and had no food. So all we got was a few biscuits and much whisky. They offered me a couch in the room and there I went asleep for five hours. We had arrived at 11 p.m. I babbled all night, they say, about a house I was going to buy. Next day, I woke up early and found a depressed lot of officers in the room. There was no food except biscuits and brandy. I had some of both. The senior officer, Colonel Pickthall, told me there were rumours that the Mole had been closed and anyway no ships had come in. The beach was crowded. This was obvious. "Couldn't I do something?" A messenger from the Naval Signal Station then came in and, fortified by the brandy, I sent an insubordinate wire to the War Office for more ships, food and Bofors ammunition. It was a lovely misty morning and just the best for embarkation without air interference. And yet nothing was happening. I got to 3rd Corps HQ and found General Wason (temporary commander) and Brigadiers Watson and Gale and Harding. They were shaved and spruce. I was not. They said they were glad to see me alive and fed me on tinned salmon.

On his way there Osborne had taken a hard look at the crowds on the beaches and had seen one of his senior officers, Brigadier Whitty, in the vicinity of the Mole trying to organize parties for embarkation against the arrival of further ships. It all seemed, he thought, a hectic muddle, requiring immediate and firm action:

> Wason told me the 44th was not for duty on the perimeter and that it was top for embarkation and that I had better go and embark. I said that I had seen such confusion on the beaches that I felt I had better try and take control. He told me that the French were to embark in the harbour and on part of the Malo-les-Bains beach and British on the Mole and the rest of the beach. I went off in a car with Gale and Kelso to go back to the Casino. Gale promised to send food up to the Casino. I made a plan that Kelso and the 3rd Corps party would control the flow from that end and

that I would go and work from a central point and make Whitty do the Mole.

They gave me a car and a very good officer of the Royal Welsh Fusiliers to help me. I made a plan with Whitty that I would not let any more come up to the Mole until he had cleared the congestion there. I went back to my central position and with the help of a megaphone got to work. I was afraid of the French coming and rushing the Mole, so I put a cordon to divert them into the town and to the harbour. I put out another cordon across the beach to stop any more going to the Mole and started getting everybody into parties of fifty or so under an officer. I made them sit down and from time to time told them what was happening. They were very good and quite safe if I did not let them stand up. Then I collected a party of lieutenant colonels as a reserve. Among them, Ledingham and Guy Cubitt of the Surrey and Sussex Yeomanry were A.1.

All day individuals came to me with pleas to go up through my cordon. I refused everybody from lieutenant colonels downward. Then the French came. I met the heads of their column and with much oratory diverted them to the route I intended them to follow to Dunkirk. Twice during the day I had to address them again when the head of the column halted with one eye on the destroyers at the Mole and one on Dunkirk, which was being shelled. It was a near thing but they got on the move again in the right direction.

Achieving some kind or organization produced a better atmosphere and created greater confidence among the waiting troops:

The men were sitting quite quietly in parties. Twice, enemy aeroplanes appeared and I directed them to go to the ruins of houses for shelter, but we were not bombed. It was a wonderful quiet day. About 3 p.m., destroyers having come in, the crowd at the Mole got smaller and Whitty said he could do with more. I told the men that they were to stay sitting down and only get up when their party was described and that I would select them at random from front, middle and rear. I changed my cordons and let the first cordons go up at once as I had promised. They were very good and all the parties close to me gave me the "eyes left" as they passed. Then we settled down to wait. Once there was nearly a panic when a newly joined mob from the east started to come through. I rushed out my lieutenant colonels and got my parties to sit down and sent the others behind. They all felt confident of fair play then and remained good.

The retreating Army had done its part. They, or at least as many as had been able to do so, had made their way to the Dunkirk shore. Before them lay the English Channel. It was now up to others to take them across it so that they could draw breath, regroup and prepare to continue the war.

CHAPTER THREE

Operation "Dynamo": Escape from Dunkirk

O N SATURDAY MAY 25, the Reverend William Purcell, curate of St Mary's Church, Dover, felt profoundly depressed. Just fifteen days earlier he had been stunned by the news of Germany's invasion of Holland and Belgium. "I heard of it first," he had confided in his diary on May 10, "having spent a peaceful morning, on going down to church for Litany, where Watkins the verger told me all about it."

Dover was a particularly sensitive place at such times, the continent where these terrible developments were taking place being clearly visible in good weather. People were suffering and dying over there, not many miles away. His diary note of May 10 had continued:

> This afternoon I was down by the docks, visiting, where there was an indescrib-able atmosphere of strained normality about the brilliantly fine, deep day. This evening there were troops with Bren guns barricading the Folkestone Road. Now the velvet night has come, and all is profoundly still. "What next?" is the unspo-ken question millions must be asking themselves. *In manus tuas, Domine.*

Now, on the 25th, there were numerous fearful developments to report. That evening in the quiet of his study he wrote:

> The feeling of nightmare has been very strong these 15 terrific days. 15 days and Holland is conquered, Belgium and Northern France over-run, the Germans in the Channel ports and 19 miles from this house, the BEF cut off and the Empire tottering. All of us are waiting for bombs to drop, sirens to wail, parachute troops to invade us. Horror and inconceivable disaster on all sides. The sun has shone all the time, there is a hard drought, the spring is most beautiful. We can hear the guns.

Matters, it seemed, could hardly be worse. Unknown to him, however, strenuous action of an outstanding kind in which Dover would play a vital part was about to begin.

The following day, Sunday May 26, was the 39th birthday of Commander R.C.V. Ross RN, captain of the fleet minesweeper, HMS *Gossamer*. The 5th Minesweeping Flotilla, which he commanded, had just successfully completed the task of sweeping in an old minefield off the Tyne. The fine weather added to the satisfaction of a job well done and he made a grateful signal to his ships, "A good day's work has given me a happy birthday". The flotilla was in harbour by teatime, and he gave his crews leave till midnight, while he went ashore at North Shields for a brief walk. An hour or so later, as he was returning to his ship, he was met by an officer from the base who startled him by saying "Goodbye"; this, thought Ross, seemed rather odd, especially as the officer was so full of the secrecy regulations that he refused to say anything else. On going aboard Ross received a signal which made him somewhat wiser, though not by much. It read: "5th MSF to sail for Harwich for operations under orders of V.A. Dover".

"V.A. Dover" was shorthand for Vice-Admiral Bertram Ramsay, Flag Officer, Dover. As Ross wrote in the account he prepared for a lecture on Dunkirk to an audience of "Wrens" in 1942: "From that day to this, I have never received any further written orders for the operation now known to History as 'Dynamo'. Those 16 words were the key which kept six ships wound up for over a week". In the course of that week Ross's own vessel would succeed in evacuating to Britain no fewer than 3,214 British and French servicemen.

The overall figure of those lifted from the beaches would be 388,226, when no one had expected more than 45,000. Ably supported by his Chief of Staff, Captain Day, Ramsay was the chief architect of this achievement. Recalled from the Royal Navy retired list in 1939, he was to prove precisely the man for the occasion in May–June 1940. Working from the former dynamo room of Dover Castle – a location which offered a ready answer to the question as to how the task ahead might be code-named – he ran the evacuation with skill and imagination, and on a light rein. His philosophy was not to fuss his captains, but to trust them to make their own judgements and decisions.

"Salt-horses" was one way of describing such a breed; intelligent and experienced officers of the Navy's executive branch who would know instinctively what to do and would then proceed to do it. Commander, later Captain, Ross was a genuine salt-horse and therefore well able to play a vital role in the forthcoming operation. As a sailor of much experience, with, as it happened, a German wife, he had among other things been present at a notable earlier Anglo-German occasion: the scuttling of the High Seas Fleet in Scapa Flow in 1919. Then he had inevitably been more witness than participant; in this new confrontation he would play an extremely active role, which would result in his being awarded the DSO.

His minesweepers spent the rest of that May Sunday evening topping up with coal, oil and stores and then, "At midnight the little smoky Tyneside tugs came and hauled our bows round to seaward and off we steamed".

In fact, even as HMS *Gossamer* was making her preparation to sail, Operation "Dynamo" had begun. The first ships left at 6.57 p.m. that Sunday and on the following day 7,669 men were brought back from Dunkirk.

On the evening of Monday May 27 the destroyer HMS *Sabre* was implementing orders to proceed to Dover with a view to escorting a westward-bound convoy down the English Channel. Arriving off the eastern entrance of the Harbour at about 11 p.m., she was told to wait. As her commanding officer, Commander Brian Dean, who also won a DSO, would later write:

> A few minutes later a somewhat dramatic signal was received: "From Vice-Admiral, Dover. The last chance of saving the BEF is tonight. You are to proceed with all despatch to beaches two or three miles east of Dunkirk and embark troops in your own boats. Return at your discretion not later than 0330".
>
> So it had come to that. Gosh, things must be worse than we had thought! There was little time for meditation, however, and within a few minutes we were heading at 28 knots for the green light buoy off Calais.

Sabre was one of forty-one destroyers which would play their part in the Dunkirk evacuation. She would be credited with bringing home 5,675 survivors, a figure only exceeded by *Codrington* with just two more and *Malcolm* with 5,851. In all she would make ten trips to the Dunkirk beaches.

Earlier that same Monday evening the officers and men of HMS *Princess Elizabeth* rejoined their ship after boiler-cleaning leave. They had enjoyed seven gloriously sunny days away from responsibility, though their time ashore had inevitably been troubled by anxiety about what was happening on the other side of the Channel. That other shore was in sight as they returned, because their ship had been undergoing its spring-clean in the docks at Dover. But more on their minds as they went aboard was the strange fact that the harbour was practically deserted. Where were the six other paddle steamers of the 10th Minesweeping Flotilla of which *Princess Elizabeth* was a member? As one of their crew, Signalman Les Mallows, put it: "There was no one to ask, so that caused the usual crop of 'buzzes' to circulate round the mess-decks".

The situation was made clear when they steamed out of the dock area next morning and came in sight of the signal-station on the cliff top in front of Dover Castle. Wrote Mallows:

> An Aldis lamp flashes down at us: "Have you received Vice-Admiral Dover's message?" "No", I reply. "Pad", says the Castle station, meaning a long message to come. My oppo [i.e. mate] writes it down as I read the Morse. "Proceed forthwith to La Panne and embark as many Allied troops as possible from the beach...etc." So now we knew where everybody else had gone.

By now Commander Dean on HMS *Sabre* was already well into his first foray to Dunkirk. As he described it in his low-key but vivid account:

1st trip: On the night of May 27. Dunkirk was already a blazing inferno and it seemed impossible that anyone could be alive in the town. We pressed on for two miles past the darkened lighthouse which could be seen silhouetted against the flames. Then we turned towards the shore steaming dead slow and taking depth soundings continuously. When the depth was a bare foot more than our propeller draught we dropped an anchor underfoot and lowered our three small boats. The 1st Lieutenant went in charge – and we wondered whether we should ever see him or our boats and their crews again. It would be no easy task for him to find the darkened ship again, steering across the tide. It was thus with considerable relief that, about 1½ hours later, I recognised the 1st Lieut's voice hailing "*Sabre* ahoy!". All three boats were laden far beyond their life-saving capacity, but we got the troops safely on board and sent the boats in again.

During our second wait two steam drifters came alongside and transferred about 100 troops to us. We could hear a lone Messerschmitt flying around, loosing off bursts of machine-gun fire at any ship he sighted. The ships were of course all darkened, but it was an easy matter for a low-flying aircraft to get them silhouetted against the flames ashore. We were amused to see him wasting a lot of ammunition on one of the few channel buoys that was still showing its light.

Before long, however, it was *Sabre*'s turn. A stream of tracer came at us and rattled against the ship's side and deck. My Leading Signalman, who was standing beside me on the bridge, crumpled up with a groan. He had got a machine-gun bullet through the leg. It was not a severe wound and he re-joined us a few weeks later – much annoyed at having missed all the "fun". This proved to be our only casualty during the whole operation.

By 3 a.m. most of the ships had left for home. The first streaks of dawn were appearing in the eastern sky and I was getting worried lest our boats should not show up before 3.30 – the latest time by which we had been told to return.

Another thing was worrying me. We had received a signal that the direct channel had been mined and that all ships were to return via the Zuydecoote Pass – a narrow channel through the sandbanks some miles to the eastward. To negotiate this channel it was necessary to use a certain chart – and we had not got that chart! Our boats duly turned up at about 3.20. To attempt the Zuydecoote Pass without the chart would have been to court disaster. There was nothing for it but to risk the mines and go direct. We did so and got away with it, reaching Dover at about 5.30.

Meanwhile, Commander Ross in Gossamer had joined Operation "Dynamo", after experiencing at Harwich what he would describe as "a little piece of business which is so typical of every seagoing officer's experiences in wartime". In view of the urgency of his summons from the Tyne he had expected the prompt arrival of a boat to take him ashore at once. When nothing happened he made a signal: "Does Admiral wish to see CO?" Back came the reply: "No, revert to two hours notice for steam". Puzzled but grateful for a moment or two in which to relax, he started to draw off his heavy bridge coat and sea boots. He had got as far as cleaning his teeth when the next signal came: "Raise steam for full speed. Report to Admiral forthwith". He hurried to respond, but this was not to prove as straightforward as he assumed. When he reached the shore he was not allowed on to the pier because he had no pass; passes, he learned, were only issued to base personnel, not seagoing people. However, as he put it, pithily, "I said a few words which convinced them I was a naval officer" and he was allowed through:

> After a short interview with some staff officers, I was shown in to a very old and tired Admiral. Had I known all that he knew then no doubt I should have looked old and tired too. He said we were to sail at daylight for Dunkirk. I said, was it for minesweeping? No, he said, almost inaudibly. I stepped close to him, and murmured, "Evacuation?". He nodded, without speaking.

Now at last HMS *Gossamer* was on her way. Soon she became part of the great motley armada that was to play so vital a role in the history of the Second World War:

> A few hours after leaving Harwich we turned at right angles into that extraordinary stream of traffic which has so often been described – then in its first flood and all untouched by casualties: coasters, life-boats, yachts, destroyers, sloops, Dutch barges. "Look!" I exclaimed, as we sighted their endless procession.
>
> We left them later, to thread our own way through the shallow channels and arrive, as we had been ordered, off Bray, a little resort three or four miles west of Dunkirk. As I gazed through binoculars at the coast, looking for landmarks, I noticed several dark square woods growing among the sand dunes. We came gradually closer, and they were not woods but men – the British Army. Silent they stood there, some on the shore and some in the water, backed by the peaceful *plage* with its little hotels and casinos.
>
> There was then no sign of enemy activity, but a signal had just been received which seemed to give a sinister air to the whole picture: "Any tanks seen approaching the beach may be assumed to be hostile". The more one thought over that signal, the less one liked it, but I did not have long to think. The destroyer in charge

of the beach asked me to send two ships into Dunkirk harbour, and I decided we would go in as one of them. The rest of the flotilla, all of which survived the evacuation, I did not see together again for several weeks. From now on, I had my hands full with my own ship.

It must have been evening twilight as we rounded the pier-head and took our first look at Dunkirk harbour. On our left was a hospital ship, and beyond it a vacant length of pier with an officer and a sailor on it. There was a strong tide sweeping through the pier, setting us off, but I got alongside all right. The pier was undamaged at that time, and soldiers could come down it two or three abreast.

The soldiers began trickling on board in a steady stream. But they couldn't come on board fast enough for me. I had not learnt the Dunkirk lesson of patience in dealing with men who were just simply exhausted, and, of course, soldiers on board a ship always tend to find the narrowest gangway and stand in it. So it was in a fever of impatience that I watched them file on board and gradually stow themselves away – 500 in half an hour or so. Little did I know that another time it would take five hours to load the same number. At last we cast off, and the tide, helping this time, carried us out sideways clear of the pier and the hospital ship till I could ring down "Full astern".

It was dark as we got through the sandbanks again. A ship called us up and signalled: "Can I enter Dunkirk this way?". Very reluctantly I eased engines and closed her. It turned out she was one of the Harwich-Hook steamers, the *Prague*, in which my wife and I had actually travelled on our honeymoon. She had no large-scale chart of the approaches. I was all impatience to go on, but Lieutenant Manisty, my navigator, said it seemed a pity to let her services go to waste and he had a spare chart, so we sent a boat over with it.

When the ship finally got under way, Ross left the Officer of the Watch (OOW), Sub-Lieutenant Phipps, to look out for a vital buoy, the Quint, and retired to his bunk, which was in a steel hut on the bridge, for a brief rest. Soon after, however, the OOW called out, "Sir, there's something going on ahead". Ross rapidly returned to the bridge, to be confronted by a sight of a kind that would always give the gravest anxiety to any ship's captain in circumstances of high danger:

The water was full of men. Here was that old problem over again – are we to risk our own ship and 500 soldiers to rescue survivors? The official answer is always, "No". But what are you to do? At any rate, we stopped and sent away three boats. I did not know that an officer went in each one, but so it was – so that there were only two of us left aboard.

Soldiers were shouting "Help", and some just bubbling and sinking, in the darkness all round. Someone put on a searchlight and lit up the two halves of a destroyer sticking up from the bottom. It was an old "W" class: *Wakeful*. Just then a fishing boat came out of the darkness and hailed us. She had the captain of the sunken ship on board and he hailed me: "We were torpedoed: I think it's a submarine and she's still about; you'd better get away". Good advice, with all my boats away in the dark. By now there were fewer shouts from the water; fishing boats had picked up a number – the wind had driven us gradually away from others, and some had sunk. How many? How shall we ever tell? At last I got my two bigger boats back; the skiff could not find us, but got to the fishing-smack which promised to look after her. We shaped our course to keep as clear of the Quint Buoy as we could and thence for Dover. Our young cook nearly missed the ship when she went ahead – he was hanging on to a net over the side. He had been swimming round on his own, rescuing soldiers. He made a practice of it and I'm glad to say he afterwards got a medal for it.

HMS *Wakeful* was one of five destroyers lost at Dunkirk; she is nevertheless credited with having secured the safe evacuation of 639 men.

Delayed already on account of her boiler cleaning, the paddle-steamer *Princess Elizabeth* was unable immediately to carry out the orders of Vice-Admiral, Dover, as she had to adjust her compasses following what Signalman Mallows described as "several metallic changes in the bridge area. So for hours we were towed slowly round a mooring-buoy while experts did clever things to the binnacle." Then at last they were on their way. The direct approach to Dunkirk being denied them since the Germans had captured the French coastal guns, they took a roundabout route through the Downs to North Foreland, then east for several hours steaming across a surprisingly empty sea. But as they turned west following the line of the Nieuport sandbank, dull thumps and crumps could be heard up ahead, increasing the tension and speculation as to what they would shortly experience. As they moved carefully shoreward they were cheered by the sight of a vessel well known to them already heavily engaged in the task assigned:

> We got a preview of our task from our own sister-ship and flotilla-mate, the *Gracie Fields*, approaching us from the west packed with troops and passing us on her way to England. The peacetime base of both ships was Southampton and many of those crew members were still part of the wartime complements. So much waving and cheerful ribaldry was exchanged as we passed close by.

Such pleasantries over, all eyes and thoughts were on the French coast looming up ahead:

Now for us, the first unforgettable sight. Six miles of beaches leading westward up to the distant port of Dunkirk, and this long stretch of light sand appears spotted and blotched with small groups and larger formations of soldiers. The lorries, trucks and Bren-carriers which have got them there are standing abandoned around the dunes that lie along the top of the beaches, except where the smart white hotels of La Panne intrude on the scene.

Along this seafront there are something like forty ships, anchored as close inshore as their draught will allow; "pusser-built" naval vessels such as destroyers and fleet-minesweepers are mixed up with small merchant-ships, trawlers and drifters, smart motor-yachts and a goodly number of paddlers. All their small boats are plying to and from the beaches, and as some ships move away with crowded decks, others like ourselves are constantly moving in to "join the club".

To make this panorama even more spectacular, the last daylight air attack is in full swing. Some thirty or forty bombers are wheeling and darting over and around the rescue-fleet, who being at anchor are sitting ducks. But all ships' guns blaze away as an aircraft approaches within range, the bombers having split up to circle the area while they select their targets and the moment for a run-in. One of the most vivid memories is the battery of Bofors guns firing from somewhere just behind the elegant hotels of La Panne – so redolent of peacetime holidays, except that they have tracer shells streaming over their roofs. The clips of Bofors shells make a glorious rhythmic thumping sound, like a giant beating a huge bass drum; and the sinister black bombers jink and weave to avoid the line of the tracer.

So we nudge in as close to the beach as we dare. A paddler has some advantage in this, as they are vessels of particularly shallow draught, in relation to their overall size. In fact, we anchor near a large paddler, the *Waverley*, who sadly was destined soon to be sunk.

It was quite dark when the first of our two boats, rowed by a mixed volunteer crew of seamen and stokers, grounded its bows close to the shore. Nobody seemed to be aware of their arrival and the Sub-Lieutenant in charge was surprised to find himself splashing ashore and groping along the beach for some time before he found a column of soldiers and led them back to the boat. The first arrivals disposed themselves in the bottom of the boat between the four pairs of oarsmen and soon afterwards they were being helped up on to the ship's port sponson – the entrances on the paddle-box. And so we welcomed aboard the first soldiers that the *Princess Elizabeth* was to bring home during that week.

Boat no. 2 met a very different situation. Her arrival at the water's edge was now keenly looked for, but she grounded on a hump of sand some distance out. To the Army, the prospect of having to do more than paddle did not appeal – especially with the greatcoats and slung rifles that most of them still retained. Some persuasive hollering by the Subby in charge induced a steady wading-out, but within a yard or two of the boat the water was up to their armpits and they feared any further move. The boat's crew got impatient, but the dimly-seen heads stayed put.

At last the Subby thought of shouting, "Who wants to go *home*?", and this highly emotive word was only too effective. The nearest soldiers threw themselves at the shoreside gunwale, tipping the boat sharply on its side and throwing two of the oarsmen into the sea. A wild time was then had by all. Several more troops floundered forward to cling to the side now pulled down to their level, while the Navy fought them off, stamping with their seaboots on the gripping fingers. It had to be done, to avoid this large boat from turning turtle and being lost to the use of all concerned.

The Sub-Lieutenant and Petty Officer finally brought the party to order. The more capable swimmers were persuaded to work their way round slowly to the seaward side, the boat was gradually brought back to an even keel, and then both sides were ordered inboard at the same time, so that they could be dragged over the gunwales while the craft remained balanced.

Looking out for enemy aircraft was not just the concern of the naval men. Any that strayed near the *Princess Elizabeth* were met by an angry greeting from the newly embarked troops, however ineffective that response might be. Nor, Mallows conceded, was the ship's own response more than a token one:

> Our passengers amused themselves by propping up against various parts of the upper deck and firing their rifles at any bombers that cruised even vaguely within range. The ship's own light armament consisted of one twin and one single Lewis-gun, and there was rather a peashooter feeling about it. Oh, for the Oerlikons and Pom-poms of two years later!

At last the ship's bows swung round and they headed for home, though oddly this did not bring the sense of easy relief they had expected:

> In fact our steaming away from the beaches and the ragged line of shipping brought a kind of disquieting silence. The Bofors guns ashore, plus whatever guns were sported by the assorted rescue-vessels, had formed a very spirited Ack-Ack club. Now we had left the club premises, so to speak, we felt very alone.

The exact order of events is somewhat difficult to establish but it would seem that by now the crew of the *Princess Elizabeth* had been informed that their sister-ship, the *Gracie Fields*, had not continued on her cheerful way to Dover but had been bombed not long after their chance meeting with her outside Dunkirk. Indeed, the *Elizabeth* was apparently ordered to her assistance but then sent back to the beaches when other ships reached the stricken vessel first. The *Gracie* had already successfully evacuated 281 men to Dover and on this, her second and last voyage, she had set off bravely with another 750. Hit in the engine-room, her upper decks swept by steam and with her rudder jammed, the paddle-steamer began circling uncontrollably at a speed of six knots. Showing notable seamanship, two Dutch skoots – small fishing boats – managed to get alongside and take off some of the men while the minesweeper HMS *Pangbourne* saved the rest. *Pangbourne* then took the Gracie in tow, but the latter began filling with water and, her skeleton crew having been taken off, she sank. The fact that their sister ship was in trouble, even though her fate was not then fully known to them, concentrated the minds of the crew of the *Princess Elizabeth* as she attempted her own home run: "Certainly we had no shortage of lookouts on bridge or upper deck as we paddled along at our best speed – about ten knots". In fact they were to have far better fortune:

> We had the luck of a six-hour journey back along the roundabout route that was trouble-free. Various crumps and bangs were heard at intervals somewhere over the horizon. This was to remain a frequent occurrence, and we could only gaze around with a wild surmise. Eventually, North Foreland came into view and an hour later we were disembarking our troops at Margate Pier. It must be almost second nature for a paddle steamer to be moored at a seaside pier – but this time with a very different crowd of trippers.
>
> When the last of the soldiers was shuffling down our gangway, a Lieutenant-Commander in spick and span uniform came to the pierhead, smiled sweetly at our CO and said, "Another trip, please?" "Ay, ay," growled the Old Man.

So the *Princess Elizabeth* backed away from the pier and turned to plod back to Dunkirk. She would ultimately be credited with having brought home 1,673 men.

Some soldiers on the Dunkirk beaches were themselves involved in the evacuation process. Among them was Driver A.O. Bennion of the Royal Army Service Corps, who on the late afternoon of May 29 learned that he had "volunteered", along with the rest of his platoon, to act as stretcher-bearer and helper to a group of wounded men who had been given priority and were waiting at the water's edge. They were duly ordered to go down to the sea, where they found a medium-sized rowing boat with a set of oars:

> We assisted some of the wounded on board and as I had done a bit of "holiday" rowing, I took over the oars. I suppose there were about half a dozen wounded and perhaps the same number of our lads – it certainly seemed a heavy load as I pulled away from the shore. Fortunately, the sea was very calm and there were no planes about. Our destination was a small cargo boat moored about half a mile from the

shore, and I suppose it took about half an hour to reach it. On arrival the crew quickly hauled the men on board and I found myself alone, still at the oars, and I realized that I would have to return to the beach for another load. This time, with an empty boat, the going was much easier. On arrival at the beach I took on another batch of walking wounded and a few more from 3 TCC. Again, it was an uneventful trip back to the boat, which was Greek and called the *Patria*. History repeated itself and once again I found myself rowing alone for the shore. Again I took another batch and this time I decided that "enough was enough", so when we reached the *Patria* I made sure that I was one of those who scrambled aboard. I have no idea who, if anyone took over "my" boat. By now it was late evening and on deck I sat down in a corner and promptly fell fast asleep. I have no idea what time the *Patria* left the beach, but it must have been some time during the night. We were lucky and the crossing was uneventful. I was woken by a shout that land was in sight and we docked at Margate some time in the morning.

The ships of the Royal Navy, assisted by over two dozen foreign warships, mostly French but also including one Dutch vessel and one Polish, took off the greater proportion of those evacuated from Dunkirk. But the legendary heroes of the story have always been the men, and sometimes the women, of the small ships, some of which were barely fit for river work, let alone the crossing of an exposed seaway under serious threat. Commander Dean's account of the adventures of HMS *Sabre* contains a remarkable sighting of one such vessel, name and name of owner unknown.

Back at Dover after his third trip, Dean had just settled down for an hour of much-needed sleep when he was called to the telephone on the jetty:

> The Duty Staff Officer was on the line. "Is that you *Sabre*? Two Captains, RN, and four other officers are on their way down to you. They are to open a Naval HQ in Dunkirk and we want you to land them on the Mole. We are also sending down two large packing-cases of wireless gear and two telegraphists. These are to be landed on the beach at Bray Dunes five miles east of Dunkirk, OK?" I replied, "I can manage the first part all right but not the second as I have no boats left. My 1st Lieutenant has been left over there with my only remaining boat." "Sorry about that, old boy, but there's nobody else to do it. You'll have to pinch a boat when you get over there. Cheerio!" And he rang off. In due course the naval party arrived, and the crates – huge affairs weighing at least 3 cwt. each.

So it was that not many hours later Dean, having landed his human cargo, found himself looking for an appropriate vessel to commandeer for the task of getting his crates on shore:

> Off Bray Dunes were ships of every description from cross-channel steamers downward. All were milling around at their best speed in their efforts to avoid the attentions of squadron after squadron of bombers. We joined in this crazy dance, searching all the while for a boat of some sort that we might press into service. At last we spotted a small motor launch of a type seen on the upper Thames. She was heading away to the northward and would be crossing the sandbanks in a minute or two. We headed her off and hailed "Oy! Come alongside". At the wheel was a little man in pin-stripe trousers, spectacles and a bowler hat. (A very sensible head-wear, after all, with bomb-splinters and bits of wreckage continually dropping out of the sky). He was obviously "something in the City" and looked as if he had stepped straight out of a solicitor's office – as indeed he probably had. In response to my hail he raised his hat and replied, "I'm sorry sir, but my boat is holed and I am trying to get home". He got as little sympathy from me as I had had from the Duty Staff Officer: "Sorry about that, old boy, but you must get your crew to sit on the hole. I've got a job for you here". So he came alongside and we bundled the great packing cases into his boat, nearly capsizing her in the process. We told him where to land them, pushed him off and wished him luck – and he disappeared into the murk to the southward.

For his part Commander Ross was far from having a quiet time in *Gossamer*, as he explained, dramatically and with numerous vocal sound effects, to his audience of Wrens two years later:

> And now we come to the "Glorious 1st of June", a date I shall never forget. We arrived off the far beaches just after midnight and anchored as close as we could get: every ship was given her exact berth for that night. It was, as usual, the "Final Evacuation". The shore was absolutely silent, a little distant shelling on the left beyond La Panne. I sent the Sub-Lieutenant inshore in a little motor boat we had pinched in Dover Harbour – the *Billy Boy*. (I got an official letter six months later, asking if I knew where it was!) No one to be seen. We sat and waited. An hour later the shore was suddenly alive with shouts and torches, and we started to get them in driblets; no boats, of course, except this *Billy Boy* and she was soon swamped. We used rafts, and some swam, and in the end a destroyer lent us her boat. It took hours.

The darkness was now fading fast. Fearing an air attack might undo all the good work done, Ross made a signal calling urgently for a fighter patrol at dawn.

Now it was 5.15 and just light. Five aircraft flying straight down the coast at us. "Look," I shouted, "our dawn patrol." Just then the aircraft started spraying out what looked in the early light like silver sparklers. "Messerschmitts, sir," called the yeoman. The foremost 4-inch gun opened up, the aircraft swayed this way and that like angry gnats and dodged close over the sand dunes and out of sight. By about 7 we were ready to leave, when a destroyer came up and asked how many I had. "675." "Go into Dunkirk and FILL UP," she replied. We had quite enough but, not knowing if it was an Admiral, we complied. On the way, another Minesweeper, HMS *Skipjack*, asked us for some morphia and we went in alongside her and passed it over. I am afraid she was blown up two hours later. We ran into the harbour and back to our old berth.

It was all French soldiers this time, with their exasperating habit of carrying little trunks with them (belonging, I think, to the officers). This was the last straw. "What's trunks?" I asked Manisty. *"Colis." "Pas des petits colis,"* I shouted out, and *"Courez!"* – "Run": a cry which the Yeoman soon learned to repeat with gusto. But the occasional howitzer shell which made us want to be off passed unnoticed by these hardened warriors. Would they *"courez"*? No. Once on board every man apparently opened a small tin of pâté and a bottle of brandy. Meanwhile, a lot of aircraft had suddenly appeared and were diving on the town. Our fo'csle gun opened up again but I shouted out, "Keep your ammunition to protect the ship," and it was as well I did so.

We now had 700 and really were full up, and cast off. The moment we were clear, I rang down "Full ahead both engines", which remained on the telegraphs till we reached Sheerness.

But Sheerness lay some hours ahead. In the meantime *Gossamer* had to survive another attack from the air, this time one that called for adroit seamanship if there was to be any chance to survive:

There was still that horrid swarm of dive-bombers overhead – a great circus of them, Junkers 87. Great ugly bent-winged gnat-like creatures. We were looking for the buoy where you turn out of the coastal channel, when the Yeoman sung out (almost cheerfully), "Here they are, sir," as one of them detached itself from the circling ring and came straight down at us, in a screaming roar. "Enough water to turn?" I asked Manisty. "Yes, sir, just high water" – trust him to know. So I put the wheel hard over. Round we went. You could see the five bombs leave the aircraft, and the white lines round her black swastikas as she swung sharply away; an obvious miss. Bang, bang, goes our gun. "Take the next one," I shout over the front of the bridge and point up to where the second aircraft has already pulled off into a dive. "Hard-a-port." I don't know now whether it made any difference steering as I did, but at the time I was convinced that I judged each case on its merits and conned the ship clear of the bombs. Aircraft after aircraft screamed down at us: salvo after salvo fell in the sea close by – then a pause – then a terrific BLOOMPF as they burst under water. Eight aircraft – then a pause which we used to get steady on our course.

Then seven more came at us. The last made up his mind to get us. I can see him now. He did a sort of little war dance high up in the sky, then came down almost vertically. I swung the ship, but he seemed to keep steady against the masthead. It all goes so slowly. As he let go, I said to the Yeoman, "I think they've got us this time". "Afraid so, sir." Down slanted the bombs. "Lie down!" Whish! Woompf! Missed! I got up and looked round. No more in sight. "Just two rounds left", said the foremost gun. I felt a little sick and sat down. It was 9.30 and I'd still had no breakfast.

At last Ross had time to visit some of his passengers to find how they had fared during the voyage:

My steward told me he had been sitting on the ladder from my cabin to the mess-deck during the air attack, telling the soldiers how safe they were. They can't have felt too bad, for they certainly had eaten all our food.

We got into Sheerness early that afternoon and spent all the rest of the day renewing our food and fuel and ammunition, and sweeping up sand and bullets and bandages and more sand. Even my cabin was full of it.

I remember two other things about that day: (1) that when I was alone in my cabin I once found myself in tears, from sheer exhaustion; (2) that when I did try to get asleep for a few hours I was wakened by a doctor who said he'd heard I was wounded and was quite annoyed when I told him he was mistaken.

The captain and complement of HMS *Sabre* were just beginning to contemplate the prospect of a well-earned respite when they were asked to undertake what would become their tenth crossing:

We had expected the previous trip to be our last, but a general signal from the Vice-Admiral was passed to us. It pointed out that the evacuation of the BEF had only been made possible by the very gallant rear-guard action fought by a French division, that the majority of these Frenchmen were anxious to come to England, and that he was therefore asking every ship that could possibly manage it to make one more trip to bring them back. Each ship was to signal whether she could make the trip or not.

Old *Sabre* was sorely battered; she had chips off both propellers, a hole in her port bow just above the waterline, her compass was still very inaccurate, and her company well nigh exhausted. Also her engines and boilers had been run to death, were badly in need of overhaul, and might be expected to break down at any moment.

And yet… I felt that if we said "No" we could never hold up our heads again. I cleared lower deck, read the Admiral's signal and said, "I think we ought to go, chaps. What do you say?" Their roar of assent was most inspiring. So the reply was sent "*Sabre* can do". (This became quite a catchword in the ship for some time afterwards.) Thus at 8. 20 p.m. on June 3 we set forth once more.

On the way northward through the Downs we overtook another of our Yangtse gunboats. She was doing her best speed of about 15 knots and, as we flashed past at about 30, she signalled "Ride her, Cowboy!" I was puzzled at first to think of a suitable retort, but just before we lost sight of her astern we signalled: "I'm headin' for the last round-up"!

And what a round-up it was! Although a time table had been carefully worked out, there was a mass of shipping of all kinds trying to get alongside, to get into the harbour, or to get out; French, Belgians and Dutch all mixed up with our own ships. We entered at 10.50 p.m. and lay off until there should be a berth for us. A small minesweeper shoved off from between two transports. Would there be room for us there? Just about. We crept gingerly in, got the bow alongside, and warped it along the pier until within a foot of one of the transports, then worked the stern in. It cleared the other transport by a few inches.

Dean was soon confronted by the phenomenon that had troubled Commander Ross, that of overloaded allies taking their time when coming aboard:

Immediately the Frenchmen began coming on board over the foc'sle. I wanted to get them down on to the upper deck to make room for more. But each man seemed to be carrying an eiderdown on his back besides other impedimenta, and it was only with difficulty that they could get down the narrow ladders. I sent our old friend the Coxswain down to try to speed up the traffic. Finding little response to his English words of command and knowing not a word of French, he hailed the bridge: "Captain, sir, 'ow d'yer tell these 'ere Froggies to get a move on, sir?" I leaned over and shouted in the best French I could remember: "*Depêchez-vous! Passez à bas! Passez vite!*" The Coxswain picked up the last phrase and the general hubbub was drowned by a stentorian Cockney voice: "Pawsay veet! Pawsay veet! Dunno wot it means, but pawsay blinkin' veet!" (Naval readers will not need to be told that the operative word has been paraphrased.)

By 12.30 a.m. on the 4th we had embarked about 600 *poilus* [French soldiers], and soon afterwards we shoved off for the last time from Dunkirk East Pier. The engineers who built that pier had designed it purely as a breakwater and not for ships to berth alongside. They would have been surprised, to say the least, had they known that a quarter-million men were to reach safety along its six-foot gangway!

We threaded our way astern, through the mass of ships waiting to berth, avoided a number of collisions by inches and got out of the harbour to find that our compass had stuck! There was nothing for it but to wait until another home-ward-bound ship should come along and to follow her. Our first pilot was a 10-knot minesweeper; so we were glad when a 20-knot transport came up from astern.

We transferred our allegiance to her but, when half way home, lost her in a fog. Soon afterwards, however, we heard the fog signal of the North Goodwin Light Vessel. Having found this we were able to pass through the Downs by hopping from buoy to buoy – for all the world like a drunken man staggering from one lamp-post to another.

We reached Dover at 5 a.m. on June 4 and while the Frenchmen were waiting to land, I went down and practised my somewhat rusty French on them. They were in surprisingly good spirits and appreciated my feeble jokes about the compara-tive comfort of *Sabre* and [the famous French liner] *Normandie*. As one of them put it: *"N'importe. On arrive"*; "No matter. One arrives."

Private Sidney Leach was also among those who arrived, though his diary does not make clear on what date. He had not had an easy time in France and the same was true of his return journey across the Channel:

We reached the pier, about 4 a.m., and as we were walking up it, a shell burst right in front of us. Some French soldiers put a railway line across the gap and we proceeded on our way once more. The enemy had our range by now and the shells were pouring into us. Piles of French dead were stacked on the pier, which was about three miles long. I was practically asleep on my feet, but a chap at the back of me kept pushing me along, or I should never have made it. About 6 a.m. we boarded a minesweeper, and put out to sea. We had not got far when a bomb or a shell hit our stern. We made for the boats and boarded another minesweeper and started for home. Planes followed us about halfway, continually bombing and machine-gunning us, but we made it. We landed at Ramsgate at 10 a.m., and were we glad! England at last, and home.

Gunner Mace and his comrades also made it back to England, despite his fears during their final night on shore that their chances of doing so were fading:

The grey, misty dawn found us still far from any boat. The number of men was amazing. A few bombs were dropped about dawn but still the expected mass of planes did not come. Nolton and I decided to wait until that evening and then put our private plan into execution. Many of our regiment were together, well back in the long file. I wondered how soon the Germans would appear. Some system was working, so many men at a time went past on to the Mole and so aboard; the others waited calmly and without panic. Then Sergeant-Major Spilling told us to come forward and we went up to the head of the file – a pretty good moment. Then another long wait, with several false starts and then, at about nine o'clock, it was my turn. We went through on to the Mole, snatched a drink of water from a can the sailors had, and ran towards the destroyer, the *Wolsey*. She was already casting off as I sprang aboard. We raced clear of the Mole and were away, full speed, for some three hours. We were lucky, for we were not attacked, though we ran suddenly into a minefield. I, Dawson and Cullen sat together, but I was restless and soon walked about, talking to people and, oddly, enjoying the trip. Then I fell asleep suddenly and woke with Dawson shouting in my ear, "Dover".

Second-Lieutenant Strother Smith's party were fortunate in that they virtually went straight from beach to rescue vessel without the usual agonizing wait:

On we trudged in single file until we were on the boat. The sailors were great and what I thought was typical was the way they helped us on. We had to climb on to some planks. They told us to jump clear and they would catch us, so from the middle of the planks I jumped and the weight of my kit crumpled me up on the ground, but before I had landed a second I was pulled to my feet and pushed on my way with a few encouraging words from the sailors who had caught me.

I was shown downstairs and in a few minutes after having a drink, I was in a bath and then asleep on the bed in one of the two cabins. The ship was a converted passenger boat, armed with two or three guns. They shook the boat from stem to stern when they fired. I never knew exactly what went on, but we were on the boat 12 hours from about 4.00 p.m. on the Tuesday afternoon. Apparently we brought down one Messerschmitt and in the early morning we hit something but there was no alarm.

At about 5.30 [on Wednesday May 29] we were landed and the nightmare was over. A train took us to Aldershot where we were encamped. The same evening I went down to the hospital where I was detained as I was suffering from complete exhaustion and had collapsed.

Lieutenant-General Osborne also made it back home safely, counting himself most fortunate to do so:

About 5 p.m. I got a message to say I would be relieved by a Brig. of 2 Div. later on. I then fixed for relief of my doctors and later when Kelso came in and said he was relieved I sent him up. At the time we were passing up a lot more parties and the beach was clearing. The Mole was being shelled but mostly overs and shorts. When all was fixed I collected all my assistants, went to the Café Jouval and brought out Dowse and Barratt. We walked to the Mole. There were three destroyers in. As we went up the Mole we were straddled by shells but no harm. On board, Dowse, Barratt and I went to the Skipper's cabin where his steward gave us coffee and sandwiches. About 8 a.m. we got into Dover. My divisional HQ had not been bombed but, of course, at Dunkirk we never found each other. Was very thankful when they gradually reported from various places. Also Crawford and Joyce. We really hit a very lucky day. All the other days there was much more bombing and trouble generally. Nearly everybody had wading or swimming episodes. I was very lucky.

Commander Dean was later to learn that HMS *Sabre* had made more crossings than any other ship, even omitting an abortive one when she had to return empty-handed. Even so, the 5,000 troops that she brought back were but a minute proportion of the total number lifted. And so much was owed, he felt, to the smaller vessels – the several hundred "little ships", which *The Times* would describe as "such an armada as can scarcely have been assembled for war since the Crusades," and which had made so splendid a contribution:

> While the naval ships were responsible for a large proportion of this total and the cross-channel steamers – with their huge carrying capacity – probably for more, a great number owe their safety to that great band of amateur sailors who responded so magnificently to the call for volunteers, lending their services and, in only too many cases, giving their lives. Our little friend in the bowler hat was but typical of thousands. When, shortly afterwards, the list of awards was published, one wondered how many whose names were not even known had done things far more deserving of recognition!

Controversy would continue, however, about the role of the RAF at this time. A Spitfire pilot of 92 Squadron, Tony Bartley, who had himself flown in the skies over France, wrote to his father in India on June 25,

> Dear Pop,
> I'm afraid that the fighter boys are in very bad odour at the moment over the Dunkirk evacuation operations. The BEF have started stories that they never

saw a single fighter the whole time that they were being bombed. The feeling ran very high at one time, and some fighter pilots got roughed up by the army in pub brawls. Well, whatever you may have heard in India, this is the true story as I saw it over Dunkirk and Calais. Fighter Command were at first disinclined to send the Spitfires out of England at all. We are primarily home defence. Anyhow, we went, and at first just as single squadrons (twelve Spitfires). You have had my accounts of how we used to run into 50 and 60 German machines every time we went over there, and fought them until our ammunition ran out. While this battle was going on up at 10,000 feet, the dive bombers, which did the chief damage, were playing havoc down below us. The fact was that they had layers of bombers and fighters, with which twelve Spitfires had to cope. When eventually Fighter Command decided to send over more than one squadron at a time, they forbade us to fly below 15,000 feet.

We were over Dunkirk on the second last day of the evacuation with more than our squadron. We went over in layers between 15,000 and 25,000 feet. Our squadron led the armada. We disobeyed our orders and came down to 9,000 feet where we ran into thirty He 111s, which we drove back, destroying about eighteen of them. However, below us the dive bombers were operating the whole time.

No wonder the soldiers did not see us up at 10,000 feet but little do they realize that we saved them from the "real bombs", 500 pounders carried by the Heinkels. What reasons Fighter Command gave for forbidding us to go below 15,000 feet I don't know.

Perspectives would certainly change later when the RAF became the front line of defence during the Battle of Britain, and meanwhile questions about its role in France simmered rather than came out into the open. The mood of the nation, in any case, was for praise, not blame. On June 5 the BBC broadcast the first in its series of Sunday night "Postscripts", the speaker being well-known Yorkshire novelist and playwright J.B. Priestley. His subject, inevitably, was the homecoming from Dunkirk and he was out to celebrate it. What particularly excited his admiration were those ships which in normal circumstances would have been bent on helping people to enjoy their summer holidays but which had just been engaged in an operation of war undertaken at great risk:

Yes, those *Brighton Belles* and *Brighton Queens* left that innocent foolish world of theirs to sail into the inferno, to defy bombs, shells, magnetic mines, torpedoes, machine-gun fire, to rescue our soldiers. Some of them – alas – will never return. Among those paddle-steamers that'll never return was one that I knew well, for it was the pride of our ferry service to the Isle of Wight, none other than the good ship *Gracie Fields*. I tell you we were proud of the *Gracie Fields*. She was the glittering queen of our local line and instead of taking an hour over her voyage, she used to do it, churning like mad, in forty-five minutes. And now, never again will we board her and go down into her dining saloon for a fine breakfast of bacon and eggs. She has paddled and churned away for ever. But now – look – this little steamer, like all her brave and battered sisters, is immortal. She'll go sailing proudly down the years in the epic of Dunkirk. And our great grandchildren, when they learn how we began this war by snatching glory out of defeat, and then swept on to victory, may also learn how the little holiday steamers made an excursion to hell and came back glorious.

Many of the troops who came back from Dunkirk, however, did so feeling that from their point of view things were far from glorious. Jack Thraves, of the Royal Corps of Signals, North Midland Corps, spoke for countless others when he wrote: "We arrived at Dover, relieved to be home, yet ashamed to have left so much valuable equipment in France and Belgium. We looked a mess, haggard, bearded and scruffy." On the instant, however, the atmosphere changed. "To our surprise we were given a welcome suitable for a victorious army! The WVS* were there on the railway platform at Dover with tea, sandwiches and buns."

It was the normality of the reception that changed the atmosphere for so many. Thirst, fear, exhaustion and the scream of bombs one moment; the next tea, sandwiches and buns being handed out by smiling English ladies. One day during the course of the evacuation William Purcell, the Dover curate, was pushing his bicycle up the East Dockside road, his profession clearly declared by his dog collar, when, as he described it, a "convoy" of troops appeared:

> They were obviously very tired and shocked, but surprisingly cheerful. "Ah, hello vicar. Now we know we're back again. How are you vicar?" And these were the chaps just rescued from the beaches. We're back home again and here's the vicar! Things were normal. Here was the vicar pushing his bike.

Necessarily, individual soldiers responded to their recent ordeal in many, widely different ways, not always with cheerful resignation. Some were clearly traumatised. The future "Brain of Britain", Mrs Irene Thomas, would recall an encounter with a clearly distressed Dunkirk survivor in her part of south London:

> The first time the war seemed really menacing was one day when I met a boy who had been a couple of forms above me at school. He had been picked up from the Dunkirk beaches two days before and was walking down our High Street on his

---

* The Women's Voluntary Service, best defined as angels of mercy and caring throughout the war.

way home. He was a weird sight, his battledress stained with sea-water, old plimsolls instead of boots, no forage cap, and all his kit gone except his knife and fork sticking out of his top pocket. He was still shaking, and stared past me as I chattered on about how good it was to see him and how pleased his parents would be. Maybe it was just as well that I didn't think of offering sympathy, he looked near to tears as it was.

By contrast Driver Bill Collihole of 79 Company Royal Army Service Corps, to judge from a letter written to his sister and brother-in-law on June 3, had come through his ordeal with little physical or psychological injury, although he had spent two anxious days on the beach before getting on a boat, and then had had to wade up to his waist into the sea encumbered with full pack and overcoat:

> I must confess that at one time I felt there was little chance of getting away, but the opportunity came quite unexpectedly and here I am feeling very fit and well and with nothing worse than sore heel – due not to enemy action but to a badly fitting pair of boots which I recently acquired. I certainly never thought we should be back home so quickly but they will doubtless soon send us off again. I can even say I have had a seaside holiday.

He was writing from Bristol, where to go about the city as a returnee from Dunkirk was to experience the sensation of being a national hero:

> Everybody here has given us a hospitable welcome. We ride upon the buses free, and I had no sooner put my foot on the steps of the hall where a BBC concert was being given when somebody put a five shilling ticket in my hand.

So much for the story of Dunkirk: often told, but with so many people involved in so many ways, so well worth repeating. It gave a word, or more than a word, a concept to the language. The "Dunkirk spirit" will continue to be referred to, or evoked, for a long time yet. Popularly it means the snatching of some sort of victory from the jaws of defeat, or more generally the kind of resilience in adversity that confronts what seems to have the makings of a tragedy and turns it into a triumph. In a sense the deliverance of Dunkirk can almost be seen as a modern version of the biblical parting of the Red Sea, with the "righteous" crossing to safety while the "wicked" remained thwarted on the other side. There is surely a hint of such an interpretation in that other, often used, phrase "the miracle of Dunkirk". But in its original context it was, to use a phrase famously applied to a battle fought not far from Dunkirk, Waterloo, by the man who won it, Wellington, "a damn near run thing". It might so easily have gone the other way. This was history on a knife edge. Yet it was so tempting to see the event, as J.B. Priestley did, in glowing terms. Another who took the same view was the then Poet Laureate, John Masefield, who published a brief euphoric account of Operation "Dynamo" in 1941 under the title *The Nine Days Wonder.* "Knowing some of the difficulties," he wrote, "I should say that the operation was the greatest thing this nation has ever done." In the circumstances of the time, maybe; in relation to a country with the great, if chequered, reputation of Britain, absurd. One man who immediately put Dunkirk into rigorous perspective was Winston Churchill himself, speaking in the House of Commons on June 4, the day on which the last British ship to leave Dunkirk sailed home. As well as praising the positive achievements of so many involved, he also emphasized the other side: the 30,000 of the Army killed, wounded and missing, the agony of the bereaved, the anxiety of those uncertain as to their relatives' or friends' fate. Above all he warned: "We must be very careful not to assign to this deliverance the attributes of a victory. Wars are not won by evacuations."

CHAPTER FOUR

"If Necessary, Alone"

I F EVER THERE WAS A KEYNOTE SPEECH in modern times, it was surely that just discussed. It was almost as full of what would become memorable quotations as Shakespeare's *Hamlet*. This is the source of the famous promise: "We shall fight on the beaches, we shall fight on the landing grounds, we shall fight in the fields and in the streets, we shall fight in the hills; we shall never surrender". But a few sentences earlier, at the start of the peroration, he said something that was perhaps even more significant:

> I have, myself, full confidence that if all do their duty, if nothing is neglected, and if the best arrangements are made, as they are being made, we shall prove ourselves once again able to defend our island home, to ride out the storm of war, and to outlive the menace of tyranny, if necessary for years, *if necessary alone* (author's italics).

That sense of being "alone", curiously, would become for most British a matter of relief, almost of satisfaction, even strength, rather than a cause for anxiety. Earlier in the year King George VI had expressed himself as "very worried over the general situation, as everything we do or try to do appears to be wrong, and gets us nowhere". Now he was more cheerful, as he noted with something approaching relish: "Personally, I feel happier now that we have no allies to be polite to and to pamper". In a cartoon by David Low, entitled *Very Well, Alone*, showing a defiant British Tommy staring out across a wild and stormy sea – as much a brilliantly appropriate metaphor as a symbol of the actual English Channel – the word became a virtual battle cry. British xenophobia, much criticized in more peaceful times, was suddenly granted legitimacy. The other teams were out of the frame; now Britain was in the final (though it should not be forgotten that she had a strong supporters' club in the countries of the Empire, already armed and committed to come to her aid). It is small wonder that later that summer a film went into production which took its title from the famous speech of John of Gaunt from Shakespeare's *Richard II* and which celebrated:

> "This precious stone set in a silver sea
> Which serves it in the office of a wall
> Or as a moat defensive to itself
> Against the envy of less happier lands:
> This blessed plot, this earth, this realm, this England."

By the time *This England* reached the cinema screens in 1941 the immediate danger was past, but it evoked powerfully the spirit of the nation, and not just that of England, as the British people found themselves standing alone.

But there was another side to that miracle all too easily ignored. When describing to his audience of Wrens in 1942 his first trip to Dunkirk, in which he and his crew reached the beaches to find them oddly quiet, Commander Cyril Ross made this important comment:

> Let me remind you why it was quiet; because the Rifle Brigade and Royal Marines and a few others at Calais were holding up two German armoured divisions; because Vice Admiral Abrial was organizing the French troops defending Dunkirk itself; because the Guards were fighting back step by step to the sea, and lastly because the RAF, which we in our ignorance blamed because we couldn't see it, was fighting the Germans on their own aerodromes and did so till it had lost 25 per cent of its own aircraft.

While Dunkirk became the icon of the unexpected success, Calais became the largely forgotten symbol of the sacrifice of a relative few to allow the safe departure of the many. Poor Calais rarely rates a mention in Second World War histories; effectively it is the Third Division story as opposed to the Premier League saga of Dunkirk. Similarly, on June 1 six battalions of the BEF holding the Bergues-Furnes Canal faced the impossible odds of being confronted by four German divisions. The fact that Captain Harold Ervine-Andrews won a Victoria Cross during this unequal encounter does not disguise the fact that the men who fought there were basically, perhaps inevitably, sacrificial decoys. The famous "few" of 1940 are of course the pilots of the Battle of Britain, but earlier there were those others, in khaki this time, not air force blue, who held the line as long as they could with little prospect of escape. In the cruel game of war, they were pawns to be sacrificed, doomed either to be killed or captured. One of the latter was Sergeant Stephen Houthakker (the name was of South African origin) of the 1st Queen Victoria Rifles, King's Royal Rifle Corps, captured at Calais. Repatriated in 1943 he would write what he called a "private and confidential report" on his experiences as a prisoner of war, which began with the following terse description of his capture:

> On Sunday May 26 I became a captive of the German Army and, in company with several members of HQ Company, was marched off to a concentration area for prisoners of war. At this place in Calais, overlooking the English Channel, I found several of my regiment who had suffered the same fate and, like myself, they were all in an exhausted condition. The commanding officer, Lieutenant-Colonel Ellison McArtney, joined us later, accompanied by a number of other regimental officers.
>
> An hour before dusk we got an order to march. Hundreds of weary, thirsty and

hungry British soldiers, too worn and too exhausted to realize the drama that was being played, rose and, with bowed heads, started on what for many was the march to Germany.

We trudged along, our eyes nearly closing for want of sleep and food. All through what had been our lines of defence but a few hours previously, seeing our brave dead, lying mutilated across their weapons, some not dead, crying out for water. The Germans would not allow us to tend them, and it was with heavy hearts that we left them behind. The destruction exceeded all possible conception all through Calais. Hundreds of trucks and mechanical vehicles of all descriptions piled high with Bren guns, parts of tanks, debris and rubble from devastated houses, presented a nightmare panorama to our already overtaxed bodies.

Slowly, as darkness fell, the scenes of our struggle against the German divisions were left behind, and in the cool of the evening, amidst death-like quiet, we found ourselves on the open road to Guines. We arrived at this town in complete darkness and, for the first time for close on a week, I lay my head on the cobble-stones of the churchyard and slept the sleep of one who was completely oblivious to his surroundings. What pleasure was that sleep! Dreams of pleasant days that seemed centuries ago. Thus ended my first day of captivity, but the dawn of horrors was only just starting. Little did we realize what fate had in store for us.

At daybreak the Germans started. The horrible words "Raus, raus" ("Get moving") were heard for the first time. These same words were to haunt us for three and a half years. Without food or water, the slightly sleep-refreshed column, now thousands strong, as we had been joined by numerous French, plodded on.

Attempts at evacuation were not confined to Dunkirk. Further west, from Brest, Cherbourg and St Nazaire, the dispirited troops made their way home, though the enemy had no intention of allowing them an easy or safe passage. A particularly horrific event occurred on June 17, one so distressing that Churchill ordered that all news of it should be suppressed.

The days before had been one long series of disasters. On June 10 Italy entered the war, with the British responding the next day with a token bombing raid. On June 14 the Germans entered Paris. On June 16 a British offer of union with France – a desperate last-minute gesture by Churchill to steel the courage of a fail-ing ally – was barely considered before it was rejected.* Seeing no alternative the

---

*This proposal produced little support among the British either. The historian and broadcaster Robert Kee, one of a troop of recruits being taught RAF drill on the front at Hastings, would recall that the flight-sergeant training them reacted to the offer with the comment: "Cheer up, lads! You're all going to be effing Frenchmen by midnight!", and then proceeded to rubbish the whole concept with a dismissive "***kin' 'ell!", after which the recruits continued their bashing up and down the front.

embattled French Premier Paul Reynaud resigned and authority passed to the 84-year-old Marshal Pétain, hailed a generation earlier as the "Saviour of Verdun". Hoping to spare his country further suffering he sought an armistice, believing that his status would be respected by Hitler and that their two countries might reach an honourable accommodation. (In fact a long humiliation lay ahead, with France divided and Pétain heading from Vichy a virtual puppet state, while later, after the war, lay the shame of the then 89-year-old soldier being convicted of treason and exiled to an island off the west coast of France from which there would be no return.)

The battle of France had had its lack-lustre aspects, but it also had its moments of brave defiance. Yet guts and determination alone could not hold back the German advance. On Monday June 17, as the French will to fight disintegrated, the last of the British troops still in France attempted to make their exit by way of the Breton port of St Nazaire. Some six thousand of them were crammed into the 17,000-ton troopship *Lancastria*. Being anchored three miles off shore, the soldiers were ferried out to it by a fleet of small boats. For some of them, there was an immediate and surprising touch of luxury. As Sergeant Trevor Williams of the Royal Army Ordnance Corps put it:

> After a short rest we were told that breakfast was ready. What a pleasant surprise was in store for us! We ate, like first-class passengers, at tables with white table-cloths, glasses and jugs of water and were served, yes served, with sausages and mash and coffee. This was grand and we were all much elated, but little did we know of the suffering and privation which were soon to befall us, with death taking its toll of more than half of us.

Their breakfast over, Williams and his comrades attempted to make their way back to the hold to which the "other ranks" had been assigned, to find progress almost impossible owing to the huge crowd on the ship. Nevertheless the boats were still collecting troops from the shore and bringing them to the anchored liner. They were soon to learn that they were in very grave danger:

> Air-raid warning bells rang and within a matter of minutes planes swooped down over the ship. Word went round that the enemy planes were attempting to machine-gun the decks, but that three Spitfires were at hand to protect us. Sporadic raids continued all morning, during which the rattle of machine-gun fire could distinctly be heard and sometimes splashes, made by bombs that had missed their target, could be seen in the sea. Low-lying cumulus clouds undoubtedly aided the marauders and the chances of our fighters bringing them down in combat appeared to be slender.
>
> I was enjoying a long-delayed rest on my improvised bed when, at about

3.30 p.m., the air-raid warning bell suddenly sounded once more. This alarm raised two questions in my mind. Should I take a chance and remain, as most of the others appeared to be doing, completely relaxed in this communal bunk in the bowels of the ship, or should I answer the call and go on top deck? By providence I decided on the latter course. The first wave of enemy planes came over and machine-gunned the deck. Just as an order was being passed round that we were to fetch our rifles and open fire on the planes a second wave of bombers approached and someone shouted "Keep your heads down".

These latter planes bombed with precision. Two bombs, it transpired, scored direct hits on the hatchway and others landed on equally vulnerable parts of the ship. While I was crouched up, keeping my head down, with my eyes closed, there was a terrific explosion nearby and debris started to fall almost at once on to my steel helmet which was on my head. Momentarily, I thought that the ship had been split wide open, and at any moment I expected to feel the sea rising upward. Nothing more happened, however, and, when the crashing noise had subsided, I could see nothing but dense smoke and dust through a red-hot glow. Previously there had been plenty of company around me but now there appeared to be no one near. I moved away towards the clear air. The ship had by now listed considerably and thick volumes of smoke were issuing from the funnel. Everywhere men were abandoning the crippled ship, lifeboats filled to overflowing were quickly being lowered and rafts and lifebelts were hastily thrown into a sea which was gradually being coated with oil.

Rescue boats appeared almost at once from all quarters; lifeboats, schooners, fishing smacks, destroyers and larger vessels. It seemed as though someone with a foreboding of the disaster which was to befall the *Lancastria*, with its glittering prize of over 8,000 fighting men on board, had specially detailed these rescue boats to stand-by.

I was badly burnt about the hands and face and was in no condition to face a test of endurance in the sea but time for action was too short to indulge in any form of self-pity. There was no alternative but to follow the action of others and seek safety in the wide open arms of the sea. I first removed my heavy boots and steel helmet and then tried to lower myself into the sea by means of a rope hanging over the side of the ship, but my hands were unable to grip and I fell about eighty feet into the water. Fortunately, there was a raft nearby and I joined ten other survivors on it. Our greatest fear, at this stage, was of being sucked under by the sinking ship. We therefore kicked out as much as our tired limbs would allow and were soon well clear of the wreck. Not too soon, though, for the *Lancastria* sank within twenty minutes of being bombed. There was still, however, constant danger attending the scene for German planes were always about, hovering overhead under cover of low-lying clouds, swooping down now and again to machine-gun the mass of men in the sea.

Never before have I witnessed such courage and spirit among men under such severe tests. I shall always remember, with pride, as a Britisher, the many instances. More especially, the ship's Bren gunner who was still firing away at the planes even when the *Lancastria* was almost submerged; the last men on the ship immediately before it finally sank who, while waiting to be taken off in due turn by rescue boats, were singing *Roll Out The Barrel*, and a rescued army lieutenant who, although a non-swimmer, on seeing a woman in the sea (one of about a dozen women who were on the *Lancastria*) insisted on jumping in to give any possible assistance.

It was by good fortune that the sea was fairly calm all this time and the sun was hot. Those on my raft were in the water for about two and a half hours before being picked up, and had the conditions been adverse it is extremely doubtful whether we would all have survived. As it was most of us by this time were exhausted through lack of sleep, injuries and exposure and, in fact, one of the men on our raft was unconscious when lifted out of the water.

Williams was ultimately picked up by a lifeboat, transferred to a French schooner and later to a British destroyer, where he was immediately given first aid for his burns by the ship's surgeon and, to counteract the intense cold through exposure, was given a double ration of rum. Next day they reached Plymouth, Williams being taken to the Royal Naval Hospital where he remained under treatment for a month. Compared with the homecoming celebrated away to the east a fortnight before, the arrival of the men of the *Lancastria* made a sorry spectacle:

The survivors undoubtedly presented a pitiful picture to the people of Plymouth when we arrived. Most of us were far from being fully dressed and many were barefooted. The matron, when enquiring where our boots were, was told "In the Bay of Biscay!".

While I was in hospital I learnt that, of the six thousand passengers on the *Lancastria*, less than three thousand were saved. It was one of the major single disasters of the war, and, for security reasons, the news of it was not released to the public until six weeks later.

War is a brutal task-master and it has to be said that a prime reason why the *Lancastria* disaster did not make the headlines on June 18, 1940 was that Churchill was planning a major speech – possibly the most important speech of the year – for that very day. The coincidence of events was cruel, but there was no avoiding the imperatives of the situation. The speech had to go ahead. It was broadcast on the BBC that evening. It ended with a peroration which has rung down the years and given an unforgettable title to the dangerous period lying immediately ahead. Sad as it might seem, it would have been impossible to cloud this *Henry V*-type

A famous image of 1940: massed troops on the beach at Dunkirk awaiting rescue.

The Dunkirk evacuation: exhausted troops on the deck of a ship heading for home.

A different kind of evacuation: children leaving for
safe areas because of the fear of invasion, summer 1940.

The real "Dad's Army": a sergeant of the Home Guard quietly preparing to give any invader a run for his money.

"Saucepans for Spitfires": one of many mountains of aluminium
accumulated in response to Lord Beaverbrook's famous appeal of July 10.

The Operations Room of No 11 group Fighter Command at Uxbridge,
as it was in 1940; a reminder of the key role of women in the Battle of Britain.

Menace in the sky: a formation of
Heinkel He-111 German bombers.

Draughts between dog-fights. RAF flyers, kitted up and ready, relaxing between sorties.

Confronting the menace: a flight of Spitfires Mark 1a, July.
Richard Hillary praised "the clear-cut beauty, the wicked simplicity of their lines".

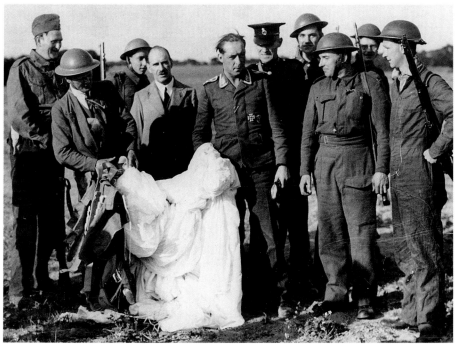

A German airman shot down in an air battle over the south-east coast
photographed by his captors, August. On the whole captured airmen were well treated.

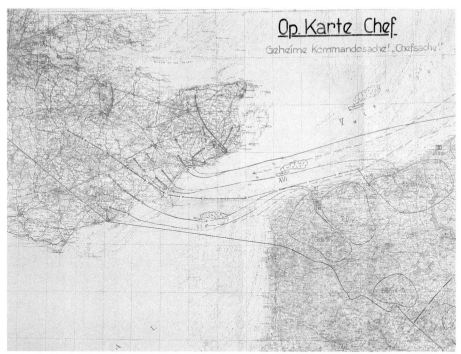

Operation "Sealion": the invasion that never was:
"Secret: for the Chief's [i.e. Hitler's] eyes only."

Map prepared for the German naval high command showing the development of German
army units in France and Belgium, the area in which the troops were to land in southern
England and the scope of the initial objectives of the forces involved in the invasion
planned for the late summer of 1940 under the code-name Operation "Sealion".

Scene on the Thames during the first mass air raid on London, September 7, showing fierce fires raging in the areas of the London docks.

The Battle of Britain as a test match: a London newspaper seller chalks up the latest score.

A London barber's response to the challenges of the Blitz.

The result of a night raid, October 14. Balham station
in the background; in the foreground, a London
Transport 88 Bus almost engulfed in a bomb crater.

Soldier guarding the wreckage of a Messerschmitt 109 shot down near the Channel coast, October 25.

utterance with the tragic news of the *Lancastria*. Referring to France's last
Commander-in-Chief before her capitulation, he said:

> What General Weygand called the Battle of France is over. I expect that the Battle
> of Britain is about to begin. Upon this battle depends the survival of Christian
> civilisation. Upon it depends our British life and the long continuity of our insti-
> tutions and our Empire. The whole fury and might of the enemy must very soon
> be turned on us. Hitler knows that he will have to break us in this island or lose
> the war. If we can stand up to him, all Europe may be free and the life of the world
> may move forward into broad, sunlit uplands. But if we fail, then the whole world,
> including the United States, including all that we have known and cared for, will
> sink into the abyss of a new Dark Age, made more sinister, and perhaps more
> protracted, by the lights of perverted science. Let us therefore brace ourselves to
> our duties, and so bear ourselves that, if the British Empire and its Commonwealth
> last for a thousand years, men will still say, "This was their finest hour".

So the first tragic stage of the drama was over. The inevitable next question was:
would Hitler attempt to crown his success by launching his forces, now holding the
coast of Denmark, Holland, Belgium and France, across the English Channel? That
possibility would hang in the air for many weeks, and would dominate the climate
of much of 1940. The fear of it would never quite go away. William the Conqueror
had achieved it in – what was that year that no-one in Britain could ever be allowed
to forget? ah yes, – 1066. The Spanish had had pretensions in 1588 when their task-
force, the "Spanish Armada", had sailed grandly up the Channel, to be decimated by
the fireships of Gravelines or lashed on to the rocks by the storms of the Scottish
coast. Napoleon had glowered across the Channel in 1804; a tradition of that year
even had him visiting in person Lulworth Cove in Dorset with a view to assessing
the feasibility of a landing in that mid-Western county. But in the end his ambitions
had failed disastrously and the only British territory he set foot on was the prison
island of St Helena. Would Adolf Hitler succeed when such predecessors had failed?

For the moment there was no question that he was in the ascendant. On June
22, in a brilliantly dramatic gesture intended to cause maximum humiliation, Hitler
forced the French to sign the instruments of surrender in the railway coach at
Compiègne where Germany had agreed to the Armistice terms of November 11,
1918. Where Marshal Foch had reluctantly allowed a photographer to take a
single group picture of the Allied delegates outside the coach, Hitler gave the
event full "media" coverage with cameras inside and outside the coach and with
himself playing a brief but starring role. The story went round the cinemas of the
world, making France's shame complete.

It is worth noting the countervailing protest of two defiant voices, one French, one British. The first was to become instantly famous and to affect the future of Europe for many years to come; the other was considerably less resonant, but highly typical of the British reaction to the hammer blows of 1940. Four days before the surrender was signed, on the same day as Churchill's "Finest Hour" speech, a former junior minister of the French government, who had also played an honourable part as a fighting soldier in the recent campaign, one Brigadier-General Charles de Gaulle, as he had now become, broadcast from London to the citizens of France, effectively claiming for himself the leadership of his people and vowing that France would fight on. And on Sunday July 2, as Britain drew its breath and waited for the next shock, a Member of Parliament, Mr George Hicks, speaking in the postscript to the BBC nine o' clock news, stated, "I have never yet asked a favour from the Führer – I hope he is listening. It is this: 'Will you please preserve that railway coach – we shall want it again.'"

As if in echo of such sentiments, just four days later a letter in *The Daily Telegraph* made the following remarkable comment:

> Sir.
> To prophecy for 2,000 years ahead is difficult – or it may be too easy. But I venture this: round about AD 3940, when the history of these times shall have become classical, the word "British" will be a synonym, just as "Spartan" is today. It will be equivalent to "unconquerable".

Such sentiments in the circumstances could seem almost absurd, and the request for the ultimate return of the Compiègne coach the veriest pipe dream. In fact, the railway coach would not be required again. Taken to Germany it would eventually be destroyed, during the RAF raids of November 1943. There would indeed be a surrender, but of a very different kind. When the instruments of humiliation were duly signed, the Führer who had preened himself at Compiègne would not be present to face the final music. Instead, he would already have withdrawn from the scene by killing himself in his bunker beneath the Chancellery amid the ruins of devastated Berlin.

Some weeks earlier, on May 22, before Dunkirk and the fall of France, Churchill's Minister of Information, Mr Alfred Duff Cooper, had broadcast to the nation. This was the kernel of the message:

> The news is grave. There is no pretending it is not. But there is no cause for serious alarm, still less for panic… Meanwhile it is the old story – sudden advances,

unexpected weight of the attack, initial gains far greater than expected – it is the story of August, 1914, of March, 1918, and let us hope that it will have the same ending.

As we know, the "old story" had a very different ending. But the basic doctrine, as expounded in that broadcast, held: "No cause for alarm. No panic". In an extraordinary way, Britain seems to have taken to heart the reassurance of that and similar messages. Thus behind the shock headlines, there was a mass of minor events, incidents, efforts, initiatives that were to become as essential a part of the "Spitfire Summer" as the battles on land or the fighting in the air. It was almost as though Britain was determined to carry on in the summer of 1940 as though nothing extraordinary was taking place. On Saturday June 8, for example, the Cup Final took place at Wembley. The BBC broadcast a commentary by Raymond Glendenning on its Home Service. Admittedly, it was called the "Football League War Cup Final", but in essence it was a championship final like any other. The two competing sides were West Ham and Blackburn Rovers and the victory went to West Ham by a single goal. What the game lacked in finesse, apparently, it made up in commitment. One newspaper reporter commented: "If the standard of play fell a little below expectation, the 45,000 crowd…were compensated by the fierceness of the fight". This was reported on page seven of the newspaper; on page one the headlines reported a more lethal kind of fierceness:

FIERCEST ONSLAUGHT BY THE GERMANS
1,500, 000 Men Flung in Offensive
Ground Won At Cost of Terrific Losses
Non-Stop Raids by RAF on Enemy Lines

The reference was to the fighting still going on at that time in France, where one of the main centres of action was the Somme, a name that would have permanent resonance in the British psyche from the earlier war. Meanwhile, on the same day as the Cup Final, G.O. "Gubby" Allen, famous cricketer and one-time English captain, took nine wickets for 28 runs at a match between the Eton Ramblers and the Forty Club at Lords. Cricket would continue, if in a limited way, throughout the summer. Thus Eton would beat Harrow at Lords on July 15, while that debonair batsman *par excellence* Denis Compton, also at Lords – the Oval had been taken over for war purposes – would score 100 in seventy minutes on August 19. By this time larger headlines would be claiming a different kind of score: thus on August 12 *The Daily Telegraph* reported 65 German Planes shot down, noting that Spitfires had been particularly impressive in the actions which had produced so encouraging a result.

Inevitably there were voices of dissent. The BBC's *Radio Times* for the week of the cup final, and of The Oaks, still being run if in "the unfamiliar surroundings of Newbury" printed the following letter by a Mr John Wilkins of Beaconsfield, Bucks:

> I beseech you to cease broadcasting races and sports news at this very grave time. While thousands are dying at the front we are asked to listen to news about dogs and horse racing and all kinds of matches – shame, shame, shame.

The BBC was perhaps happier to air Mr Wilkins' protest because the same edition carried the following paragraph in its regular feature *Both Sides Of The Microphone*:

> Have you noticed how radio has responded to the intensification of the nation's war effort? Almost every day seems to bring a broadcast that makes vivid a new phase of the struggle. Look at the programmes in this issue and you will find *Works Canteen* on Sunday, *Balloon Barrage* on Monday, *North Sea Trawlers* on Wednesday, *Marching On* on Friday; with a tribute to our French Allies in the second *Home Front In France* on Wednesday night.

Effectively, the mix of serious and lighthearted continued. Indeed, clearly conscious of the varied reactions of its listeners, the *Radio Times* of June 21 tackled the subject head on, with an article entitled *Radio in Wartime: should it be GRAVE OR GAY?* It ended with this forthright statement:

> Do not forget that the words "entertainment", "amusing", and "frivolous" mean different things to different people. There are some listeners to whom a Beethoven sonata is the best form of entertainment, though the ordinary man might not agree. At the other end of the scale are the people who think that everything but jazz and theatre organs is highbrow and dull. Then there are listeners who think that in time of war religious services and war news are the only things that ought to be heard on the air. The BBC cannot cater for all of them all the time. It has to try its hardest to please most of them most of the time.

The determination to carry on with a deliberate bow towardss normality affected the theatres too. Though some of them had initially closed because of the crisis, they soon began to flourish again. By late July Marie Tempest was playing in Dodie Smith's sentimental family drama *Dear Octopus*, while Shakespeare's *A Midsummer Night's Dream* was entertaining open-air audiences in London's Regents Park.

It was about this time that a Madrid newspaper commented: "No foreigner could but marvel at the tranquillity, self confidence, self assurance of the British people at times like these".

All this did not mean, however, that Britain, ostrich-like, was putting her head into the sand. On the contrary she was preparing, with energy, enthusiasm and gusto, to defend herself.

On May 14, Churchill's new Secretary of State for War, Mr Anthony Eden, made an important broadcast on the BBC. Its purpose was to announce the creation of a new force to be called the Local Defence Volunteers. This was to be, he told his listeners, "a part-time job, so there will be no need for any volunteer to abandon his present occupation… When on duty you will form part of the armed forces… You will not be paid, but you will receive a uniform and you will be armed…" Within twenty-four hours, a quarter of a million men had enlisted. The spirit of the country that had risen to the challenge of the Spanish Armada and Napoleon was ready to rise against the threat posed by Hitler.

The proposed new force instantly became known as the "L.D.V." – and as rapidly the initials were translated to mean "Look, Duck and Vanish". Within weeks, Churchill would rename it the "Home Guard" and thus it would remain, eventually, to be immortalized in the public mind as *Dad's Army*. But the original name, reluctantly abandoned by Eden and many of the first recruits, was not forgotten. Some wits even suggested that the Home Guard should adopt the catchphrase: "We'll give 'em L., D.V." – i.e. "We'll give them hell, God willing" – as its motto. Before that the relatively advanced age of some volunteers produced the following newspaper report on June 10, which stated: "A number of ex-servicemen, including majors and captains, have joined the L.D.V. They are known as 'Long Dentured Veterans'." At the other end of the age scale, many teenagers also flocked to the designated places of recruitment.

The account by an Essex volunteer, L.F. Edwards, only seventeen in 1940, convincingly evokes the atmosphere of these heady times. Local newspaper announcements stated that those interested in joining should assemble in the Moot Hall, Colchester, on certain evenings according to their electoral wards:

> I went to volunteer on a fine sunny evening. I found the hall crowded with men, mostly middle-aged ex-soldiers from the 1914–1918 war. Several of the older men present had also served in the South African War of 1899–1902. Various official-looking persons were seated at a table and were asking questions regarding experience and were taking names and addresses. Nearly all the men could refer to experience in one war or another. I implied that because my grandfather managed a farm I had fired a shot-gun; a lie actually, but I had read the theory of holding and firing a rifle. (I had actually taught myself to swim in this way.) I later heard that I had been selected to act as a "despatch rider" as I had a bike.
>
> I was asked to report to the Drill Hall in Stanwell Street one evening. There was a scene of great activity as the Colchester Battalion was being organized under a

retired officer, Major-General Kirkpatrick. A number of us lads were put in a group to learn drill and we were instructed by an ex-NCO in the arts of standing to attention, at ease, turning and marching. On a later evening we were instructed in arms drill.

Weapons were extremely scarce, but there was a store of Martini-Henry carbines in the Drill Hall. None were fit to fire and there was no ammunition anyway. It was with these weapons, 1871 model for cavalry, that we were taught arms drill and the correct way to sight a rifle.

The first uniform was an armlet, coloured khaki, which bore the letters LDV in black. Within a few weeks we received uniforms of khaki denim battle dress. These were really army fatigue or working dress. We had also a forage, or side, hat made of khaki serge. The first weapons distributed to us capable of being fired were long, heavy Canadian Ross rifles of .303 calibre. They had a straight pull back bolt and a safety catch on the bolt handle. The magazine held five rounds and the bayonet was a short sword type.

Summoned one mid-summer evening for his first real rifle-practice, Edwards was looking forward eagerly to demonstrating his abilities:

We reported to a 25-yard range, which was at Reed Hall just behind Gujerat Barracks and near the old garrison fire station. We fired Pattern 1914 rifles of .303 calibre which had been made but not issued during the 1914–1918 war. When my turn came to fire I lay down, resting my forearm on a sandbag and sighted at the very small bull. Mr. H.O. Cousins, the former Borough Treasurer and a well-known Bisley shot, spotted my shots with binoculars. I fired. "Miss," said he. I fired again. "Another miss," Mr Cousins reported scornfully. Five times I fired and five misses were reported. Disconsolately, I went to retrieve my target at the end of the detail. I reached it. There, crammed together in the black, semicircular bull were five shots. The best shooting of the evening! "Good shootin' boy," said Mr Cousins.

The force's name change, marked by the distribution of a piece of khaki drill cloth printed with the words "Home Guard", seemed to speed up the process of preparing for war. Soon steel helmets appeared, together with army boots and a haversack of khaki drill cloth, which could be worn slung across the shoulder or on the back as a small pack; it was usually worn as a small pack. They had no ammunition pouches but carried ammunition in a cotton bandolier. Gradually, these amateur soldiers from a wide mix of backgrounds and generations came to feel themselves more like the real thing:

At first, my post in the event of a German invasion was at a concrete strong point, or pill box, at the end of Spring Lane, Lexden, just where it joined the by-pass road. The Home Guard officer in charge was a Captain Potter who wore the ribbon of the Military Cross and the three 1914–1918 ribbons. I remember him and all the other men with great affection. I suppose most were about 40–50 years old. They were very determined and intensely patriotic. They would have resisted the Germans to the last. I know we wouldn't have stopped them, but each Home Guard post would have delayed them and enabled the Regular Army to counter attack.

Exercises were undertaken with the greatest seriousness and it was not long before they were being trained in the use of small-scale but nevertheless serious weapons:

We did section training in Lexden Park, then owed by Mr Percy Sanders, the Mayor. We learned to use [some] American weapons and the improvised ones invented in England, such as the sticky bomb (an anti-tank bomb which had to be stuck on the side of a tank by hand – a suicide weapon if ever there was one), the Blacker Bombard, the Spigot Gun, both kinds of horizontal mortars and the simple "Molotov cocktail", which was a bottle full of yellow inflammable liquid, which, when it hit a tank, burst into flame.

Another early teenage volunteer was H.A.J. (Tony) Stiebel, later to serve as a tank commander in Italy but who in 1940 was a schoolboy at Beaumont near Windsor:

Everyone over 16 at Beaumont volunteered and, having an OTC [Officers' Training Corps], we were rather envied as we had .303 rifles, our cadet uniforms and an organisation. Many units of the LDV literally had their own clothes with an armband and pitchforks. Initially, we did guard duties on the slope of Priest's Hill behind the school with vague orders to look out for parachutists. Quite what would have happened if we saw one we luckily never found out.

Beaumont Home Guard platoon had the honour to be in the Crown Lands Battalion and to wear the Grenadier Guards badge as we were so near to Windsor Castle that we came under the general plan for the defence of that key installation. Most Home Guards were controlled by their county authorities and wore the badges of their county regiments. Eton envied our status because being in Bucks they wore the Buckinghamshire Battalion badge. One weekend we had a big exercise with the Parachute Regiment dropping in Windsor Great Park and advancing on the Castle. For we boys this was as near the real thing as we could imagine. Officers of various units were referees and one went up to the company commander of The King's Company of the Grenadiers and asked if they had been captured. The reply was "The King's Company is never captured," which put him down a bit!

Young as he was, Tony Stiebel and another young volunteer – as it happened, from the despised Buckinghamshire Battalion – were shortly to prove their worth and show a courage remarkable for their age, though this was at the later Blitz stage of the Spitfire Summer. In the Home Guard's early months, however, the inexperience of the new recruits could lead to bizarre situations. Thus *The Daily Telegraph* report of July 15 carried the following story.

An LDV man in a lonely spot cried "Halt" to a man in a car, who promptly halted. "Halt," said the LDV man again. "I have halted," said the motorist. "'What do you want me to do next?'" "I don't know," said the LDV man, "my orders are to say 'Halt' three times and then shoot."

There were more serious events when volunteers actually did shoot, with tragic consequences. In late June a motorist was shot and killed in Gloucestershire. Earlier in the month in the same county a lady ARP warden had been shot because she did not heed, or rather because of a slight deafness did not hear, an LDV order. Later in the summer even Battle of Britain heroes were not safe. On August 16 Flight Lieutenant James Nicolson, the only Battle of Britain VC, having bailed out of his burning Hurricane near Southampton after a dog-fight with a group of German Messerschmitt fighters and already suffering from serious burns, was shot at and wounded by some LDVs who had assumed he was a German paratrooper – though in fairness it should be added that this reaction might have been triggered by an over-eager officer of the Royal Artillery. A pilot officer who jumped at the same time was hit and killed. There were attempts to restrain the gung-ho attitude of some volunteers, but it was inevitable that such zeal would have its aberrations.

One early unofficial name for the new volunteers – not surprisingly in view of the incident just described – was "parashots". The meaning was clear: should German parachutists, or paratroops, invade, British parashots would attack them. There was a kind of grammatical tidiness, even alliteration, in the two related terms: "you parachute; I parashot". Unfortunately, there had been so many tales of enemy parachutists landing in disguise across the Channel that some members of the community began to feel distinctly nervous. *Picture Post* carried the following letter by a correspondent from Colchester, in its edition of June 1, under the heading "Close Season for Bishops":

> May I make a plea for sanity in this problem of paratroops and parashots? Ever since the Germans were reported to have dropped paratroops disguised as clergymen on Holland, respect for the cloth has in some parts of the countryside given way to odium and suspicion. Parsons are eyed narrowly in lanes and stalked over fields by sportsmen with rook rifles. A rural incumbent of my acquaintance, who is in the habit of cycling round his parish, feels that he is nearer to martyrdom than any Christian since the days of Nero – and this in a district where he is known. Imagination shrinks from the probable fate of a visiting bishop. Rustic

intuition would at least diagnose his hat as a portable wireless transmitter and blow his head off.

Challenges difficult to accede to also worried the magazine's readers at this time. Its edition of June 22 published a letter by a reader living in London W.1, under the title "Dark Encounter":

It is right that sentries should be posted at vital road junctions and outside depots. It is proper that civilians should be stopped and challenged. It is, however, alarming on a dark wet night, to be halted so that the point of a bayonet is resting on the bottom button of your waistcoat, and then be told, "Advance, friend, to be recognized". Yet this happened to me. Had I obeyed blindly, I would surely have been impaled. But I exercised my initiative, I live to serve my country, and write this letter. There is a moral here.

Other related subjects troubled the magazine's readers. Thus, for example, a resident of Derby, writing in the edition of June 8, raised the matter of the status of those who would command the various elements of the new force. Would they be (in cricketing terms) old-fashioned gentlemen or new-style professional players? *Picture Post*'s sub-editors titled the letter "Your Bird, Sir George":

The British are a sporting race with an amateur tradition, but that does not mean that it would be disgraceful for us to use professional help. The parashots are being put into the hands of the squirearchy and septuagenarians in many districts. There is a danger that some of these people might be inclined to visualize a Nazi invasion as a sort of sporting afternoon, potting paratroops from the butts with a gamekeeper to load for them, and the butler bringing up the lunchbasket at noon. One admires the spirit of these gentlemen, while advocating that the "Players" might put up a better show.

This letter drew a spirited response a correspondent in Caversham, Reading, in the edition of June 22, under the heading "Tally-Ho":

Writing under the title, "Your Bird, Sir George" (June 8), your correspondent, B.J.Greene, is pleased to be facetious about the service which country gentlemen are giving to the LDV. He appears to be afraid that the joy of combating paratroops might be undertaken in a sporting spirit. And why not? There is no finer spirit, and sportsmen have no scruples about destroying vermin. These men know the lie of the land, and the only alternative would be to employ a gang of poachers. I, for one, would like to see some of our famous hunts suitably armed against invaders.

Earlier, *Picture Post* had started a weekly course in French, to show solidarity with Britain's key continental partners. That solidarity, which, alas, was all too soon to evaporate in the wake of coming events, had produced back in the middle of May the following letter by a reader in London NW11, under the title *"Entente"*:

> As I was walking through Trafalgar Square, I was struck with the thought that it would be courteous to our great allies if we changed the name of the square and also that of Waterloo Station. Hardly had the thought entered my mind when I saw a French Staff Officer walking down Whitehall. He appeared to me to be looking up questioningly at Nelson's Column. I felt overwhelmed with embarrassment and longed to leap forward to speak for the nation. I cannot talk French, yet felt an urge to do something, and so sprang to attention and saluted smartly although I was in civilian clothes. The officer halted. Our eyes met and a look of understanding seemed to come into his. He returned my salute and, with a charming smile, passed on.

By June 1, however, the magazine's instant French course was being treated with tongue-in-cheek mockery by one reader, who affected to see it as providing a potential "linguistic defence" against an invader. A resident of Regent's Park Road, London, wrote:

> Your "Ready French" (May 18), with its directions for pronunciation, have caused a fearful epidemic of grimacing in our family, what with pushing our faces this way and that. In the event of Nazi paratroopers landing in Regent's Park, we shall go out in a body and talk French at them. To hear us talking the language of our allies would bewilder them, and the faces we pull should do the rest.

This kind of off-beat, light-hearted response to what was undoubtedly a genuine hostile threat would not be without its parallels when the struggle came closer to home later in the year. Thus Reverend Lynn Ashley, an officiating chaplain of the RAF attached to the Kidlington base near Oxford, could write of the early autumn of 1940, when the invasion scare was still not entirely discounted:

> I was cycling round the airfield, when at one point on the perimeter I saw at some distance what seemed to be a defence post, manned by a man with a Bren gun. Closer to I saw that the "man and gun" was in fact a plywood cut-out. Back at headquarters I commented to the staff-sergeant in charge of the Orderly Room, "Not much of a defence if the Germans landed!" "Don't you worry, Padre," he said, "we have a secret weapon. On the word of alarm our clerks here will march out with fountain pens at the ready – and with forms for the Germans to fill in. That will keep them busy till the Army comes."

All this did not mean that the defenders of the realm did not take their task seriously. The LDVs of Maidenhead, Berkshire, for example, took themselves very seriously indeed. George Ward, a schoolboy evacuated late in 1939 from St Stephen's School, Paddington, London, was drawn into the unit's activities. For him it was all part of a strangely exciting new life, or, to quote his own words, "a big adventure".

> I was billeted with an elderly couple at a house in All Saints Road, joining a fellow pupil of my school; we were both twelve years old. The excitement of being in a new and interesting country environment, with the bonus of being at war, made it very acceptable for a boy of my age. School at this time was limited to alternate mornings one week, afternoons the next, sharing the building with the local children.
>
> In 1940, I joined the Boy Scouts, and we were busily engaged with the collection of waste and sometimes, I think now, quite valuable paper and books, etc., for recycling. This we did with a "Trek Cart", going to the many affluent houses in the Pinkneys Green area. I suspect much valuable reading-matter was lost to our heritage at this time.
>
> I remember the crisis of Dunkirk, with Winston Churchill's "fight on the beaches" broadcast, and the call for volunteers to join the LDV, shortly to be renamed the Home Guard. One of our teachers, a Mr Crocker, formed a mounted platoon. They would often be seen exercising on the Thicket.

Maidenhead Thicket, a small forest of ancient trees to the north of the present M4, is well noted now for the speed with which cars progress along the former London-Bath Road, that famous highway along which coaches once proceeded at their best pace while coachman and postilions looked out anxiously for the sudden appearance of a highwayman or footpad. In 1940, the anticipated dangers were of a different kind, though the area offered its pleasures, and its possible dangers, too:

> The Thicket at that time was more extensive than it is now. I spent many happy hours there both with school walks and in my leisure time. Our headmaster warned us of the probability of German parachute troops invading, and told us that in this event we should hide in the dense bracken. We were very reluctant regarding this as there were large colonies of adders on the Thicket. Though the Home Guard now are regarded with some derision, I am sure they would have acquitted themselves quite well had they been called upon.

George Ward's reminiscences also touch on a very important part of the culture of 1940, which, while it had much time for optimism and high spirits, could also produce an almost irrational fear with regard to strangers, or anyone whose name might suggest, however remotely, an "alien" origin. Thus he commented: "My

Father at this time became quite paranoid regarding the 'Sir' I was billeted with, as he was of German ancestry – Crumplin or Krumplin. Dad thought he could be a spy. In fact, he was very much on our side."

For many foreigners living in Britain, especially those with some contact, whether close or distant, with the countries of the enemy, there was an all too easy assumption that they were "not on our side".

The Spanish Civil War had added a graphic concept to the language that was now in constant use; at the siege of Madrid in 1936 General Mola had ominously stated that there were four columns outside the city and a fifth one inside it. In Britain in 1940 everybody was on the lookout for such traitors. The terms "Fifth Column" and "Fifth Columnist" became two of the year's key phrases; as well as the obvious enemy without, there clearly had to be an enemy within. The situation was not helped by an important precaution which came into force at this time with a view to causing confusion and dismay to the enemy in case of invasion: the removal of all road direction signs. Even milestones surviving from the coaching age could be cemented over. At the same time there was much overpainting of the names of the nation's railway stations; the signs stayed, but being all in white they could not, or at any rate not easily, be read. This could leave the train traveller uncertain as to whether he had reached his destination or the stranger in his car or on foot baffled as to his whereabouts, and thus with no alternative, whether his intentions were honourable or not, but to ask the way. There was an all too easy assumption that any stranger who did not know where he was must be an enemy, a member of the dreaded Fifth Column. A letter in *The Daily Telegraph* of July 9 sounded a note of caution:

> Some people think it their duty to refuse information to those who ask the way… Unity of feeling…will be impaired if suspicion is allowed to corrode the natural instinct of the Englishman to treat everybody in a neighbourly spirit. All the Fifth Columnists in the country cannot do as much harm as would be done by any general tendency to regard strangers as probable foes and traitors.

But such voices were very much against the prevailing wind. Already in 1939 there had been a rounding up of aliens who were deemed to be potential enemies, either by virtue of their country of origin or merely the un-British sound of their name. This had happened in the First World War and it was almost automatic that it would happen again in the Second, the assumption being that such people might well be pro-enemy, or that if they were not it was nevertheless better to put them behind barbed wire just to be on the safe side. The crisis of 1940 produced a further substantial crop of arrests. In mid-May, three thousand so-called aliens were interned in a nation-wide round-up, two thousand of them refugees from the horrors of a turbulent Europe. Four hundred were seized in Liverpool, and a similar number in Glasgow. The entry of Italy into the war instantly put another nationality under suspicion. Countless shopkeepers, businessmen, chefs, waiters and restaurant staff of Italian origin were seized as a result, many of whom had been resident in Britain for years.

The Cabinet attempted a less than entirely blunt-edged reaction to the situation, aware that too hasty a combing-out process might entail much unfairness, but the Prime Minister would have none of it. "Collar the lot!" was his impatient, if in the circumstances of a national crisis, understandable reaction. Almost inevitably it was widely assumed and reported that many of the aliens combed out in this purge were thought to be potential members of the Fifth Column. This was particularly tragic in the case of people who had fled for genuine reasons from one tyranny, only to find themselves victims of another, in a country which they had seen as a sanctuary and which they had long admired for its decency and fairness. For some this was too much. There were a number of suicides, to add a distinct if often overlooked shadow to Britain's generally honourable reputation at this time. One inmate of an internment camp wrote of two comrades who had succumbed: "The two men who had succeeded in committing suicide had already been in Hitler's concentration camps. Against these they held out, but this camp has broken their spirit." Not that such camps compared with Dachau or Buchenwald in terms of conditions; it was the sheer fact of yet again being behind walls or barbed wire that produced the tragic outcome.

Another internee who would also fail to survive the summer of 1940 was a young Berlin-born German Jew, Friedel Sittner. His father was a Berlin pharmacist who had been decorated by the German government in the First World War. Sittner had left Germany in the 1930s in the hope of trying to persuade the US Food and Drug Administration to permit the marketing in America of a rejuvenation drug patented by his father. In the event he got no further than England, where he managed to support himself by teaching German and, as more and more of his background, racial origin and political persuasion fled the continent, helping with refugee work.

Before the outbreak of war he had found his way to Loughborough, Leicestershire, where he was befriended by a kindly Christian couple, Mr and Mrs Albert Priestley, who took him under their wing. He was arrested in the first wave of internment in 1939 and dispatched to a camp at Paignton, Devon. His story emerges from a clutch of letters and other material retained by the Priestley family in the wake of his untimely death. One particularly moving relic is a copy of E.M. Forster's novel *Howards End*, which he gave to Mrs Priestley, his special friend and champion, later that year. It bears the inscription:

Grateful for knowing you
When there was peace for us
And now in the darkest moment of all
And in days to come
Were it not for you I might sink
And I will not forget.
F.S. to M.P
R.44102
No 24 Internment Camp
Wednesday, Nov 15, 1939

The letters, all to Mrs Priestley and dating from June 1940, were written in a minuscule hand on the special paper allowed to internees – the smallness of the writing dictated by his wish to cram as much as possible into the limited space allowed. They suggest an intelligent, sensitive mind getting near the end of its tether. Thus, on June 6:

My Dear Mrs Priestley,
Thank you for your letters of May 21 and 22. On Sunday I will conduct the Jewish Service of Intercession, like every other Jewish community in England (we are not many – ten out of fifty) we will pray for the Allied cause, and in my own heart I will pray that the day may not be too far when logical reasoning takes again the place of instinctive and prejudicial thinking…

They have now taken the wireless from us and we may have no papers. We were also told that walks in the future would be made in the company of fully armed escort and we declared unanimously not to be interested. Today, huts were searched. We may no longer send special letters to solicitors, they are now counted among the few private letters we are allowed per week.

Evidently, Mrs Priestley had intended to visit him in the camp, but had then become anxious as to how in the present climate such a gesture might be interpreted. This caused Sittner much distress, tempered by a concern not to offend the person whom he saw as his best hope and support:

So you are afraid they may think you are a member of the "Fifth Column", because your friendship "may easily be misunderstood" and believe nothing will get me out. You feel you have done right not to come last week and the town council passed a resolution that all "enemy aliens" be interned – I don't know what to say or to think or to do… You are honest and put things down as they come into your head…in writing it looks so cruel. I am not very diplomatic, [but] I would say nothing which might annoy you, for I need you and if you are cross you may not come. Shall I make a last appeal for you to come? …I often wonder if the last blow to all my hopes and all that makes life endurable will come from you…

If you do visit do you think you might arrange to bring the typewriter and lots of carbon paper as well? This change from mental talk to material requests must seem funny – perhaps detestable – to you. Am I to hope for Wednesday? Perhaps visits are no longer possible, who knows?

In a letter postmarked June 19 he told her that he had found an echo to his situation in the writings of a noted hero of the previous war, at that time just five years dead, who had himself gone through many periods of travail and depression:

I have just read the letters of T.E. Lawrence ("of Arabia"). Do we both feel like this? "You wonder what I am doing? Well, so do I, in truth. Days seem to dawn, suns to shine, evenings to follow and then I sleep. What I have done, what I am doing, what I am going to do, puzzle and bewilder me. Have you ever been a leaf and fallen from your tree in autumn and been really puzzled about it? That's the feeling."

Somebody has written a poem about the gates opening one day, and freedom and no hatred when the war is over. We all cheered wildly. Sometimes I feel as though this is not life, but I a figure in a novel, reading it at the same time and wondering whether the end will be happy.

Friedel Sittner's last letter to Mrs Priestley was written on June 24, by which time he had been moved to a camp at Huyton, near Liverpool. Daringly, he addressed his correspondent as "My Dear May" adding "Please, dear, don't be shocked that I call you so. I never dared when I was free, not in my correspondence. If you think it's too familiar or presumptuous tell me. I only want you to know you are my best friend."

He sensed that this might be his last chance of seeing Mrs Priestley. Like many other aliens he might be sent to the Isle of Man or there might be other even more punitive possibilities:

Tuesdays and Fridays are visiting days, but if you can manage only Sundays say so, an application should be made to the commandant in any case. It may be better to come by rail. You must know that I have constantly asked myself since Easter why you had not come and if you were reconciled to the idea not to see me again. Never have I appealed to anyone to come to me as I did to you – you will remember the letters. There may be bombs. If you feel you should not take the risk I will not grumble. If I go away without seeing you, you know what this will mean to me but then, whatever the end of it all, I would be quieter in the knowledge I tried to do what little I could. I have often wondered what I should do and how, if I were you. I feel there are many things which I ought to know to understand every reaction of yours so well as I used to – and vice versa – but instead I trust you blindly and in the end always agree. Perhaps it will please you to know I had one or two indications that had my case come up earlier release would have been likely, but all this is academic now. If the story should end in tragedy it would well fit in with those moments of depression and nightmares I've always had. I wrote a letter to my parents on the last day of my stay in Paignton, telling them how well I was treated and that we must all be brave, etc., they must not know what happens if happen it does. You have always been so kind to me and your temperament appealed to what was best in me. I so wish I could find the proper words to thank you for it all and to help you over these dark days and the sunless ones to come. It is a pet idea of mine that you should adopt a little boy. Will you do so if the worst comes to the worst? If nothing else perhaps we will learn to pray. I'll bless you and all you are doing.

Kindest regards.
    Ever yours,
        F Sittner

On June 30, just six days after sending this letter, 712 Italian and 478 German internees, Sittner among them, were embarked for Canada on the Blue Star cruise liner, SS *Arandora Star*; there were also 374 British soldiers on board. The ship sailed from Liverpool at 4 am on July 1. At 7am the next day she was torpedoed off the coast of Donegal by the German U-boat U-47, commanded by Gunther Prien, who had been fêted in Germany for sinking the battleship HMS *Royal Oak* in Scapa Flow in the preceding October. For such a crew and captain the SS *Arandora Star* was an easy target. Two thirds of the Italians aboard her, about one third of the Germans, forty-two of her crew and thirty-seven soldiers were lost. The survivors, picked up by a Canadian destroyer, were landed at Greenock on July 3. Sittner was not among them. By way of a sad footnote to an already sad story it has to be recorded that both Sittner's parents perished in Germany as victims of Hitler's "final solution" of the Jewish problem.

A happier footnote is that the Priestleys did adopt a son, a young evacuee from a broken family who came to Loughborough and found a new life there; it was he who many years later, following his adoptive parents' deaths, offered the Sittner papers for preservation, including his late mother's precious copy of *Howards End*.

An internee of Italian-Jewish origin who narrowly escaped Sittner's fate was a BBC employee named Uberto Limentani, arrested immediately after Italy came into the war despite impeccable anti-Fascist credentials. The corporation made strenuous representations for his release, and an order to that effect was obtained some days before the *Arandora Star* was due to sail. Unfortunately, Limentani could not be traced, and the next his colleagues heard of him was when his name appeared upon a list of Italian casualties following the ship's sinking. A reader who told the story to *The Times* added: "I should have thought that the fact that he was employed by the BBC was sufficient to show that he was a friendly alien. Fortunately, some three weeks later Mr Limentani reappeared from the dead, having been rescued and in a Scottish hospital suffering from shock." The letter, printed in the edition of August 12, indicated that the order for Limentani's release had finally been acted upon.

A second case reported by the same reader was that of a Mr G. Cantoni, a young man who had been studying in Oxford as a research student. He made up his mind to emigrate to the United States with his elderly mother and his sister:

> The party was stopped at Liverpool the day Italy entered the war – I believe they were actually on the boat – and Mr Cantoni was interned. For some time now nothing has been heard of him, and his mother has been informed by a friend that he has been sent to Australia. In this case all the papers for the United States, including British exit permits, were in order and the Italian Department at Bloomsbury House was applying for his release to proceed there. It will now be necessary to communicate with Australia before this can be done.

The unnamed reader added, clearly in some anger:

> Both these men were Italian Jews, who were unable to carry on their professions in Italy owing to the laws of September, 1938. Their feelings towards the government that persecuted them can well be imagined, and one of them was playing a part in the war effort of this country.

If Cantoni was by then in Australia, he presumably travelled there on the SS *Dunera*, on which he would have endured what has been described as "a nightmare two-month voyage". The *Dunera* herself was dubbed "a prison ship" – 2,550 deportees sailed on her in appallingly overcrowded conditions, with the hatches battened down for weeks at a time and the portholes closed throughout the whole voyage.

It is good to report that, in its August 1 edition, *The Times* offered one modest silver lining to this otherwise grim saga, under the heading "A Hero of the *Arandora Star*":

> It is now disclosed that Brevet Major C.A. Bethell, whose death in the *Arandora Star* was announced in *The Times* yesterday, gave his lifebelt to one of the internees as the ship was sinking, walked on to the bridge and went down with the liner alongside the captain. "It was the finest thing I have ever seen," one survivor said.

Major Bethell was the officer commanding the military guard in charge of the Italians and Germans who were being taken to Canada.

For many internees there was a much shorter voyage: to the Isle of Man. The island had been used to house aliens in the earlier war and was an automatic choice for the same function in the second. Ultimately, no fewer than six camps were opened there. It was the Isle of Man that was to produce perhaps the best "happy ending" among the numerous stories that emerged out of this often forgotten aspect of a world conflict. Three of the four musicians who were to form the Amadeus String Quartet met there: Norbert Brainin, Sigmund Nissel and Peter Schidloff, all of them born in Vienna in the early 1920s but only brought together by the accident of internment. Later, after their release – for though "enemy aliens" they were recognized as "friendly" ones – they took up various jobs in support of the war effort in London, where they were also able to take an active part in the capital's musical life. Here they met a sympathetic cellist, Martin Lovett, and together formed what has been generally recognized as one of the world's greatest chamber-music ensembles, which would only cease its activity on the death of one of its founder members, Peter Schidloff, in 1983.

CHAPTER FIVE

"Go To It"

"**G**O TO IT" became one of the great rallying cries of 1940. It was first voiced by the Minister of Supply, Herbert Morrison, on 22 May and in early June it gave the title to a series of important programmes on the BBC Home service, in the opening edition of which Morrison himself addressed the nation. The future war-reporter Robert Reid, in an article in *Radio Times*, hailed the venture as Morrison's "stirring radio call to the workers of the country to put their last ounce of energy into the struggle".The series ran fortnightly until early September. In the final edition Morrison would appear again at the microphone to urge the nation to continue its efforts with a second slogan: "Keep at it".

This was no mere routine exercise. One of the Corporation's best and most innovative producers, D.G. Bridson, was appointed general editor of the series, and he and his team of producers set zealously to work, tackling such subjects in the programme as the manufacture of tanks, aircraft and heavy armaments and the building of ships. Nor was this done by sitting in offices and studios in Broadcasting House, as Reid indicated:

> Bridson has travelled over 2,500 miles and has visited dozens of factories in search of material. One souvenir of the series he carried about with him for a day or two was a scar on his forehead – a souvenir obtained during a tour in a particularly frisky tank before Bridson had had time to acquire his "tank legs" or whatever the landship equivalent to sea legs may be.

The basic idea was that the workers of Britain would tell their story to the nation, "not for the novelty of appearing before a microphone, nor for a broadcast fee, but because they were proud of the job they and their pals were doing". Above all what the series attempted to do was to bring out the underlying drama of what Reid described as "the greatest arms drive ever":

> What could be more dramatic and farther removed from normal peacetime industrial life than the story told, for instance, by a young girl fuse-maker from a factory in the North? The girl told listeners that her sweetheart is a rear gunner in a bomber. One day during a fight with fifteen German planes he discovered that he was firing shells made in the factory in which his sweetheart works. "I feel I am making fuses for him now" was her comment.

Inevitably, for all its high purpose, the "Go to it" campaign put the slogan instantly into general phraseology, making it liable to creative interpretation in the most unlikely contexts. Thus on August 3 *The Times* reported that one John Thomas Heywood, a Brixton van driver, summoned at Horsham for speeding, admitted to the policeman who stopped him that he was "shoving it along", but explained that Mr Herbert Morrison had urged everyone in Great Britain to "Go to it", and he was doing his best to carry that out. His plea clearly failed to move the examining magistrate. Heywood, who was transporting food supplies, was fine £1.

A more obvious use occurred in the correspondence columns of the same newspaper in September when a resident of London W14, clearly an animal lover, raised the matter of providing sanctuary for the nation's favourite pets. He saw this as a task to be undertaken by the Home Secretary, Sir John Anderson, whose name had already been assigned by its inventor, William Patterson, to the build-it-yourself corrugated iron air-raid shelter to be found in countless thousands of British gardens. *The Times*'s letters editor headed his contribution "Job for Sir John":

> After all the un-British talk of killing our dogs after the Nazi model I was over-joyed to read that Hyde Park and Kensington Gardens are giving a lead to the nation by the construction of air raid shelters for animals. There is a lesson here for the ordinary dog-loving householder. Beside each Anderson shelter (which is in essence nothing more than a human kennel), there should be a sandbagged and earth-covered kennel. Here is a job for Sir John Anderson. Tell him to "Go to it".

"Go to it" was one of the key phrases of the time, backed up by its later variant "Keep at it". "Stay put" was another. It was one of the basic instructions to the British people in case of invasion. This apparently contradictory combination of exhortations would produce an amused tongue-in-cheek response by a London reader in a late August edition of *Picture Post* in a one-sentence letter published under the heading "Quandary".

> How can we stay put and go to it?

It was indeed a quandary, but one to be lived with nevertheless. June saw the printing and distribution of an important document of the Spitfire summer, published by the Ministry of Information in co-operation with the War Office and the Ministry of Home Security. In it the "Stay put" message came clearly across, but there was no suggestion that the only reaction to a German invasion was to be a passive one. There would be much to be done. It was headed in large print "If the

INVADER comes" and the following were its opening paragraphs, clearly much influenced by the refugee problem which had so bedevilled the recent fighting across the Channel:

> The Germans threaten to invade Great Britain. If they do so they will be driven out by our Navy, our Army and our Air Force. Yet the ordinary men and women of the civilian population will also have their part to play. Hitler's invasions of Poland, Holland and Belgium were greatly helped by the fact that the civilian population was taken by surprise. They did not know what to do when the moment came. You must not be taken by surprise. This leaflet tells you what general line you should take. More detailed instructions will be given you when the danger comes nearer. Meanwhile, read these instructions carefully and be prepared to carry them out.
>
> When Holland and Belgium were invaded, the civilian population fled from their homes. They crowded on the roads, in cars, in carts, on bicycles and on foot, and so helped the enemy by preventing their own armies from advancing against the invaders. You must not allow that to happen here. Your first rule, therefore, is:
>
> 1) IF THE GERMANS COME, BY PARACHUTE, AEROPLANE OR SHIP, YOU MUST REMAIN WHERE YOU ARE. THE ORDER IS "STAY PUT".
>
> If the Commander in Chief decides that the place where you live must be evacuated, he will tell you when and how to leave. Until you receive such orders you must remain where you are. If you run away, you will be exposed to far greater danger because you will be machine-gunned from the air as were civilians in Holland and Belgium, and you will also block the roads by which our own armies will advance to turn the Germans out.
>
> There is another method which the Germans adopt in their invasion. They make use of the civilian population in order to create confusion and panic. They spread false rumours and issue false instructions. In order to prevent this, you should obey the second rule, which is as follows:
>
> 2) DO NOT BELIEVE RUMOURS AND DO NOT SPREAD THEM. WHEN YOU RECEIVE AN ORDER, MAKE QUITE SURE THAT IT IS A TRUE ORDER AND NOT A FAKED ORDER. MOST OF YOU KNOW YOUR POLICEMEN AND YOUR A.R.P. WARDENS BY SIGHT, YOU CAN TRUST THEM. IF YOU KEEP YOUR HEADS, YOU CAN ALSO TELL WHETHER A MILITARY OFFICER IS REALLY BRITISH OR ONLY PRETENDING TO BE SO. IF IN DOUBT ASK THE POLICEMAN OR THE A.R.P. WARDEN. USE YOUR COMMON SENSE.

Altogether six "rules" were spelt out in the document. As well as those already quoted, there was advice as to what to do if members of the public saw anything suspicious: "Keep watch… Do not rush about spreading vague rumours"; how to cope with parachutists, "Do not give any German anything. Do not tell him anything. Hide your food and your bicycles. Hide your maps…"; how to help the military, "Do not block roads until ordered to do so by the military or LDV. authorities"; how to make sensible preparations in factories and shops, "All managers and workmen should organize some system now by which a sudden attack can be resisted"; and there was one rule more:

> Remember always that the best defence of Great Britain is the courage of her men and women. Here is your seventh rule:
> 7) THINK BEFORE YOU ACT. BUT THINK ALWAYS OF YOUR COUNTRY BEFORE YOU THINK OF YOURSELF.

It was all stirring stuff and clearly not just the product of some lowly civil servant. There have in fact been rival claimants for its authorship. Sir Kenneth Clark, Director of the National Gallery (and later to be well-known to television audiences as "Lord Clark of Civilisation") was one. Another was Harold Nicolson, MP, a junior member of the Government, long famous as a diarist, letter-writer and broadcaster. If that were the case, there is an extra interest in the fact that about this time, on May 26, Nicolson was writing from London to his wife, Vita Sackville-West, expressing himself as deeply concerned about the future. Their country home, historic in its own right and additionally famous for its superbly designed garden, was Sissinghurst Castle, Kent, and Nicolson and his wife were likely to be high on any German black list:

> The government may decide to evacuate Kent and Sussex of all civilians. If, as I hope, they give orders instead of advice, then those orders will be either "Go" or "Stay". If the former, then you know what to do. If the latter, we are faced with a grave predicament. I do not think that even if the Germans occupied Sissinghurst they would harm you in spite of the horrified dislike they feel for me. But to be quite sure you are not put to humiliation I think you really ought to have a "bare bodkin" handy so that you can take your quietus when necessary. I shall have one also.

His wife, he knew, would understand precisely what he meant. In the most famous of the soliloquies of Shakespeare's *Hamlet*, "To be, or not to be", the Danish prince muses whether there is any point in a man confronted by "a sea of troubles", or plagued by "the whips and scorns of time", continuing to put up with such hazards: "When he himself might his quietus make/with a bare bodkin".

A "bodkin", an archaic word now, is a short dagger or alternatively a blunt needle. In brief, Nicolson was proposing that he and his wife should each equip themselves with the means of suicide. He was not, he added, "in the least afraid of such sudden and honourable death. What I dread is being tortured and humiliated… I shall ask my doctor friends. I think it will be a relief to feel, 'Well, if the worst comes to the worst there are always those two little pills.'"

Another person of note – though his comet-like fame was yet to come – whose mind was firmly concentrated by the new "If the INVADER comes" policy was the future Spitfire pilot Richard Hillary. In his book *The Last Enemy* he would write:

> The government's appeal to the people to stay put and not to evacuate, printed on the page of every newspaper, roused England to the imminence of disaster. It could actually happen. England's green and pleasant land might at any moment wake to the noise of thundering tanks, to the sight of an army dropping from the skies and the realization that it was too late.

One other means of stiffening the sinews of the nation, and attempting to make the population aware of, but not dismayed by, the gravity of the situation, was to use the most popular mass medium of the time, the cinema. A propaganda film aimed at achieving that result appeared in July, under the title *Britain At Bay*. It was meant to be one of a series of five-minute films to be inserted into cinema programmes almost (as we might now describe it) as a kind of commercial, a party political broadcast on behalf of the nation; an item long enough to catch the audience's attention, not so long as to anger it by getting in the way of what most of it had come for, the often escapist main feature. As it happened, this film exceeded its proposed norm; it ran for eight minutes.

It came with the best of credentials. It was produced by the illustrious GPO Film Unit, now best known for its later masterpiece, *Night Mail*, and was written and narrated by J.B. Priestley. In it arcadian vistas of an idealized Britain were contrasted with *blitzkrieg* scenes from the recent fighting in France, while the message pressed home emphasized the nation's crucial role in the present crisis: "The future of the whole civilized world rests on the defence of Britain ... Britain must become an impregnable citadel of free people." Scenes of soldiers on guard accompanied Priestley's voice quoting Churchill's famous lines about fighting on the beaches, on the landing grounds, etc.

For some, however, the film clearly had precisely the opposite effect from that intended. An anguished citizen of Gosport, Hampshire, wrote to the editor of *Picture Post*, dismayed especially at the film's title:

> The moment the title was flashed on the screed I thought, "Good Lord, is it as bad as that?" I do not know what definition is given to the term "at bay" in the Oxford Dictionary, but of the two dictionaries that I possess the first gives: "In a position of defence, in great straits, at the last extremity"; and the second, "said of hunted animals surrounded by dogs and unable to escape". It struck me as strange that use should be made of this term when there are so many alternatives. In these days words cannot be chosen with too much care.

Presumably the correspondent would have been happier with the title of the American version, distributed "perhaps more wisely" (to quote Clive Coultass. the author of the work from which most of the above evidence is quoted) as *Britain On Guard.*

The concept of *Britain On Guard* would have certainly appealed to young Brian Poole, just seventeen and therefore old enough to join his father in the Cheshire Home Guard. Far from being uneasy at the nation's plight, he was looking forward to whatever might happen with the greatest excitement. Writing to a female pen friend in America, and gleefully playing the card of a hero in danger while his correspondent slept safe beyond the steep Atlantic, he told her, clearly with the greatest relish, and an undoubted desire to shock:

> I am practising bomb throwing every night now. We are to fight guerrilla warfare and will be taught how to kill a sentry without making any noise and such as that. Oh boy, what fun!

There were many ways in which the people of Britain could help the war effort other than by the taking up of arms or working in shipyards or factories. One was by attacking the enemy indirectly by supplying the materials out of which the necessary weapons of war could be made. On July 10 the nation's newspapers carried a message to the women of Britain from the Minister of Aircraft Production, the masterful and energetic Lord Beaverbrook, barely two months into his job but already a formidable power in the land. It was entitled "Appeal for Aluminium":

> We want aluminum and we want it now. New and old, of every type and description, and all of it. We will turn your pots and pans into Spitfires and Hurricanes, Blenheims and Wellingtons. Everyone who has pots and pans, kettles, vacuum cleaners, hat pegs, coat hangers, shoe trees, bathroom fittings and household ornaments, cigarette boxes, or any other articles made wholly or in part of aluminum, should hand them over at once to the local headquarters of the Women's Voluntary Services…

The response was immediate and enthusiastic. The War Office alone offered 500 tons of saucepans. Countless thousands of families, from the humble and ordinary to the highest and most noble in the land, not excluding the Royals, cheerfully stripped their cupboards and kitchens. The appeal also produced one of the most delightful poems to emerge out of the national emergency, by Elsie Cawser, from Staffordshire, who spent her war as a dairy laboratory worker and helping in voluntary organizations. She called it *Salvage Song (or: The Housewife's Dream)*:

My saucepans have all been surrendered,
The teapot is gone from the hob,
The colander's leaving the cabbage
For a very much different job.
So now, when I hear on the wireless
Of Hurricanes showing their mettle,
I see, in a vision before me,
A Dornier being chased by my kettle.

David Low celebrated the same idea in a cartoon showing a lady with her nose in the air striding proudly past two ordinary working-class women, one of whom comments to the other, "It's the stuck-up woman she is since Lord Beaverbrook brought down two Dorniers with her frying-pan".

A parallel initiative led to the nation's railings being removed from parks and private houses. The roar of the oxy-acetylene burner was heard in the land, and lorries lugged their allegedly vital loot away leaving countless low-slung walls looking like gums from which teeth had been untimely wrenched. Visually destructive, the scheme had a genuine psychological advantage. It was helping the war effort; it was spreading the burden of sacrifice, though there was some resentment when, as could happen, the defences remained around the domains of certain people of influence. The present author can recall experiencing a surge of the patriotic spirit when his family's railings were duly removed; surely now Hitler had no chance! He was a little dismayed some considerable time later when passing the area of his northern town managed by the municipal cleansing department to see bonfire-size piles of such railings still apparently awaiting their finest hour.

One other means of concentrating people's minds on the seriousness of the nation's plight had already been given the force of law. The sounding of sirens, factory hooters, whistles and noisy rattles had been forbidden since the previous year, but the pressures of the post-Dunkirk crisis were now to silence what in normal times was perhaps the ultimate symbol of peace and calm. Under the Control of Noise (Defence) Order, which came into effect on June 14, church bells were to be rung only in the event of invasion. On July 15 an unfortunate rector in Lincolnshire, who claimed not to have heard of the regulation, was sentenced to four weeks' imprisonment for "sounding his church bell other than for the purpose authorized".

Suggestions were made to soften the order, one practice proposed being that bells might still be rung as usual for normal occasions, but would be tolled in a jangling manner if the enemy were at the gates. The regulation remained, doubtless causing numerous churchgoers to find a special irony in the verse of the well-known hymn, which read:

Whene'er the sweet church bell
Peals over hill and dell,
May Jesus Christ be praised!

The regulation produced a wry, elegantly expressed word of warning by the poet John Betjeman in a BBC broadcast of September 4:

There have been many changes in our countryside of late. The removal of those hideous tin signs of place-names, for instance, while conversely the rumble of iron-rimmed cartwheels has taken the place of the endless gear-changing of motor cars, now thankfully garaged by petrol rationing.

One particular sound we will miss in the country are church bells: the mellow lin-lan-lone across the hay. And here I would like to put in a word of advice. If any country air raid warden thinks he is going to be able to ring the church bells as a warning of invasion, let him be sure he knows how to handle a bell.

I picture to myself an excited warden running up the belfry stairs, giving a colossal pull at a bell-rope, and finding himself either hauled up to the belfry roof and crashing down unconscious on the floor with his skull cracked open, or else I see him with skin ripped off his hands as the bell rope slides through it, or else I see him hanged by the neck as the rope end coils itself round him!

Bell-ringing is an art, and I wonder how many country wardens have learnt it? As this is not a talk on bell-ringing, and I have not the time to tell you how to ring a church bell, I beg all wardens who contemplate ringing to consult a ringer immediately.

The emergency also forced a rethink of some of the regulations of civilian life already adopted. The blackout had been instituted on September 1, 1939. On the roads this had resulted in a spate of accidents and numerous fatalities. By now people had become accustomed to it, but with the threat of air raids a new culture was required. On August 7 the papers would record the official response to the obvious questions that had been raised: in the event of a raid, car headlights, meagre though they were, were to be extinguished, but side and tail lamps never. But there had clearly been much confusion up to that point. On June 27 a letter written to the press by the actor David Niven from Boodle's Club, London, had raised the question as to what taxi drivers should do in the event of a raid. It was sensible to despatch their clients to the shelters, but was it a good idea to sit outside the shelters with headlights on having done so? Meanwhile, Niven also noted, traffic lights continued to function as usual. As this was a time when it was thought even the glow of a cigarette could be seen by an approaching German raider, Niven's protest was far from being a frivolous one.

Offenders against the black-out regulations rarely reported themselves, but one guilty lady, who had been so absorbed in what she was doing that she had not noticed the passage of time, sent 10 shillings to the Minister for Aircraft Production, Lord Beaverbrook, by way of apology. She told her story to *The Daily Telegraph*, which published her confessional letter on August 1, though she gave only her initials, not her full name or address.

One of the first signs of a possible invasion was an intensification of air activity over the English Channel. In particular, the area of Kent around Dover was being especially targeted, becoming known as "Hellfire Corner" because of the vulnerability to attack of any shipping attempting to make safe passage between the Channel and the North Sea. Clearly the Germans were attempting to claim air mastery and this was a key sector. An early witness of the increasing tension was Signalman Les Mallows of the paddle steamer *Princess Elizabeth*, which had done such excellent service during the Dunkirk evacuation:

> Having lost two of its number at Dunkirk, the 10th Minesweeping Flotilla reassembled with just four paddlers – *Sandown, Medway Queen, Princess Elizabeth, Ryde*. We recommenced sweeping different areas along the South Kent coast – but trouble was brewing.
>
> Now operating from French and Belgian airfields, the Luftwaffe set about neutralizing Dover as a naval base. From the French cliffs, powerful telescopes could pick out shipping movements; sometimes a prowling single bomber would sneak up, drop a stick of bombs and high-tail it back home. But worse could be expected when there was sufficient British shipping around to warrant a whole bomber-group.
>
> I was never more terrified throughout the whole war than on July 12, 1940, (if memory serves). In the late afternoon we finished a sweep near Dungeness and headed back east towards Dover. Passing between the two lightships known as Folkestone Gate we overtook a convoy of some 15 coasters plodding towards the Thames estuary. At the same time – horrors! An approaching westbound convoy of similar size. Just our luck to be in the middle of the whole shebang.
>
> Sure enough a cloud of some 40 black bombers soon loomed over us. These were not dive-bombers; it was "carpet bombing", releasing the sticks in quick succession. It was stomach churning to watch the sea all around us erupting in dozens of waterspouts. But worse still, it seemed to me, was the sheer noise. The loud droning of the bomber formation passing over head, the steady rumble of bombs exploding in water, and the sharp crack of our 12-pounder gun below the

bridge – it was more mind boggling than what the eye was witnessing.

As the first formation cumbersomely wheeled to turn for France, we were utterly dismayed to see another bomber group approaching. At this point I for one began to think solemn thoughts. If I was shortly to meet my Maker – which I felt was increasingly likely – what a pity I was dressed like a pirate. (Dress at sea on small ships was please yourself; come-as-you-are seemed to sum up the situation.)

But thankfully at this dire moment a squadron of our fighters shot out from the Folkestone cliffs – presumably from RAF Hawkinge – and tore into the bombers. We now had a ringside view of a spectacular air battle. In no time planes were falling in flames; and one bomber had been parted from its fuselage, the black wings and engines twizzling into the sea like a sycamore seed. Very soon these two black clouds were disappearing south to safety.

Two days later, on Sunday July 14, the BBC reporter Charles Gardner found himself a surprise witness of a similarly vicious fight between the Luftwaffe and the RAF in the same vicinity. At a time when most broadcasts, apart from sporting ones, were made from prepared scripts, Gardner opted for an instant running commentary. Even as transliterated text, his broadcast – not actually transmitted at the time, but recorded and played shortly after – shows an immediacy and excitement which are standard, even commonplace, now, but then were capable of gripping and galvanizing the audience in what seemed a totally new way:

…Ah! here's one coming down now! There's one coming down in flames! There's somebody's hit a German, and he's coming down. There's a long streak and he's coming down completely out of control – a long streak of smoke. Aah! – the man's baled out by parachute – the pilot's baled out by parachute! He's a Junkers 87 and he's going slap into the sea, and there he goes – SMASH! – a terrific column of water! – and there was a Junkers 87. There's only one man got out by parachute, so presumably there was only a crew of one in it.

Now then – oh, there's a terrific mix-up now over the Channel. It's impossible to tell which are our machines and which are the Germans. There's one definitely down in this battle, and there's a fight going on - you can hear the little rattles of machine-gun bullets.

[CROOMPF] – that was a bomb, as you may imagine. Here comes – there's one Spitfire, there are the little bursts – there's another bomb dropping. The sky is absolutely patterned now with bursts of anti-aircraft fire, and the sea is covered with smoke where the bombs have burst, but as far as I can see there's not one single ship hit, and there is definitely one German machine down, and looking across the sea now I can see the little white dot of parachute as the German pilot is floating down towards the spot where his machine crashed with such a big fountain of water about two minutes ago.

Well, now, everything is peaceful again for the moment. The Germans, who came over in about 20 dive bombers, delivered their attack on the convoy, and I think they've made off as quickly as they came. Oh, yes, I can see one, two, three, four, five, six, seven, eight, nine, ten Germans haring back towards France now for all they can go, and here are our Spitfires coming after them. There's going to be a big fight, I think, out there. You can hear the anti-aircraft batteries still going.

Well, that was a really hot little engagement while it lasted – no damage done except to the Germans, who lost one machine, and the German pilot is still on the end of his parachute, though appreciably nearer the sea than he was. I can see no boat going out to pick him up, so he'll probably have a long swim ashore.

There are about four fighters up there, and I don't know what they're doing – one, two, three, four, five fighters fighting right over our head now. There's one coming right down on the tail of what I think is a Messerschmitt, and I think a Spitfire behind him. There's a dogfight going up there; there are four, five, six machines wheeling and turning round now. Hark at the machine-guns going! – one, two, three, four, five, six – now there's something coming right down on the tail of another.

At this point another voice interposed: "Here they go! They're goin' back home!," then Gardner resumed:

Yes, they're being chased home, and how they're being chased home! There are three Spitfires chasing three Messerschmitts now. Oh, boy! Look at them going! And look how the Messersch… eh! that is really grand! And there's a Spitfire just behind the first two – he'll get them! Ah, yes! Oh, boy! I've never seen anything so good as this! The RAF fighters have really got these boys taped!

The broadcast produced a mixed reaction. There were those who responded with the greatest enthusiasm. Thus, a resident of Woodbridge, Suffolk, wrote to *The Daily Telegraph* on July 17:

Please tell Charles Gardner to do it again. It stirred the blood of millions who heard him. War is much too serious a thing to be taken seriously – ask any fighting man.

But a titled lady, writing from Whitchurch, Hampshire, on the same day took exactly the opposite view:

Bullfights are forbidden in this country. Is then the courage and selfless daring of our sons to be made into a sensational entertainment? Are the dangers of deaths of brave men to be treated like a football match? Mr Gardner's running commentary on an air battle filled me with a sense of shame and revulsion – that their splendour should be so belittled. We need to lift up our standards not to lower them.

It was the start of a debate that would run to the present day. On the whole, however, there were far more in favour of the BBC's response to the war than against it. There were, inevitably, as there always are at any moment of crisis, those for whom there was just too much news, too many bulletins. *The Daily Telegraph's* Peterborough column published this quatrain of protest on July 9:

> A quiet man was Mr Brown,
> A clerk of forty-three,
> But his life was marred by the "blah, blah, blah"
> Of his neighbour's BBC.

For most people, however, and increasingly so as the war continued, listening to the BBC news, especially the evening nine o' clock news, became a necessary ritual. Silence would be mandatory as the strokes of Big Ben pronounced the hour. Before the war the corporation's newsreaders had been anonymous; now they gave their names at the beginning of each bulletin. The reason for this was that it was assumed that there might be attempts by the enemy to cut in on the BBC's frequencies with counterfeit news or misleading instructions. The result was that a handful of well-spoken Englishmen were rapidly transmuted into national heroes; all of them speakers of what the first Director-General of the BBC, Sir John Reith (himself a Scot) termed "educated southern English", alternatively known as "received pronunciation". Listeners felt instantly reassured and at ease when they heard the familiar formula spoken by voices they had come to know and trust: "This is the nine o'clock news and this is Alvar Liddell – or John Snagge, Frank Phillips, Bruce Belfrage, Alan Howland, Joseph McLeod or Frederick Allen – reading it". In the following year an attempt was made to broaden the spectrum by including the Yorkshire actor, Wilfred Pickles, in the team, but his "Good neet" and other northern interpretations were not appreciated – indeed were seen as what would now be condemned as "dumbing down". He withdrew after five controversial months to return to those areas of broadcasting where his northern wit and breezy good humour were rightly celebrated. But the news was a thing apart; it was almost as though the news could be accepted only as true if it were spoken with a whiff of the West End, Oxbridge and the established church.

The letters columns of the *Radio Times* saw much heated debate on the subject of the BBC's announcers, and this went on throughout the summer. A resident of Weston-super-Mare thought them all far too dull, as his letter of May 24, under the heading "Colourful News" made abundantly clear:

> The BBC announces the news several times a day with the enthusiasm and verve
> of a schoolboy reading "The Lays Of Ancient Rome". I suggest that some colour
> should be given to the news. A cheery voice might start "Another good day for the

Navy", or "The RAF are doing it again". The news all through should be alive and appealing, and the people should be shown how to think by listening to the news.

A counter view appeared in the edition of June 7, with the following comment by a York reader:

I admire the imperturbability of the men who announce the news. Every evening I hear a voice say "This is the BBC Home Service – here is the news", and try to guess from its tone whether the news is good or bad. I have never yet succeeded.

A housewife from Birmingham was equally admiring of the announcers' cool, unruffled delivery and the sense of confidence it instilled in the listener:

A word of appreciation to all BBC staff and announcers, who are doing yeoman service in this grave time. Surely, there should be a special Order instituted for them, for I believe they would go on just as calmly as long as the mike would trans-mit, whatever happened.

Responding to what effectively was becoming a cult of celebrity, the BBC eventu-ally published the photographs, with mini-biographies, of its front-line team. This delighted many, but for some listeners it was a step too far. Two disappointed ladies from Essex wrote in protest:

The *Radio Times* has delivered a shattering blow. Why publish photos of your announcers and so disillusion our "mind's eye" pictures to fit the BBC voices over the air?

It is interesting to record that the idea of women announcers reading the news was raised at this time but received little support, the most outspoken objections came from the sex that stood to benefit from the proposal:

I think it would be unbearable in these critical days for a woman to read the news. It is well known that our voices do not carry as men's do; we cannot help that, but the women announcers sound so weak and tired, and at times patronising.

There was no doubt that the vast majority of listeners wanted the clear well-spoken tones of male announcers capable of coping with the highs and the lows of a continually changing national situation. Later in the year a bomb fell on Broadcasting House while the news was being read. That the newsreader, Bruce Belfrage, carried on with only the slightest hesitation surprised no-one. It was part of the expected code of behaviour.

As it happened, Belfrage and another popular newsreader, Alan Howland, were also special constables and when not on duty in Broadcasting House directed traffic in the neighbourhood of Whitehall and Trafalgar Square. Meanwhile the corporation's most senior announcer, the illustrious and much admired Stuart Hibberd, who rarely read the news but was always present for high occasions, was no longer wearing his dinner-jacket when on duty as in pre-war days. The *Radio Times* made a special point of mentioning this, adding, "nowadays he announces either in ordinary clothes or in the uniform of the Home Guard".

The BBC voice had a curious competitor throughout this period: the distinctive quasi upper-class accent of William Joyce, American born of Irish-American extraction, living in Germany and broadcasting from Hamburg as part of the team of the Propaganda Ministry of Hitler's close ally, Dr Joseph Goebbels. His notorious, much imitated call-sign "Germany calling, Germany calling, Germany calling" (though his "Germany" sounded more like "Gairmany") could pull in an audience of six million listeners. His consciously cut-glass tones, and the air of sneering condescension which he adopted, won him the nickname of Lord Haw-Haw. (Strictly, it should be added that, according to BBC records, though he was known as Lord Haw-Haw from September 1939, he was not officially identified as William Joyce until April 1941, when, doubtless with a touch of hubris, he gave the game away himself.) Much of his so-called news – for example his claim that famine was stalking the streets of England in 1940 – was palpably absurd, but he could fascinate and chill his audience by his clear assumption of Teutonic superiority. Curiously, claims for which he became famous, for example, that he knew for a fact that a certain clock in Hull, or Lewisham, was so many minutes slow, have not been substantiated by later research, but then rumour and "disinformation", as it might now be called, had a field-day in wartime. The BBC's five minute talk after the nine o'clock news was a strategic response to Lord Haw-Haw, deliberately aimed at holding the audience where previously people had been tempted to switch across. Joyce, who ironically had a brother working in the BBC's civil engineering department until he joined the Army, was sealing his own death warrant by his pro-German efforts. Never a British citizen he nevertheless had a British passport, issued in 1933, and liked to claim himself to be British until formally becoming a naturalized German in September 1940. Tried for treason after the war, he attempted to save himself by claiming, with justification, American and German citizenship but his British passport secured his conviction and he was hanged in Wandsworth Prison, London, in 1946.

Many, of course, refused to be tempted by Lord Haw-Haw, staying faithful to the BBC – indeed seeing him almost as a satanic figure, a kind of fallen angel, in contrast to his benign opposites in London. To switch elsewhere after the nine o'clock ritual would have carried a whiff of betrayal. The Sunday night bulletin was given an extra odour of sanctity when from October onward it was preceded by the playing of the national anthems of Britain's allies. To begin with the list comprised France, Poland, Norway, Belgium, Holland and Czechoslovakia; though later it became so long – and politically difficult when the Soviet Union became an ally – that the idea was dropped. While it lasted, however, the nine o'clock news could only gain from this ritual. If people were unable to listen, they were eager to hear the latest from those who had. Sometimes, however, this desire to know could fall foul of another mantra of the time: the instruction not to indulge in careless talk. Hence the following letter, published in *The Daily Telegraph* on July 16 under the title "Telling The Enemy":

> Sir.
> The other night in a Devonshire inn I heard the following conversation between two villagers:
>
> A.   Have 'ee heard the nine o'clock news?
> B.   Yes.
> A.   Was there anything in it?
> B.   Can't tell 'ee.
> A.   Why not?
> B.   'Tis giving information away.
>
> Who says we are not a disciplined nation?

In the debate about women broadcasters, performers of a different trade from that of the announcer could also receive short shrift from some writers to the *Radio Times*. Thus a reader from Cheshire, in a letter published in the issue of June 6 under the title "Moo!":

> One suggestion to the new government. Send all women crooners into the new Land Army – their chief job "to call the cows home".

This provoked a stiff reply from a correspondent from Rolvenden, Kent, in the edition of June 28:

> I sincerely trust the government will not permit this. Cows are sensitive creatures, and it is a fact that they give less milk if annoyed or disturbed. The nation needs all the milk it can possibly produce today.

The Women's Land Army might have been the butt of good-humoured badinage in the columns of the *Radio Times*, but the women who belonged to it saw it as offering a genuine and serious challenge. A similar organization had operated, if on a small scale, in the previous war. It was re-formed in June 1939, and by the outbreak of war there had been a thousand volunteers. The crisis of 1940 produced a further surge, many of the women moving to a world of which they had no knowledge and which inevitably had its shocks and problems. Clearly, however, they were keen to show that they could cope as well as anybody else responding to the national emergency.

Grace Chawe was a junior sales girl in London in 1939, who volunteered to help get the harvest in when war was declared. It was not, however, until the summer of 1940 that she received formal instructions, with accompanying railway ticket, to report to Evesham Station, Worcestershire. The following is her brisk account of her first season as a Land Girl:

> We were taken to Charlton Manor, Charlton. Quite a surprise we had. There were about 100 girls: about half came from the North and the rest were southerners. In our room there were eighteen camp beds and bare floors. We had to climb over beds to get to ours. The first few mornings we dressed under our blankets but we soon got used to the lack of privacy. There were no curtains, no electricity, but we were allowed candles. There were only two bathrooms and toilets but plenty of privies in the garden. To get a bath we had to organize: one dashed to get the room; the others the towels. The bath had a huge shower end. The toilet was grand, built for the lady of the house. You walked up steps, the walls were padded silk and the seat all wood.
>
> We had no training: our only orders were not to dress in a manner likely to offend the local people. No short shorts were to be worn, neither were blouses to be skimpy. Evidently previous girls had tried to glamorize their uniforms. We had full uniforms, but were auxiliaries.
>
> Meals were very poor at the manor. Breakfast was porridge and bread and jam. The porridge was made in advance. We saw big earthenware jars full of porridge with a leather-like top. Many girls had intestinal problems. I didn't eat much for two weeks but by then it was eat or starve. We took sandwiches for lunch, prepared the day before. No refrigeration, so bread was dry and meat was often rancid so we threw away the meat. It got so bad a complaint was made to headquarters at the insistence of the local doctor, who had become a regular visitor. Officials came and we got a pep talk, "For our King and Country", but with a promise things would improve. The staff did try so we settled down and got on with the job.
>
> We went to work wherever we were needed. It was all market gardening. Our first week was hand hoeing. We could hardly stand up straight after a few hours but the local women told us to keep bending, "then you will get used to it". That

was our first lesson. Once we worked on a fruit farm. When we finished there we were given a basket of fruit each. These we sent to our families.

We used to gather at the local pub. The local boys would treat the girls. Some of us took part in a film to promote the Land Army. It was hoped it would encourage more girls to join up. Our part in the film was to show what we did after work. It was taken near the pub. I was told it was shown in London as I was asked if it was me in the film.

After the harvest, she returned to her London job, but knew she would have to join up soon, and decided to return to the WLA, first as an auxiliary, and then in 1941 as a regular: "It made no difference whatsoever in pay or status". She eventually became a GI bride, living on a farm and still working in her WLA overalls. Returning to the UK after her husband's death she continued to work on the land until she retired from poultry farming in 1978. She looked back on her rural war with considerable pleasure, despite some of the early problems:

> I enjoyed my life in the Land Army; I was made so welcome by the local people I feel I became one of them. A wealth of experience; I do not think I would ever have got that anywhere else. Perhaps it would have been nice to have got a medal like my brothers, but then my life could not compare with their experiences.

Rosina Davies, the daughter of a Welsh farmer, decided in June 1940 to volunteer for the WLA:

> The representative for the district was certain I could do the work. One friend, however, admired my "pluck", as she put it. She was certain that I would not remain an ordinary working Land Girl for long. I replied, "Have you ever heard of promotion in the WLA?". One just joins as a Land Girl and remains a Land Girl. The only move she is likely to have is from one farm to another, where the farmer might be better or worse than the last.

She was eventually to achieve substantial promotion, even – though not till after 1940 – to become a forewoman in charge of a "mobile gang" of twelve, while later still she became an Assistant Labour Officer, and, together with another WLA representative, was invited to attend a garden party at Buckingham Palace. But that lay far in the future as, on July 8, 1940, having received a postcard bearing her Land Army number, and a telegram asking her to report for one month's training on the following Monday, she travelled to the farm in Wales (not identified in her account) to which she had been assigned, feeling quite confident that she was going to like the work. There were, however, certain hazards and difficulties at first:

The farm was in the centre of a village, so the land was on each side of the village. When I arrived about 3.30 p.m. the family were having tea. I was welcomed, and told that my uniform had not arrived, but would be sent to me as soon as possible. How disappointing – after all, wearing a pair of breeches or dungarees and green pullover was going to be part of the "fun"! There was nothing for it but turn out in a dress.

After tea, I asked for something to do, so from 4.15 on that day my work began. First of all there were pigs to be fed. The "swill" was kept in a large barrel or butt at the far end of the yard. The two buckets seemed nearly as big as me. I was to put meal in the buckets and fill them up with the "swill". On approaching the pigs' sty, I heard the most deafening noise of pigs squealing and grunting. At this early stage I began to wonder what I had let myself in for. How was I going to enter this mad house? Was life ever going to be the same again? It did not seem safe to enter, but I had "signed the form" and therefore had to get on with it. The pigs were so anxious for their food that they kept knocking the buckets and me until half the contents was spilt.

At least the next job was milking by hand, which she had sometimes done at home. She soon began to realize that, being just one on her own, she was something of a sensation in the district:

At this time Land Girls were very few and far between so, needless to say, for the first few weeks I was the centre of attraction by the schoolchildren, as indeed I was with the adults, but the adults were more discreet. The children would stand and look at me open-mouthed, as if this Land Girl dressed in dungarees should be anything but a human being.

Her first field job, with an old gent in his seventies, was to cut thistles with a scythe:

After half an hour or so the scythe seemed to get heavier, and I was so pleased when the old gent suggested sharpening it. At least it meant a few minutes' break. Dinner time came none too early – my arms hardly belonged to me and every bone in my body ached. I could have cried. In the kitchen the children had arrived for their midday meal, and to have another look at their Land Girl. Anyone who knows children can imagine their pride in "owning" the first Land Girl in the district – I was really theirs. I had to be so careful what I said, as I knew it would be repeated in school.

One morning we had to collect the sheep and take them a few miles to be dipped. A few neighbouring farmers had come to help, and I suspect to see how this "girl" was shaping. It was rather a mucky job as the ground was wet all the time. For the first hour, catching the sheep was fairly easy as there were so many of them in the pen, but when we came to the last twenty or so we had to do some chasing in order to catch them. Several times I slipped on my bottom in the mud, much to the amusement of the farmers – I suspect that was why I was left on my own to catch the last few sheep!

As well as those helping on the land through official schemes, there were those who were prepared to offer their support individually. One such was quoted in *The Times* of August 1 under the heading "Harvest Volunteers". Fully prepared to exchange collar and cassock for smock – or equivalent – and Wellington boots was a gentleman of the cloth who was clearly ready and willing for an appropriate call:

> It may be that there are dozens of ministers like myself who have cancelled their seaside holiday and would be pleased to give a fortnight to a neighbouring farmer, if we knew where to apply. We may not be able to work all the day and every day, but there are many jobs in the harvest field and on the farm that we could tackle with benefit to ourselves and to the farmer.

There were indeed many ways of "going to it" in the remarkable summer of 1940.

CHAPTER SIX

Waiting for the Enemy

H OWEVER MUCH THE NATION might energize itself by the "Go to it" philosophy of the time, there was no escaping the thought that the ball was in the enemy's court and that he might strike at any moment. The ultimate horror of a desperate fight on the beaches and in the hills and, should resistance fail, of enemy occupation, might only be weeks, even days, away. Vera Brittain, best known for her First World War classic of disenchantment *Testament Of Youth*, described the fear that lurked in so many people's minds in her powerful and moving book *England's Hour*, written during 1940. Using for vividness the present tense, as she did throughout most of the book, she wrote:

> We face the ruin of those private worlds which hold all the warmth and sweetness of our existence; we contemplate the loss of our sons, the shattering of our homes, the ruthless termination of maturer lives which walked with death a quarter of a century ago. But, hardest of all, we who are part of England's faith in honesty and toleration must help to maintain her courage in a darkened world where the spiritual forces of love and truth are themselves the nearest casualties.

A similarly solemn mood as the country braced itself for the next shock was expressed by a much less celebrated but nevertheless extremely acute observer of the wartime scene, Philip Chignell, of Hessle near Hull, who wrote a series of eloquent letters to his sisters throughout the crisis months of 1940, and on throughout the war. Retired, but active as the organist of the village church, he reacted to the pattern of events with a profound sadness that matters should have come to such a pass:

> Well, I suppose they will have to go on with this bloody business until all the ammunition gets blown up and then there will be a halt for a certain number of years, that is until another store of war material has been accumulated and then we shall have the same thing all over again. It seems that mankind will have to put up with this sort of thing every twenty years or so in the future. I have seen it once, I have seen it twice, and this is my fair share of this idiotic and senseless game. This is my last turn, anyhow, and I shall not be sorry to quit life, the life that is hardly worth having nowadays because it has to be lived with such a lot of ingenious devils who have, by their ingenuity in manufacturing machines of destruction,

made life not worth the living. I, for one, shall be glad to be quit of it and I don't mind how soon, so please note.

Inevitably in the circumstances it was decided that those who were most vulnerable should be given sanctuary away from the areas of greatest danger. The war's first year had seen a mass evacuation of children, some of whom had returned home once the immediate threat had turned out to be far less serious than expected. The present crisis produced a second surge.

Many earlier evacuees had been taken to quiet seaside districts which in 1939 seemed safe havens but had now to be considered to be at risk. Starting in May the process began of re-evacuating children housed within ten miles of the sea along a section of coast from Norfolk to Sussex. South Wales was selected as a prime destination though some were also sent to the Midlands. One among thousands, in late June a young schoolboy called Dennis Heyderman, originally evacuated from London to St Leonards on Sea, Sussex, sent a postcard to his family to inform them of the impending change:

> Dear parents,
> The school will be evacuated to Wales on Sunday. I'm going too. I'll write a letter as soon as I'm there.
> > Your loving son, Dennis

A kindly teacher, clearly saddened at losing a pupil she had become fond of, added this comment to the postcard:

> We are so very sorry to lose Dennis for he has been a dear good boy all these nine months. I hope we shall see him again.

This modest little card, the spidery penmanship of the child contrasting with the mature endorsing hand of the schoolteacher, is in itself a potent and touching document of this remarkable year.

Other children, being further inland, were considered safe to stay where they were. In some cases this offered a closer contact with the actualities of war than might have been envisaged. A schoolboy evacuated to Maidstone, Roy Grimsley, saw something of the aftermath of Dunkirk and sent an excited postcard home:

> Dear Mummy,
> I saw a lot of aeroplanes go over and I saw a lorry with a piece of aeroplane that crashed and I saw some wounded soldiers.
> > Love from Roy to Mummy and Conny and Pop xxxxxxxxxxxx

On June 23 the pupils of the Mary Datchelor School for Girls, previously evacuated from Camberwell, London, to Ashford, Kent, were despatched with less than
a week's notice to "somewhere in Wales". In the school's official history the episode,
as described by the headmistress, emerges as something of a great adventure, if not
without its brief twinge of nostalgia in its earliest stage:

> We had a splendid journey, though as we went through the outskirts of London,
> not far from our homes, we had some home-sick moments; and as the long day
> wore on, home began to feel very far away. Everywhere we were greeted by waving
> crowds, and when we stopped at various stations the WVS brought us cups of
> water and tea and chocolates and papers. We ate many nameless meals – elevenses
> merged into lunch and lunch into tea and tea into early supper.

In their previous migration they had been sent to one place and ended up at
another. Now it was to happen a second time:

> Once more we did not go to the destination originally scheduled for us –
> Carmarthen – but were taken to Llanelly, where we arrived at 7.30 in a lovely
> evening light, and had a wonderful welcome. [The town's] cinemas and
> Woolworth's were loudly cheered by each bus-load of girls on our arrival. Sea (not
> safe, alas, for bathing) and lovely country were within easy reach, and a Rambling
> Club soon began to explore the district. Many girls had bicycles (we brought nearly
> 200 from Ashford) and could go further afield.

According to Miss Brock this was an evacuation without a hitch, but not all schools
were so fortunate. Gloria Bundy was a pupil at Wentworth, a private school
at Boscombe, near Bournemouth. In the aftermath of Dunkirk it was thought
possible that their premises might be requisitioned as a hospital. Fortunately, the
chairman of governors was on friendly terms with the Robertson family, famous
as producers of *Golden Shred* marmalade, who offered the school the use of their
stately home, Llantysilio Hall, near Llangollen, North Wales, for the duration.
Writing sixty years later and commenting on the school's recently published
history, Gloria Bundy (now Mrs Gloria Siggins) pronounced herself amazed at how
successfully the "awesome task" of evacuation was accomplished by the headmistress and her staff, at short notice and with extraordinary resourcefulness, the
headmistress even pronouncing the whole process as having been "fun". For the
school's young pupils fun was not perhaps the first word to spring to their minds:

> Llantysilio Hall was a startling contrast to the Boscombe premises. There was no
> electricity until a generator could be installed and I remember it was very erratic
> in performance and much of my studying for School Certificate was done by the

light of Aladdin lamps. Despite every care in the packing up of Wentworth and the despatch of loads of equipment, furniture, etc. to North Wales, the first things to arrive were desks – but no kitchen utensils or crockery! Thus pastry was made in the lids of biscuit tins, fruit salad came to the table in a washing bowl while eggs were cooked in a metal hot water jug. Then pupils started to arrive from London by train before the telegrams sent to announce their ETA [estimated time of arrival], with resulting crises of accommodation and catering!

Further memories of her two years at Llantysilio Hall were of continuous rain "and, of all things, discovering where flies go in the winter: the handrail of the spiral staircase and the walls of the forbidden territory of the clock tower were encrusted with them but it was worth the climb for the breathtaking view over the Welsh countryside".

If the coastal areas were considered to be at risk, so undoubtedly was the capital. Between June 13 and 18, 1940, nearly 100,000 children were moved from London. A fortnight or so later it was the turn of the North East. Thus on July 6 the newspapers reported the departure of 10,000 from Newcastle-upon-Tyne, 8500 from Hull and substantial numbers from South Shields, Sunderland, Gateshead, Grimsby, Jarrow and the Hartlepools, adding up to a total of 40,000.

Many evacuees flourished in their new surroundings, but others suffered from the problems inherent on being deprived of their normal background and relationships. Rosina Davies of the Women's Land Army, whose story was told in the previous chapter, herself something of a solitary in an alien environment, found herself constantly attended by one young evacuee. This became particularly evident when she succumbed to an unfortunate bout of stomach trouble:

> One compensation for being on my second farm was they had a very good orchard, and I love apples. I should mention that there were evacuees from London and Liverpool billeted at houses in the village. One of them, nine-year-old Billy, had fallen head over heels in love with me, and did promise to marry me when he would grow up. (I wonder where he is now?)
>
> However, Billy was like my shadow. Everywhere I went Billy was there wanting to help me. One day, when I had eaten more apples than was good for me, I suffered the consequences. Poor Billy was in such a state because I was ill; he clung to me more than ever. When I had to make for the toilet he stood by the door, I'm sure in case I needed help.

For many children that summer evacuation meant going to more distant destinations, under the auspices of the newly established Children's Overseas Reception Board, soon to be familiarly known simply as CORB. The story of the founding, and of the later abandonment is told in Vera Brittain's already quoted *England's Hour*:

> Towards the end of June, many conscientious parents throughout England find themselves confronted with a heartbreaking dilemma. Simultaneously with the collapse of France, the government announces an official scheme to send thousands of British children to the Dominions. Canada, South Africa, Australia and New Zealand broadcast enthusiastic offers of hospitality. In the United States, a committee is formed under the chairmanship of Marshall Field of Chicago to rescue Europe's children; it is even possible, we learn, that the adamant immigration laws may be modified in order to admit a hundred thousand boys and girls of British stock to America.
>
> We feel certain that the government would not sponsor so large a scheme unless it was convinced that horror and dislocation would come to this country with the downfall of Europe. The announcement of the plan seems to thousands of anxious parents a warning of "things to come". Earlier evacuation schemes have made no special appeal to them, for moving children from the town to the country was merely a method of redistributing the population; it assured neither safety, freedom from chaos, nor that sense of security which is the birthright of childhood. Emigration to the Dominions or America, where real freedom from war will be a gift from new territories unhampered by the evil nationalistic traditions of the quarrelsome Old World, is a proposition more hopeful and far more imaginative.

What gave the scheme a special impetus was the sense, shared by many resourceful and energetic parents, that they would never forgive themselves if the worst came to the worst and they had failed to take advantage of such a golden opportunity to send their children to safety:

> "If we must die," say these fathers and mothers, "at least we intend to save the next generation."

Vera Brittain and her husband, George Catlin (disguised under the name of Martin in her book), duly went to the offices of CORB, newly established in the Berkeley Street offices of Messrs Thomas Cook and Son under the chairmanship of Geoffrey Shakespeare, Parliamentary Under Secretary of State for the Dominions. Their concern was for their son and daughter, the son at a school in a so-called "safe area", their daughter already summoned once to an air-raid shelter and with a headmaster who felt that only across the Atlantic could there be a guarantee of a stable life and an uninterrupted education:

Two humble units in a long line of troubled questioning parents, we make our inquiries. The woman Member of Parliament who answers them happens to be a personal friend, "Don't hesitate," she advises us. "*Get them out!*"

Their adviser had a further suggestion, however: not to wait for the publicly funded scheme, but, since they had the means, and hosts ready to receive their children in the United States, to send them independently; a ship funded by private means was shortly to sail. One argument for so doing as that it would leave extra spaces for those applying for CORB places. So the decision was made. On June 24 John and Shirley Catlin (the latter being the present Baroness Shirley Williams) came up from their schools to London. On June 26 they travelled as a family to Liverpool, in a boat train filled with hundreds of children from babies to teenagers and, for this first leg of the journey, countless anxious parents. Their ship was the *Duchess of Atholl*, which made a swift and safe voyage across the dangerous Atlantic.

There were so many applications for CORB places that the scheme closed its books within three weeks. After various delays CORB sailings finally began on 21 July, the first ship to leave being the SS *Anselm*, bound for Canada. Other destinations were Australia, South Africa and New Zealand. Altogether over the following two months 2,664 children were successfully taken overseas, most of them to Canada, under the CORB scheme.

In gratitude for her children's safe arrival, Vera Brittain offered her help to Geoffrey Shakespeare, a distant cousin on her father's side. She became a member of an advisory panel interviewing would-be escorts to accompany the children registered for evacuation, eventually seeing some 15,000 applicants in order to select 500. One of those chosen, she would later recall, was a Miss Mary Cornish, a music teacher from Baker Street, who impressed the panel as being courageous and responsible. Some weeks later she would sail for Canada on the last ship to sail under the auspices of CORB, one destined to become unhappily famous, the SS *City of Benares*.

Meanwhile, as the weeks wore on and the waiting continued, the nation steeled itself for the expected ordeal to come. Conscious of its key role in not only keeping its audience informed but also inspiring it with martial spirit the BBC offered, on June 25, a major radio feature entitled *Spitfires Over Britain*. It was headlined on the front cover of the June 21 edition of *Radio Times*, and supported by a striking 4- by 8-inch photograph of three Spitfires streaking across a dramatic sky. Described on the programme page as "a radio impression of the work of a Home Defence Squadron of the RAF Fighter Command", it was written by J.D. Kinross and produced and recorded by a master of radio craftsmanship, Cecil McGivern. The invented "incident" on which it focused was a successful attempt by three Spitfires, code-named Red 1, 2 and 3, to fight off three German Heinkel bombers which had attacked a trawler, and forced her crew to take to their boats, in the vicinity of the Tyne. Much of the programme consisted of what sounded like extremely convincing cockpit- or air-to-ground dialogue, complete with genuine sound effects, but the climax was left to the narrator (whose text, on paper at least, might seem to bear more than a passing likeness to the epoch-making running commentary of Charles Gardner at Dover already quoted).

(*Narrator, fast*) The Flight Leader is moving at 400 miles per hour. He's under cloud base, and with throttle wide open he's making the nearest Heinkel look as though it's standing still… The Heinkel has seen him, and dives from 2,000 feet straight towards the sea… There's the trawler – away to the right… Her boat is standing clear and there's a glimpse of white faces looking upward. The third Spitfire's streaking like a rocket northward…up to a great cumulus which glints in the sun. A second Heinkel's in there…but it will have to come out…the sky's clearing…escape will be difficult.

(*Renewed whine of engines – dim sound again*)

Red 1 and 2 are coming down in a terrific power dive. The Heinkel sees the two black dots which mean death diving from the clouds, and, seeking speed, opens his bomb hatches. The load splashes into the water as the Heinkel dodges all over the sea, trying to get away by sharp turns…he's not 50 feet up…those banks of his are almost vertical…and it looks as though the inside wing must go into the water.

The two Spitfires flash down…400 yards…200 yards. The Heinkel's rear gunner is firing wildly. They've got him…cut him off like a whippet by anticipating a turn… [*Narrator's voice rises with excitement.*] They're nearing the bottom of their dive…

(*Narrator, soberly*) A burst from each plane – each firing eight guns at a rate of 1,200 bullets per minute, smashed into the Heinkel from a range between 50 and 100 yards. The Heinkel, ripped into pieces, went down into the sea after ten seconds. The attack began and ended within one minute.

Meanwhile Red 3 was accounting for a second Heinkel. Her pilot called the Squadron Leader:

Hello Red 1. Am about 30 miles north of where we broke formation. I got my bird. Two of the crew are in a rubber boat. Regret third Heinkel has got away. Over.

Other voices on the air, less dramatic but potent in their own distinctive way, joined in the task of shoring up morale, to instil a sense of resistance, and, if overheard by the enemy, impressing upon him the sense of a country armed and ready. The following extracts are from a broadcast by a Captain Alan Harper of the Royal Artillery, as reproduced in the BBC's magazine *The Listener* in July, describing a visit to Britain's nearest point to the lurking menace of the enemy, the vicinity of Dover:

> Along the coastline I visited headquarters of battalions and companies that, after a period of rigorous training, were now established in the front fortified system. This is a real, good reception area down here for Nazi evacuees. No possible device for their suitable entertainment has been left out. Barbed wire and machine-gun emplacements and guns, and tank traps and more guns, and ingenious dodges of all sorts – every curve and gully of this peaceful Kentish countryside is swept and garnished for the guests: those of them, that is to say, who manage to survive the attentions of the Navy and the RAF. How different all this must have looked in May last, when the gates were almost wide open!
>
> Thank God Britain is still an island, in spite of pre-war theorising by continental pundits. The obscene Goebbels and his litter in Berlin can falsify the history books, but not even Nazi propaganda can monkey with geography. Yes, but there must be no stupid belief in security. Our defences are now formidable and methodical behind these ever-blessed Straits. But only a few miles away is the giant army that has smashed its way through Western Europe, an unprecedented battering-ram at the disposal of a cunning and merciless gang. There is no trick, no treachery, no murderous invention they will not use to destroy this country, which alone stands between them and the world's loot. All this means we cannot afford to slacken for a moment.

Another element forcefully emphasized at this time was solidarity, the sense that this was a struggle undertaken by a unified nation:

> Walking about in the streets reminds me of another thing this war has done – it has wiped out any invidious distinction between soldiers and civilians. Again, that's not at all like the last war. We really *are* all in it together this time.

Singing from much the same hymn sheet was George Hicks, the MP who some weeks earlier in a Sunday night *Postscript* had advised Hitler to keep the Compiègne surrender coach for later use. In a radio talk broadcast on July 24 entitled "The Army of the Night", he portrayed a country full of eager and determined defenders only too willing to do battle with any invader:

Britain bristles these days. It is armed and alert, and never so strangely so as at night. There is something terribly menacing, mysteriously formidable in that guard kept over this land of ours, in the black night; in the quiet recesses of the towns, and along the roads of the countryside, shadowy sentinels, strange sounds and murmurs in the streets, strange sounds and murmurs by the misty hedges, under the trees, in the winding lanes, between the fields, vapoury breaths, movements, tramplings, faint ebony gleams on steel helmets, little groups silhouetted against the sky and every now and again searchlights that seem to throw pencils of light unto the very stars.

"How well they serve, who only watch and wait." I have been wanting to say that ever since this war began. If there is anything which has made me proud of being a Britisher, proud of my people, that has filled me with confidence in our strength and resolution, that makes me certain of victory, it is this "Army of the Night". This army that waits, silent and ready, prepared for any emergency, keyed up to meet any shock. This army of the people, of citizens, watching over their homes; of workers, watching over their workplaces; of countrymen, watching over their land; ARP wardens going their rounds; fire-fighters and balloon barrage men; the first aid men and nurses at their posts; anti-aircraft men by their guns; citizens and workers intermingled with the soldiers, all sprung from the people; on patrol through the city highways and byways, and all the roads that lead over the hills and down the valleys of Britain to the coast. And the coast, thronged with troops, lined with cannon courses, and, out at sea, the grey ships riding...

Herr Hitler and company, we are ready!

As already quoted in a previous chapter, Lord Beaverbrook, in his famous aluminium appeal of July 10, had made the promise: "We will turn your pots and pans into Spitfires and Hurricanes, Blenheims and Wellingtons". In the summer of 1940 it rapidly became clear that the British people did not only want its saucepans to be turned into aircraft, it wanted to purchase the aircraft as well.

As it happened, the original impulse for raising cash for planes came not from Britain but the Caribbean. A Jamaican newspaper called *The Gleaner* cabled Lord Beaverbrook's Ministry of Aircraft Production to ask how much it cost to build a bomber. A figure of £20,000 was suggested and the cheque arrived within a week. A week later the *Straits Times* of Singapore cabled £25,000. By that time Jamaica was on its way to its second £20,000 bomber while the Gold Coast cabled £100,000. This started a whole culture of sponsorship of which, as it turned out, the principal beneficiary was the Spitfire, which soon emerged as the nation's favourite aircraft. Not that the Hurricane was without its admirers,but it was the Spitfire that took the limelight and inspired what became a spate of funds to build Spitfires as the supreme defender of a people at bay. Its very name indeed was a gesture of defiance. With an assigned price of £5,000 it was a bargain compared with a bomber. Soon the BBC was including lists of the latest donations at the end of news bulletins.

Hundreds of schemes were started all over Britain and the Commonwealth. Over the following weeks letters to the press proposing or supporting Spitfire Funds of various kinds became legion, though sometimes the Hurricane was also given honourable mention, while in other cases money was offered simply to the Royal Air Force as the hero service of the hour. The following letter to that effect appeared in *The Daily Telegraph* on August 14:

> Sir.
> Kindly send the enclosed £1 to Lord Beaverbrook's fund for aircraft production as a mark of the donor's appreciation of the glorious work of the Royal Air Force.

The same edition included a somewhat more specific proposal (with the Hurricane not forgotten) over the signature of a gentleman (clearly) who wrote from Wimpole Street, London, under the name of "George the Nought":

> Sir.
> It has occurred to me (being a George) that all Georges throughout the kingdom might like to subscribe towards the purchase of a Spitfire or a Hurricane named "George".
> Not to be outdone, no doubt the Arthurs, Charleses, Lucys and Marthas, etc. would like to follow suit and purchase a machine to be named after them. I have much pleasure in starting the ball rolling by enclosing my mite.

In fact, despite the implication that "George the Nought" had hit on a unique idea, it has to be said that sadly he was not the first in the field with such a "name the plane" suggestion. Several days earlier *The Times* had carried the following item (in this case with one of the aircraft in question being the only beneficiary):

> **THE DOROTHY SPITFIRE**
> The Dorothys of Great Britain have made a promising start in raising funds to buy a fighter for the RAF to be called the "Dorothy Spitfire". The manager of the Sheffield branch of Lloyds bank has consented to act as trustee for the fund, and all amounts of £1 or less should be sent to him. Amounts of more than £1 should be paid into any branch of Lloyds Bank.

Similarly, the Spitfire was the only aircraft mentioned in a letter in *The Daily Telegraph* of August 26, which proposed: "…the setting up of a 'Home Guard' Spitfire fund to ensure, if possible, that the plane or planes be named the 'Home

Guard' than which no finer name could be given to the defenders of our homes."
However, any tendency to smile at such initiatives might well be checked if one
reads the following item, published in *The Times* on August 19 under the heading
"Spitfire in Memory of Airman Son". It began by reporting that gifts of money for
the purchase of aircraft were being regularly received by the Minister of Aircraft
Production, and that Lord Beaverbrook had just announced that he had collected
£3,052,841 for this purpose. The item continued:

> Among the gifts received over the weekend was a cheque for £5,000 from the village
> of Michaelston-le-Pit, South Wales, received through Mr. H.H. Merrett, of Cwrt-
> yr-Ala, near Cardiff. "On Sunday last," Mr. Merrett says in his letter to Lord
> Beaverbrook, "we received the tragic news that my son, Flying Officer Norman
> Merrett, had lost his life somewhere in Britain while serving with the RAF. I
> cannot provide you with another gallant son. The one who has gone was my only
> son. But I want you to accept the enclosed cheque to purchase a Spitfire so that
> one of the ever-growing number of lads from Britain and the Dominions, so
> anxious to defend us in the air, may be equipped with an instrument which,
> combined with that indomitable spirit, courage and fearlessness, will enable him,
> as his colleagues are now doing, to take severe toll of these inferior beings attempt-
> ing, with increasing failure, to demolish the moral of our people. It is not a
> personal gift, but something to commemorate the passing of my son.

The appeal of the fighter – as a shield of the threatened homeland – was obvious,
and in the light of the letter just quoted one with a powerful impact, but in late
August *The Daily Telegraph* printed a robust contribution offering a variant
perspective by the detective writer and Christian apologist Miss Dorothy L. Sayers.
She was reacting to an earlier letter by an MP, E.H. Kealing, who had deplored "our
defensive attitude of mind as expressed in gifts for fighters rather than bombers",
stating: "Our main objective is to win the war, and that can only be done by
attacking the enemy in Germany". She commented:

> Defensive attitudes and defeatist mentality be hanged. We need not rush out, like
> mad psychologists to dig for hidden ambitions, when there are plenty of good,
> human, sentimental reasons why Hurricanes and Spitfires should have caught the
> public imagination.
>
>   First, a fighter plane is, comparatively speaking, a very small machine and there
> is something irresistibly endearing about a very small thing that fights like hell…
> Second, a fighter plane is less expensive; the task before our town or name-
> groups seems a little less formidable, and our humble contribution just a little less
> adequate. Third, when a ferocious giant has been coming at one with a club, this
> impulse to send the hat round for Jack the Giant-Killer is too strong to be

restrained by any calculations of policy. Don't let us put the fighter-enthusiasts out of conceit with themselves by calling them ugly names. The only suggestion that deserves to be considered is that we must not, in our excitement, appear unappreciative of the work of bomber command. I enclose £5 towards a bomber and feel sure that your critical correspondents will subscribe lavishly.

Two days later another correspondent sprang to her support, obviously converted to the concept that there were many other "sinews of war" than those that seized the glamorous headlines:

Sir.
May I supplement the excellent letter by Dorothy Sayers…
I suggest:
1. That the public be offered a list of fighting parts, e.g. a rivet at so much, a piston so much.
2. These lists should be hung in every post office, and that stamps with an appropriate design should be issued over the counter in return for cash, showing a receipt for the particular part which has been bought.

Immediately below, another letter looked forward to the time when the realities of war might be taken to the country from which they had sprung:

Sir.
I enclose £5 to start a fund for the purchase of a tank to begin the Battle of the Bulge at Cologne, or wherever else we can get at them.

Clearly this was not a nation seriously interested in the prospect of giving in to the enemy, whatever arguments, moral or military, might be used against it.

What inevitably kept the British on edge throughout this whole period is that nobody knew what the enemy's next move would be. In the light of the surgical despatch of Holland, Belgium and France, it was automatically assumed that there would be a similarly well-honed plan already on file for the dismemberment of Britain. One of the remarkable curiosities of 1940 is that there was not.

Germany had to do something about Britain, clearly, but there was much uncertainty as to what. The basic problem lay in the mix of options swirling inside the wayward brain of the German Chancellor. He could not make up his mind as to what he really wanted. He admired the British Empire and the British people. He would have been extremely happy if Britain had produced, if not quite a compliant Pétain, at least a leader willing to acknowledge Germany's supremacy in Europe and to settle for an arrangement whereby he would not have, Janus-like, to face two fronts but could get on without disturbance in realizing his ambitions elsewhere. Britain had produced a Churchill, however, who was singularly failing to transmit the signals Hitler wanted to hear. The new British supremo seemed curiously incapable of recognizing the hopelessness of Britain's situation in the wake of the fall of France. His absurdly defiant – and clearly unrealistic – speeches sounded more like eve-of-battle rallying cries rather than attempts to educate the British people as to the true nature of their situation. Thus on June 18 he was prophesying that if the British Empire and Commonwealth should last for a thousand years, this would be their finest hour. France's humiliating surrender at Compiègne four days later might have been expected to cool Churchill's rhetoric, but on the contrary that rhetoric was followed by the most vigorous action. Thus on July 3 the Royal Navy's Force H, having failed to persuade a French naval squadron in Mers-el-Kebir, the naval port of Oran in Algeria, to come across to the British side, followed British government instructions and opened fire. Nor were these shots across bows; they were meant to inflict serious hurt. The battleship *Bretagne* was sunk with the loss of 997 lives and the *Dunkerque* was badly damaged with the loss of 210 lives; *Mogador* was also damaged, *Provence* ran aground, only *Strasbourg* managed to escape to Toulon. There was a gnomic saying current a decade or so later in the context of Stalin's Soviet Union that the best way to frighten your enemy was to kill your friends. This hardly applied in 1940 but if nothing else Oran (as the event came to be known) left Hitler in no doubt that Churchill would not allow sentimental affection for a former ally to get in the way of preventing a sizeable slice of sea-power ending up on Germany's plate. Clearly Churchill meant business.

Nevertheless Hitler still hoped Britain might relent, or rather he hoped that although Britain's leadership might be hard-line the British people might prefer a gentler option. He was also aware that there were members of Churchill's own government who were in favour of negotiation rather than confrontation, suggesting that a softer attitude was already in place in Whitehall which might conceivably be exploited. Hitler had planned a great victory speech to be delivered to the members of the Reichstag in Berlin, at a triumphal occasion during which twelve generals would be promoted to Field Marshal and a special new rank of Reich Marshal would be conferred on his close colleague, the Luftwaffe commander Hermann Goering (who would appear in a brand-new sky-blue uniform he had designed himself). He kept on postponing the event hoping for accommodating signs from London. In their absence he finally made the speech on July 19. It was a mesmeric performance lasting over two hours. When he came to the matter of Britain he warned Churchill that he was risking the destruction of a great Empire "an Empire which it was never my intention to destroy or even to harm", and then tried to reach beyond Churchill to the people whom he felt Churchill was wilfully leading astray:

> In this hour, I feel it to be my duty before my conscience to appeal once more to reason and common sense in Great Britain. I consider myself in a position to make this appeal since I am not the vanquished begging favours, but the victor speaking in the name of reason. I can see no reason why this war must go on.

Eager to promote his message he ordered that Britain should be leafleted from the air with copies of his speech, though curiously it was not until early August that the necessary paper raids took place. Headlined "A Last Appeal to Reason" thousands of copies fluttered to the ground, but he had no takers and no peace doves flew in response.

Thus the ball came back into Hitler's court and he was forced to arbitrate between various options. He could invade Britain and dictate terms as he had done in France. He could try the indirect approach by threatening Britain's interest in the Mediterranean or Far East and by stepping up the U-boat war. He could ignore Britain and win a rapid victory in Russia – after defeating France so easily he was confident this could be achieved with relative ease – thereby acquiring the security and access to the raw materials that would allow Germany to defeat Britain at his leisure, and , if it came to it, the United States as well.

The most obvious option was invasion. Even while Hitler had been playing for time, serious preparatory work had been in progress, if not quite carried out with the professional excitement and gusto that had helped to produce (to quote Alistair Horne's fine phrase) the "diamond brilliance" of Operation "*Sichelschnitt*". When General Keitel, Chief of the Supreme Command of the Wehrmacht, issued a preliminary instruction for invasion on July 2, he added the proviso: "All preparations must be undertaken on the basis that the invasion is still only a plan and has not yet been decided upon". A further major step had been taken three days ahead of the Reichstag speech, in that on July 16 the Führer had gone so far as to issue War Directive No.16, a document that would ultimately acquire the special patina of being the great plan that never was. The following were its main clauses:

> As England, in spite of her hopeless military position, has so far shown herself unwilling to come to any compromise, I have decided to begin preparations for and, if necessary, to carry out the invasion of England. This operation is dictated by the necessity of eliminating Great Britain as a base from which the war against Germany can be fought. If necessary, the island will be occupied... I therefore issue the following orders:

1. The landing operation must be a surprise crossing on a broad front extending approximately from Ramsgate to a point west of the Isle of Wight... The preparations...must be concluded by the middle of August.
2. The following preparations must be undertaken to make a landing in England possible:
(a) The English Air Force must be eliminated to such an extent that it will be incapable of putting up any substantial opposition to the invading troops.
(b) The sea routes must be cleared of mines.
(c) Both flanks, the Straits of Dover and the western approaches to the Channel...must be so heavily mined as to be completely inaccessible.
(d) Heavy coastal guns must dominate and protect the entire coastal front area...
3. The invasion will be referred to by the code-name "Sealion".

Thus the overall plan, but the questions remained. In conferences with the commanders-in-chief of the *Wehrmacht* on July 21, Hitler expressed his doubts about a landing operation: "If it is not certain that preparations can be concluded by the beginning of September, other plans will have to be considered". Among these other plans was, inevitably, an attack on the USSR.

Doubts were not confined to Hitler. Admiral Raeder, Commander-in-Chief of the German Navy, saw a landing only as a "last resort to force Britain to sue for peace", and as possible only after strong air attacks "to make the entire nation feel the effects"; one target he suggested, though far from the intended invasion points, was Liverpool, the controlling point of Britain's western approaches.

A crucial problem for the Germans was that, though adept at land invasion, they had no track record, no available culture, for an invasion by sea. (The almost ludicrous diary comment by one general that the operation would be "similar to a large-scale river crossing" speaks for itself.) Moreover, they were extremely short of landing craft. Thousands of river barges were hurriedly pressed into service, to be adapted with specially fitted ramps. Training the *Wehrmacht*'s soldiers to debouch horses, weapons, vehicles and themselves from such a motley assembly of improvised craft did not come easily; there were numerous moments of bewilderment and many of farce. More delays resulted. After Raeder had informed Hitler on July 31 that the Navy's preparations for a landing could not be concluded before September 15, Hitler decided to take that date as a deadline, insisting again that his final decision would depend on victory in the air. The "great air campaign against Britain", which would bring that about, would begin at any time from about August 5. Eight or, at most, fourteen days after the start of that campaign, he would decide whether or not "Sealion" could go ahead in 1940.

Knowledge of such equivocations and delays not being available, to the British the threat of invasion seemed real and menacing at the time and it certainly concentrated their minds at all levels. With hindsight the whole concept can almost seem like an impossible dream. As the novelist-cum-historian Len Deighton has written: "A contrast is inevitable between the Germans' feeble preparations to cross the Channel in 1940, and the vast, highly-trained machine that proved necessary to enable the Allies to do so in 1944". In other words, what turned out to be a near-run thing in 1944, would have required a maximum combination of favourable elements and the greatest good fortune for the Germans four years earlier.

Yet if "Sealion" failed to materialize, what did take place was a hard-fought conflict in the skies which tested the nation's air defences to the limit and put into the nomenclature of war one of the most famous feats of arms of modern times. Its title was, aptly, Churchill's own, when he stated, inimitably: "The Battle of France is over. The Battle of Britain is about to begin." An Air Ministry account of it published in 1941 described it as "the first great air battle in history", and claim that "future historians may compare it with Marathon, Trafalgar and the Marne".

If Churchill was the towering figure on one side in this struggle, his real opponent was not Hitler but the newly promoted Reich Marshal Goering, Air Minister and Commander-in-Chief of the Luftwaffe, the German Air Force. He had proved irresistible in Poland and, apart from a doubt or two over his handling of the Dunkirk crisis, in the Low Countries and France. He was confident that he would achieve a similar success in the matter of Britain and achieve that crucial victory in the air required by Hitler. This would not be, however, his finest hour.

But for many it would. No account of the Battle of Britain is possible without giving honoured mention of such as the Commander-in-Chief of Fighter Command, Air Chief Marshal Sir Hugh "Stuffy" Dowding; or Air Vice Marshal Keith Park, in charge of 11 Group Fighter Command, covering the area of London and the South East of England. Nor does the fact that there were major tactical, even personal, disagreements between these two and others, such as Air Vice Marshal Trafford Leigh-Mallory and Air Marshal Sir William Sholto Douglas mean that the latter should be left out of the frame. There were also disagreements with the Prime Minister. This is not, however, the place to raise such essentially behind-the-scenes issues. Here the main focus is on those men who bore the brunt of the actual fighting. For the young Irene Thomas, as for most people, these men were the nation's champions:

> Our heroes were the fighter pilots who made repeated attempts to beat off the invaders. We were encouraged to believe that carrots would improve our eyesight, and make us able to see in the dark, like night fighter pilots were supposed to be able to do. I can remember seeing a group of these young men walking along Oxford Street, with the crowds of shoppers making way for them. They wore dark glasses – reputedly so that their eyes would get used to darkness – and wore the top button of their jackets unfastened. I've never known the reason for that fashion, but it was their trademark. The names of fighter pilots ... were as familiar to

us as the names of footballers are now, and it's strange to think that the morale
of the whole country was raised more by this handful of mainly upper-middle-
class youngsters, than by all the exhortations of politicians.

The poet Stephen Spender (whose more humble yet still dangerous role in the war
from 1941 would be that of a member of the Auxiliary Fire Service working in
London) was similarly admiring. He saw in the young fighter pilots of the Battle of
Britain "a flame-like resurgence of a quality flowering throughout English history".

There is of course great truth in all this, but the authors of the prestigious *Jubilee
History* of the Battle of Britain, Richard Hough and Denis Richards, enter a
caution, in a valuable section on the "myths" of 1940 that is well worth quoting,
if only to keep a complex and controversial subject in balance. If a group of the
more persistent of these myths were to be embodied in a pantechnicon sentence
it might conceivably run something like this: "The Battle of Britain…was won by
unfailingly cheerful young officers flying Spitfires magically produced by Lord
Beaverbrook and directed by "Stuffy" Dowding, who first had to beat the Air
Ministry, Winston Churchill and the French before he could beat the Germans".

That there were substantially more Hurricanes than Spitfires in the battle has
already been mentioned. Of the myth of "the unfailingly cheerful young
officers", Hough and Richards add:

> [It] is perhaps sufficient to point out that very often the officers were non-
> commissioned ones, in the rank of sergeant; and that though these young men,
> mostly in their early twenties, were indeed incredibly cheerful, they were not
> invariably so. Particularly not when, as was always happening to someone, they
> were dog-tired from flying and long hours at readiness, or tense with nervous
> strain from repeated danger, or badly wounded, or burnt.

All this notwithstanding, the speech of the Prime Minister, Winston Churchill,
delivered to the House of Commons on the afternoon of August 20, 1940, as part
of one of his periodic reviews of the progress of the war, remains not only the most
memorable but also the most apt verdict on the Battle of Britain even though the
conflict had yet to reach its peak and had many more weeks to run. After referring
to the work and achievements of the Navy, he turned to the war in the air:

> The gratitude of every home in our island, in our Empire and indeed throughout
> the world, except in the abodes of the guilty, goes out to the British airmen who,
> undaunted by odds, unwearied in their constant challenge and mortal danger, are
> turning the tide of world war by their prowess and by their devotion. Never in the
> field of human conflict was so much owed by so many to so few.

Behind the few there were, of course, the many. Angus Calder, commenting on the speech in his book *The People's War*, adds the significant comment:

> Conversely, never had so few warriors owed so much to so many… It is sometimes most helpful to see [the battle], not as a struggle between men, but as a contest between rival technologies. Had the superb planes and the excellent (though far from infallible) radar system not been in existence that summer, no commander, however sagacious, and no daring brotherhood of pilots, however well trained, could have resisted the Luftwaffe.
>
> Besides the pilots, many unpraised heroes exhausted themselves in maintaining the brittle and intricate structure of defence. Most immediately of all, there were the mechanics, technicians and engineers of the ground crews, working round the clock to keep the planes fuelled, armed and in repair, and the women of the WAAF who, often under bombing, drove vehicles, cooked food and maintained the vital switchboards.

And, it might be added, at a range of airfields and other key establishments, sometimes plotted the flights and could even find themselves the first to be aware of the deaths of the young men they had recently been dancing or drinking with or were dating. It was that kind of war.

CHAPTER SEVEN

Battle in the Skies

T HERE ARE DIFFERING INTERPRETATIONS as to the dates of opening of the Battle of Britain. The already quoted official account, published in 1941 by His Majesty's Stationery Office, stakes its claim with the subtitle: "An Air Ministry Account of the Great Days from August 8–October 31, 1940". In his formal despatch on the battle, also dated 1941, Air Chief Marshal Dowding, while accepting August 8 as a key date, since it marked "the first attack in force against land objectives in this country", pushed the true opening back a month earlier, to July 10. "Although," he wrote, "many attacks had previously been made on convoys, and even on land objectives such as Portland, July 10 saw the employment by the Germans of the first really big formation (70 aircraft) intended primarily to bring out Fighter Defence to battle on a large scale."

The reason why he saw the engagement of Fighter Defence as the crucial factor is clear from two other simple but keynote statements in his report, statements which relate precisely to the already discussed reservations about invasion as defined by Hitler:

"The essence of their [the Germans'] strategy was so to weaken our Fighter Defences that their Air Arm should be able to give adequate support to an attempted invasion of the British Isles".

The destruction or paralysis of the Fighter Command was therefore an essential prerequisite to the invasion of these islands.

The 1989 *Jubilee History*, following Dowding, begins its chronology of the battle with July 10, for which it offers the following details:

Weather	Main target	Losses
cloudy, clearing	channel convoy, first dogfight of over 100 aircraft	*Luftwaffe* 13, RAF 6

As for the other "book-end" of the battle, the entry for October 31 reads: "Weather – rain; main target and event – the great battle fizzles out damply, the Germans having exhausted every tactical alternative after being deprived of their best chance of victory by the inept decision of their supreme command to attack London rather than continue with the direct offensive against Fighter Command and its ground installations; losses 0,0".

Thus the overall parameters and – in respect of the explanation just given – the overall plot. Supporting this interpretation, July 10–October 31 are the dates of qualification for the award of the Battle of Britain clasp to the 1939–45 Star. Between those two dates there were various phases. First there was the Channel Battle, which included attacks on coastal convoys, ports, coastal aerodromes and radio location stations; Charles Gardner's famous Dover broadcast was a product of this phase. Next, there was the attack on inland fighter aerodromes, which produced the "classic" phase of aerial combat between the two air forces. Then there was the Battle of London, usually dated September 7–30 (though the first bombs had fallen well before that start date and London was far from being the only target), when Hitler attempted not to take out the technology but to break the will of the people. Finally, there was the month of October, generally defined as a period of minor raids but which Dowding saw as a period in which the actual targets were of less importance than the attempt by the Germans at "drawing our fighters into the air and engaging them in circumstances as disadvantageous to us as possible". But Dowding was wise enough in his report not to make too much of such so-called phases, which, he cautioned, "indicated only general tendencies; they overlapped and were not mutually exclusive".

Thus the scene-set; what of the actors?

Jean Mills went to RAF Leighton Buzzard in early August 1940 to train as a plotter and tracer with Fighter Command. Towards the end of the month she and a crowd of other young WAAFs set off in high spirits to travel to RAF Duxford, Cambridgeshire, looking forward to playing their part in the Battle of Britain. She would never forget their first sight of that airfield:

> We arrived at the little station at Whittlesford and lugged our kit bags and our gas masks and tin hats behind us up the platform. And outside there was an open-backed lorry waiting and the driver stood by and said, "Shove them up here girls" and in went the kit bags and then he sort of helped us up after them. And there we were, about a dozen of us clinging onto the sides and laughing and talking. We were quite excited because we were all pretty young, eighteen or nineteen I suppose, and most of us hadn't been away from home before and life was a great big adventure and we were feeling very hyper I should imagine. And the truck bumped over the country roads and suddenly we reached the brow of a hill and we could see Duxford stretched out before us and it was a very sunny day. And there was the aerodrome, mostly grassed, and the big hangars there and you could see the main gate. To the right was what looked like a little housing estate, which was the previous married quarters for the airmen and their families. And

suddenly as we looked there had obviously been something going on because planes seemed to be landing from all directions. And as we looked one of them appeared to hover for a moment and then it nosed dived straight down into the ground. And there were smoke trails rising. The noise just stopped absolutely instantaneously and we looked at each other a bit shocked. And the mood changed and we were all very much sobered up. And I think we then realized that it wasn't a great lark and it was quite serious business that we were in for.

Actually, we were reminded of this because the pilot was killed of course, and he'd owned a large Alsatian dog which for the next few days just seemed to roam the camp looking for him all the time until somebody else took him over. It was quite sad. There were moments like that, but most of the time you were so busy that you just didn't let it get at you.

They had learned straight away the essential lesson that for all the glamour and the hero-worship surrounding the air warfare of the Spitfire summer it was for those at the heart of it a matter of life or death. Richard Hillary found himself jolted to the same conclusion when he took to the air to engage the enemy in action for the first time:

The voice of the controller came unhurried over the loudspeaker, telling us to take off, and in a few seconds we were running for our machines. I climbed into the cockpit of my plane and felt an empty sensation of suspense in the pit of my stomach. For one second time seemed to stand still and I stared blankly in front of me. I knew that that morning I was to kill for the first time. That I might be killed or in any way injured did not occur to me. Later, when we were losing pilots regularly, I did consider it in an abstract way when on the ground; but once in the air, never. I knew it could not happen to me. I suppose every pilot knows that, knows it cannot happen to him; even when he is taking off for the last time, when he will not return, he knows that he cannot be killed. I wondered idly what he was like, this man I would kill. Was he young, was he fat, would he die with the Führer's name on his lips, or would he die alone, in that last moment conscious of himself as a man? I would never know. Then I was being strapped in, my mind automatically checking the controls, and we were off.

What he anticipated duly took place. In the middle of a brisk dogfight he found a Messerschmitt at his mercy:

He came right through my sights and I saw the tracer from all eight guns thud home. For a second he seemed to hang motionless; then a jet of red flame shot upward and he spun out of sight. For the next few minutes I was too busy looking after myself to think of anything, but when, after a short while, they turned and made off over the Channel, and we were ordered to our base, my mind began to work again. It had happened.

My first emotion was one of satisfaction, satisfaction at a job adequately done, at the final logical conclusion of months of specialized training. And then I had a feeling of the essential rightness of it all. He was dead and I was alive. It could so easily have been the other way round; and that would somehow have been right too. I realized in that moment just how lucky a fighter pilot is. He has none of the personalized emotions of the soldier, handed a rifle and bayonet and told to charge. He does not even have to share the dangerous emotions of the bomber pilot who night after night must experience that childhood longing for smashing things. The fighter pilot's emotions are those of the duellist, cool, precise, impersonal. He is privileged to kill well. For if one must either kill or be killed, as now one must, it should, I feel, be done with dignity. Death should be given the setting it deserves. It should never be a pettiness; and for the fighter pilot it never can be.

No one could put the point better than Richard Hillary, but former Sergeant Pilot Charlton Haw, interviewed fifty years after the event, made much the same distinction. Asked what was his attitude to the enemy, he answered:

We didn't bear them any grudge because it's so different. I don't think I could have ever stuck a bayonet in someone. But to go and have a fight at twenty thousand feet with another chap, that's entirely different, because you're shooting at an aeroplane not him. I honestly think if I'd had to go in the Army, I don't know what I would have done because obviously you must do it. But it's much easier to put your sights on an aeroplane and shoot it than shooting a man in cold blood. I don't think I could do that. Obviously, if he was going to shoot me I'd have to have a go at him, but you're shooting at the aeroplane.

Yet there is no denying that there must have been a huge satisfaction in "taking out" a bomber intending to kill or maim one's own people, or returning home from having attempted to do just that. Writing to friends in August 1940 Flying Officer Kenneth Gundry, a Hurricane pilot, described the destruction of one German bomber:

One poor swine of a Junkers 88 was spotted while going back from a raid on Portsmouth or somewhere inland, and about seven of us whooped with joy and dived on him from all directions. His rear-gunner put up a marvellous show and was replaced later by the observer, I guess, but he finally went down in a complete inferno of red hot metal, and we could see the column of smoke rising from where it crashed on the cliffs near Bognor Regis from our 'drome at Tangmere for several hours afterwards.

The preceding accounts have included retrospective interviews, extracts from a published classic and a fragment of a contemporary letter. Perhaps closest of all to the reality are the typewritten combat reports completed as soon as possible after any sortie or action, of which many have survived. Certain abbreviations are standard in such reports, thus; A/C = aircraft; E/A, or e/a, = enemy aircraft; an ME or Me is a Messerschmitt, a Do a Dornier, a Ju a Junkers; R/T = radio telephony; 'vic' = a 'V' formation… The following is by the officer just quoted, Kenneth Gundry, then a Pilot Officer, flying as number 4 Yellow Section, A Flight, 257 Squadron, consisting of eleven Hurricanes, at 12.30 on August 8, their contact point with the enemy being eight miles east of St Catherine's Point, Isle of Wight:

> After patrolling in very loose formation at 14,000 ft for 30 mins, heard gunfire and observed Me 109 on tail of another member of Yellow Section. I gave two bursts approx two secs each in an astern attack at approximately 250 yards range and observed Me 109 to be hit and dive in gentle turn, disappearing into the sea with a trail of black and white smoke behind. Meanwhile, an Me 109 had got on my tail and I saw tracer bullets passing on my right. After making sharp left turn through 300 degs I found opportunity for two bursts of deflection shots on Me 109 turning outside me. This A/C I observed to be hit in the starboard wing, emitting a white trail of petrol or smoke. It immediately turned on its back and dived steeply but still under control. I followed for approx. one minute, but turned back to rejoin my section. After searching and identifying several single Hurricanes, none of them my section, I formated with a section of Hurricanes, markings VK. and circled at 11,000 feet over the convoy until recalled by R/T to base.

Annotations to the account show that four enemy casualties were claimed during the attack, two Messerschmitts destroyed, one damaged, and a Dornier damaged; but the squadron lost three Hurricanes, while one officer was pronounced lost and another missing.

An earlier attack by B Flight of the same squadron on July 19 off Shoreham claimed one Dornier destroyed with no losses on the British side. Three pilots, Green Section 1, 2 and 3, were involved in the kill. The following report is by Green or G1, the section commander, Flight Lieutenant Mitchell:

> Took off to intercept Raid 15 and the vectors [i.e. the ground guidance system] took the section down to the coast between Hove and Tangmere. When at 8,000 ft enemy seen to be below and near to a large bank of cumulus cloud. At that time there was a Hurricane on its tail and two other Hurricanes further behind. The e/a recognised as a Do.17 dived into cloud. Ordered the section into line astern and

stayed on the fringe of the cloud. The e/a came out of cloud in front of the section having evaded the other fighters in the cloud. E/a dived to sea level and we followed it down. I closed to 250 yards and then opened fire. Return fire noticed from the upper gun position of the e/a. It appeared as scarlet particles which appeared to shoot up from the e/a and then come straight back towards me. All my ammunition was expended, the only effect noticed was the cessation of the return fire. I broke away up and to the left and G3 closed in to make his attack. I broke away at about 100 yards. I saw the e/a crash into the sea just below G3. Wreckage was noticed but no personnel were seen in the water. The e/a was doing about 280 mph in its dive and about 200 mph when at sea level. The swastikas on the tail fin were very noticeable.

One of the RAF's most famous fighter pilots was Robert Stanford Tuck. He was a Spitfire man *par excellence*, who had fallen in love with the aircraft at first flight and who found it "an understanding and intelligent creature that responded instantly to the most delicate and suggestive pressures of its master's hands and feet". For him, in fact, the plane was almost a part of him, so that it was said of him that it became "like an extension of his own body, brain and nervous system". On August 18, while visiting an airfield not his own, he discovered there was an action in progress and hastened to join the fray. This is his rather more colourful than most combat reports:

I was on a visit to Northolt from Pembry (92 Squadron) and on hearing the Attack Action I took off at about 13.20 hrs. and made for the South Coast. Whilst patrolling over Beachy Head at about 15,000 ft two JU 88s came straight towards me flying SSE. One immediately jettisoned its bombs into the sea, and both dived straight down to sea level on seeing me. I went down shallower and came down to sea level in front of the e/a. I turned and made a head-on attack at one of the JU 88s. The e/a opened fire from its front gun at about 200 yds, but I held my fire until within range, and one short burst was sufficient to dispose of the enemy. It immediately slid sideways into the sea at a very fast speed. I turned and chased after the second, and getting in front of it proceeded to repeat the attack, but when about 800 yds from the e/a, the e/a opened fire and something very heavy hit the underside of my engine, which caused me to bump badly. A short burst was given at range, and the e/a was last seen crabbing along on its port engine, only leaving a trail of oil on the water. The e/a was almost at sea level and was then about 35 miles from English coast. My Glycol and all systems were very badly damaged, and after crossing the coast at 4,000 ft with the engine vibrating badly (the airscrew was badly damaged) I was unable to see for fumes, and baled out at about 800 ft. My parachute was still swinging when it reached the ground, and I sustained strains to my knee and ankle of my left leg. My aircraft landed near

Tunbridge and is a complete write-off.
   (Signed) R.R. Stanford Tuck

He claimed one Junkers 88 destroyed, and the second as probable. In fact, he was
not quite correct in his observations. The aircraft he had encountered were
Messerschmitt 110s, and the "something very heavy" that hit the underside of his
engine were cannon shells, not carried by a Junkers. What emerges incontrovert-
ibly from the story is that, although his radio lacked the correct frequency and he
had neither sought nor been granted permission, he had gone off on a one-man
patrol for the hell of it and, having assumed on sheer hunch that Beachy Head was
a likely place for action, had scored a considerable success, if one at some cost. What
is more, he nearly made it back to an airfield, but the cockpit fire proved too much,
so, in the parlance of the time, he "took to the silk".
   He was well received on the ground, but as the authors of the *Jubilee History*
make clear, this was not always the case. Pilot Officer Kenneth Lee, shot down near
Whitstable, slightly wounded, was taken to a local golf club to await an ambulance.
As he told the story himself: "I was in shirtsleeves, slightly bloodstained, but could-
n't help hearing members at the last hole complaining that the distraction of the
battle in the air was disturbing their putting, while once inside a voice demanded,
'Who's that scruffy looking chap at the bar? I don't think he's a member'."

There may have been much gallantry of the air during the Battle of Britain, but
there was also much ruthlessness with little mercy shown. The report of Sergeant
A.V. Clowes of an air combat near Chelmsford on August 31 makes clear this was
a surgical killing match. There was a mass of enemy planes to counter and no place
for squeamishness:

> I was Yellow leader. When travelling northeast I saw a formation of e/a in two lots
> of fifteen in close formation, consisting of Do 215s and other Bombers from 12,000
> to 18,000 ft. In among them fighters in line astern in fives and up to fifteens in no
> definite formation. I was unable to attack the formation as I was prevented by
> threatened attack of the Me 110s. Finally I got in from below, and climbed up and
> gave them a frontal beam attack on a formation of fifteen DO 215s in five Vics of
> three, with a burst of two seconds. I half rolled and climbed again for an attack
> and saw only thirteen left. One was spinning down and the other was leaving
> formation in a steep turn to the left. I was attacked by the ME 110s, and looked
> up and attacked them from underneath. I gave them a short burst at long range.
> I saw a white streak from the starboard motor. We stayed with the formation for
> a while and the engine of the e/a stopped. I continued to attack from astern

quarter until my ammunition was exhausted and killed the crew. The pilot appeared to be looking for a place to land near Martlesham.

There was no love lost between Polish pilots fighting in the Battle of Britain and the representatives of the nation that had ravaged their country. The reports of an officer and two sergeants following a clash between members of the A Flight of 303 (Polish) Squadron and an estimated sixty enemy aircraft east of Biggin Hill on August 31 were terse, cold and dismissive.

Pilot Officer Feric:

> I was Yellow 2. After about 15 minutes flying we saw about 70 e/a to N.E. On the way towards them Yellow section met 3 Me 109s, which did not see us as we had the Sun behind us. The surprise was complete. Each of us took one e/a. A higher section of Me 109s began to descend on us. I gave a short burst at my Me 109 from 70 yards at fuselage and engine. The engine caught fire. The pilot baled out and e/a crashed in flames.

Sgt. Szaposznikow:

> I was Red 3. E/a were in very tight formation in vics of three, line astern. The fighters were above and behind. To port I saw three Me 109s. I chose that most to port and fired at him before he saw me. He rolled and dived with me copying his movements. I fired again as he straightened up. He rolled on to his back and fell vertically trailing clouds of smoke.

Sgt. Karubin:

> I was Red 2: at 15,000 ft I saw enemy bombers. Then I saw three ME 109s. I attacked the lowest one with the Sun behind me. Enemy aircraft dived and I fired ½ second burst. When he straightened out I fired ½ sec. at 200 yards and enemy aircraft smoked and turned and fell. I followed and gave him another short burst. He fell in flames.

The 303 (Polish) Squadron would win for itself a formidable reputation; before the battle was over the Secretary of State for Air, Sir Archibald Sinclair, would have sent two telegrams of congratulation to General Sikorski, Commander-in-Chief of Free Polish forces and Premier of the Polish Government in Exile.

Wreaking vengeance for damage done and casualties inflicted made such killings easier. In the case of the Polish Squadron they had lost a homeland. When Kenneth Gundry described in his letter of August 27 his destruction of a "poor swine of a Junkers 88", he was aware that his squadron's home airfield had suffered only days before from a particularly determined and effective enemy attack. As he put it, perhaps with legitimate exaggeration, "We had about a week of this *blitz* at Tangmere during which we lost rather a frightening lot of fellows".

August 16 had, in fact, produced Tangmere's worst moment of the war; it was a highly successful part of the German "attack on the airfields" campaign. Tangmere's squadrons were already airborne when Junkers 87s of *Stukegeschwader* 2 made a direct assault on the base, diving out of the sun in a textbook attack which left the station in ruins. Two hangars were completely destroyed and the other three damaged. The station workshops, sick quarters, water pumping-stations, the Y (Interception) service hut and the officers' mess were wrecked and the tannoy, power, water and sanitation systems were all put out of action. Six Blenheim bombers, seven Hurricanes, two Spitfires and a Magister two-seater trainer were either destroyed or badly damaged. Ten servicemen and three civilians were killed and another twenty injured.

In the midst of the mayhem a damaged Hurricane with a terribly wounded pilot came in to land, to become an immediate target for strafing. Groundcrew rushed to extricate the pilot and get him to hospital, where he was to die next day. He was William "Billy" Fiske, of 601 Squadron, the first American to die for the British cause, a young and immensely popular addition to the Tangmere community famous for his four-litre open Bentley in British racing green. Extra detail to the story comes from the account of Billy Fiske's flight commander, Sir Archibald Hope Bt, who saw one of 601's Hurricanes lying on its belly, belching smoke, as he came in on his final approach:

> I taxied up to it and got out. There were two ambulancemen there. They had got Billy Fiske out of the cockpit. They didn't know how to take off his parachute so I showed them. Billy was burnt about the hands and ankles. I told him, 'Don't worry. You'll be all right…' Our adjutant went to see him in hospital at Chichester that night. Billy was sitting up in bed, perky as hell. The next thing we heard he was dead. Died of shock.

Squadron-Leader, later Air Vice Marshal A.V.R. "Sandy" Johnstone, of 602 Squadron, himself an "ace" at twenty-four, hurried to find out what had happened:

> I drove over to Tangmere in the evening and found the place in an utter shambles, with wisps of smoke still rising from shattered buildings. Little knots of people were wandering about with dazed looks on their faces, obviously deeply affected by the events of the day. I eventually tracked down the station commander standing

on the lawn in front of the officers' mess with a parrot sitting on his shoulder. Jack was covered with grime and the wretched bird was screeching its imitation of a Stuka at the height of the attack! The once immaculate grass was littered with personal belongings, which had been blasted from the wing which had received a direct hit. Shirts, towels, socks, a portable gramophone – a little private world exposed for all to see… Rubble was everywhere and all three hangars had been wrecked…

In spite of the smoke and craters, Tangmere's aircraft all managed to land back safely – with the one exception already described.

Even a conflict as tough and serious as this one could have its moments of light relief. Hence the following document preserved in the Public Record Office under the title "The Flight Engineer (*Bordmechaniker*) Who Jumped To It Too Quickly":

At 07.00 hours on August 13 a lone German airman (a Flight Engineer) Gefreiter Niessl was discovered near Tangmere. There was no trace of a crashed aircraft or other German airmen. Apparently, this airman was in a Ju 88 bomber which took off from St André in France on a bombing attack. After an encounter with fighters near the Isle of Wight the engines of the Ju 88 started failing, and the pilot headed for land and ordered the crew to jump. Unfortunately for him, the Flight Engineer obeyed this order much too promptly, for it later transpired that the pilot had second thoughts, and succeeded in bringing his aircraft back to base and landed safely.

This was the unfortunate Flight Engineer's first and last war flight. Two days later, on August 15, at Middle Wallop, there was the second of two airfield strikes similar to the attack on Tangmere already described. Pilot Officer David Crook recorded the following in his log book:

We shot down four Me 110 confirmed. A Blenheim attacked the German formation and I shot it down by mistake. Crew OK (save for a cut in the rear gunner's bottom) and machine landed at Wallop, looking fairly well peppered. Not a very good show.

Yet about this period the atmosphere of the air battle changed as men became more hardened. Richard Hillary would write:

During that August-September time, we were always so outnumbered that it was practically impossible, unless we were lucky enough to have the advantage of height, to deliver more than one Squadron attack.

After a few seconds we always broke up, and the sky was a smoke trail of individual dog-fights. The result was that the squadron would come home individually, machines landing one after another at intervals of about two minutes. After an hour, Uncle George [the station commander] would make a check-up on who was missing. Often there would be a telephone call from some pilot to say that he had made a forced landing at some other aerodrome, or in a field. But the telephone wasn't always so welcome. It would be a rescue squad announcing the number of a crashed machine; then Uncle George would check it, and cross another name off the list. At that time, the losing of pilots was somehow extremely impersonal. Nobody, I think, felt any great emotion – there simply wasn't time for it.

It was getting hard for others too, including those who had to cope with their awareness of the losses and the consequences without being able to show it. In early September Hillary was shot down, and, terribly burned, became one of the patients who were treated at the Maxillo-Facial Unit of the Queen Victoria Hospital at East Grinstead by Archibald McIndoe. The WAAF Jean Mills saw him when he began his slow process of returning to active service. However brilliant McIndoe's work, it could not conceal all the scars, or return a man so badly affected to normality. She commented:

I remember seeing Richard Hillary. He was the one who got terribly bad burns. And I remember he walked on to the platform and we looked up and I remember consciously thinking, "You mustn't flinch, you mustn't avert your gaze, you must look at him as if he was just like anybody else". His face was absolutely livid…

Inevitably combat reports, however vivid, give little or nothing away about the mind-set and the morale of those engaged in the fighting. Moreover, it would appear that, with some noted exceptions (such as Richard Hillary's, quoted above) not many wrote at length or in detail about their experiences while the battle was in progress. Or afterwards, because those that survived moved to other activities or other campaigns. Fortunately, later attempts to record for posterity the reminiscences of the last of the "few" have left a legacy of valuable evidence – material that arguably deserves wider circulation than it has so far received. The extracts that follow are from a handful of the numerous interviews recorded in the late 1980s and early 1990s as part of a major project undertaken by the Imperial War Museum on the air operations of 1940.

For Peter Brothers, Hurricane pilot first with 32 and later 257 Squadron, air warfare had begun during the battle for France; it was not long before he was in contact with the Luftwaffe:

The first patrol we did from Abbeville, we stumbled across a bunch of Me 109s going in precisely the opposite direction. And one of them whizzed over the top of my head so close that you could see the oil streaks on the aircraft and that sort of thing. And you did a sudden realization: "Good God, it's the enemy!". And then a combat started and I managed to shoot one of them down. It was quite strange because the chap who'd passed over my head went into a steep turn as I did to see where he'd gone. And he came round in a great curve and I was on the inside of the curve and as the Hurricane could turn much better than the 109, I got him in the sights and fired and was surprised to see that the thing caught fire and went down through the clouds burning merrily.

My first feelings were, "Goodness this is going to annoy the rest of them, I'd better look out, where are they?". But I think one of the things that was a saving of my life in a lot of respects was that when I first joined the Air Force, we were lectured by a chap called Taffy Jones, who was a First World War ace of some renown, and he stuttered terribly. And Taffy warned us that there was going to be a war and that we were going to be in it. And – I make no apology for his language – this is how he put it, he said, "When you gget into your ffirst ffight you'll be ffucking ffrightened. Never fforget that the cchap in the other ccockpit is ttwice as ffucking ffrightened as you are". And that was a very good morale booster. I thought I was pretty frightened but I thought that poor German must be even more frightened than I was.

Brothers, who would later rise to the rank of Air Vice-Marshal, came through the hard fighting of 1940, both in France and Britain, with his morale and motivation undiminished, but he was well aware that this was a war in which there would be casualties, and not only on account of the fighting. The point was to try to keep a sense of balance:

If you start taking life too seriously under those sorts of circumstances this is when people crack up. And we had cases of chaps who cracked up. One who, according to the doctors, when they pulled him off flying, wrote a report for me as flight commander and said that he had baled out so many times and he'd been burnt and everything else. Well these were all things that had happened to other people in the squadron and he'd thought they'd all happened to him. And he'd reached the stage where he'd got beads of perspiration on his head. In fact he was sitting at dispersal with us and I thought he must have pneumonia or something – he'd got beads of perspiration and looked hot and hands were shaking. And so I sent him off to the doc and thought "Oh, he's just got flu or something". And they sent a message back saying he was not even to fly his aeroplane back to Biggin Hill from Manston. They were taking him off flying. He subsequently became a test pilot testing rebuilt aircraft and had a ghastly crash. And was badly smashed up and in hospital for about six months. But went back to it. He'd got a lot of guts but not the sort of guts to face the enemy. A different sort of courage.

Brian Kingcome served as a Spitfire pilot in both France and Britain. Although he was shot down in the later stages of the Battle of Britain, on October 15, for which he blamed himself, he clearly had the right stuff for this kind of war:

It sounds perhaps callous – I don't know – but it was enormously exciting and tremendous fun. And we had every advantage. To begin with, we were flying over our own territory and this was a huge moral advantage. Because first of all it gives you a reason for being there. But normally air fighting is very detached. You're not killing somebody in an aeroplane, you're shooting down a piece of machinery. And you forget the personalities involved and it comes as quite a shock and a surprise when somebody jumps out of it. Then you realize the personalities involved. And it sounds a bit melodramatic, but when you are defending your own homeland, it does give you an added edge. So when you are flying over your own homeland with friendly faces below, if you got shot down and weren't killed, you lived to fight another day.

He believed in "head-on tactics" whatever the size or nature of the enemy force they were sent to repel. He described one especially formidable formation:

They looked like a bloody great swarm of bees. And in the distance they looked like a milling great mass of little insects. But you were approaching – not at today's speeds – you were lumbering towards each other amazingly slowly. But in those days if you were diving down from a couple of thousand feet above them, which is probably what you tried to do, you were probably doing roundabout four hundred in your Spitfire. And they were probably doing somewhere about a hundred and eighty. So you were approaching not far short of six hundred miles an hour. So the gap closed very quickly. And so very soon the swarm of bees became a lot of bloody great aeroplanes. And then the tracer fire would come out. It's a little bit unnerving when they're firing at you because every third or fourth round – whatever their mixture was – was tracer. And tracer comes out at you apparently very slowly to begin with. You see these lazy, long smoke trails coming at you. They get faster as they reach you, then suddenly whip past your ear at the most amazing speed. Luckily most of them miss.

Of course you didn't always have the time to plan because sometimes you were sent off late. Maybe you had only landed a short time ago from another sortie and hadn't had the time to rearm and refuel. It was when you were sent off in time you could do what I really preferred to do: climb to your height ahead of the enemy bombers, then turn around and tackle head on. A head-on attack did far more to destroy the morale of the approaching bombers than anything else. And it upset the driver so much, the poor old pilot. He was the chap who then turned tail. When he was sitting and couldn't see the attack and was protected by a nice sheet of metal behind him and he had the gunners and he could hear the guns going backward and all that, he was in a much more relaxed frame of mind than when you were coming straight at him and he had nothing between himself and the guns. And one would then go straight through the formation, turn round when you got through. And try and have another go from the rear then. But usually by that stage their fighters would come down. So normally you had one or maybe two jolly good goes at the bombers before you got involved with the escorting fighters. After your first attack, you did whatever you could. Wherever you found yourself, you attacked. It was only the initial attack you could take any part in the planning of. After that it was very much a free for all.

The danger time in a pilot's life was the inevitable period of initiation, though having emerged successfully from the apprentice stage could also have its risks:

If you lived through the first three or four or five or six sorties, you cottoned on very quickly. And you learnt the business of rubber necking because far more pilots were shot down by an aircraft they never saw than by one they actually did see – people creeping up on you because you weren't looking round. And in fact that was how I finally bought it. Sheer overconfidence, being *blasé*. Practising a forced landing from fifteen thousand feet after an engagement. I never saw what shot me.

One who would agree with Kingcome about the risks a first action entailed was George Unwin, sergeant pilot with 19 Squadron at RAF Duxford:

Despite the fact that I had four good years or more of flying experience, and that was a lot of experience in those days, I still regard this as the most dangerous time in any fighter pilot's life – and I've talked to many of them about being in action. The first time you're shot at – and most of them agree with me – you freeze. I did. I suddenly saw a Messerschmitt coming up inside me. And I saw little sparks coming from the front end of him. I knew he was shooting at me. And I did nothing, absolutely nothing. I just sat there – in a turn – but just sat there. Not petrified but frozen for, I don't know, ten seconds, fifteen seconds. But never again did I do that.

After that, of course, you don't hesitate; you've been…blooded. But despite all my experience I just sat there and watched him shoot at me. Stupid thing to do I know, but fortunately he knocked a few little holes in the back of my aircraft and did no damage at all. And didn't hit me luckily. From then on, of course, you realize what a mug you were and you never do it again. But I suppose it's just one isn't used to being shot at in any walk of life and I suppose most people finding someone shooting at them would freeze anyway wondering what on earth's happening. Anyway that's what happened. As I say, from then on it never happened again. Oh, I was hit again, quite often, not for the same reason, not my own fault, put it that way.

Unwin was involved in a shooting down of a Heinkel bomber while flying from Duxford in what was known as the "big wing" formation (a variation of fighter-fighting technique much associated with Douglas Bader, which involved a large number of fighters in action together):

Well this Heinkel was flying around. There was a very thin layer of cloud no more than fifty feet thick and I was wandering around above this, having lost everybody of course. An incredible thing this in air warfare. You go in as a squadron or a wing as we did eventually under Bader in '40 – the big wing fighting – and you get mixed up and then, two minutes later, you are on your own. You can't see an aeroplane anywhere. It's amazing how suddenly the sky seems to clear. You can find them eventually but it was rather strange, it always happened. Anyway I'd got split up on this particular occasion and I was above cloud looking for some fun and what have you and I suddenly saw this Heinkel come out of the cloud, climbing, and he was smack in front of me. So I closed in and gave him a burst whereupon he promptly went back into the cloud. I thought "Damn it" and I was about to go down again when he came up again. And he did this some four or five times. And I was rather puzzled on one occasion, about the third or fourth time, because he went down apparently unhurt and when he came up he had one engine blazing. I thought, "That's bloody funny, he didn't have that when he went into the cloud". Anyway, when we got back for debriefing my flight commander, Sandy Lane, repeated exactly the same story. But he was the one underneath the cloud. And so what was happening was that this Heinkel was being shot at by me above the cloud, went for cover into the cloud which was so thin he went through it. Below it happened to be Lane and he shot at him and he went back up again. And this went on until eventually he was shot down. It was a bit puzzling why he kept coming up for more. But that was the reason.

David Cox was another sergeant pilot with 19 Squadron. He also found himself curiously alone following a skirmish in which he had found himself more observer than participant:

I hadn't fired my guns or anything and then I heard over the radio that the enemy formations were making for the Thames estuary – withdrawing. So I climbed up and just near Clacton I saw about twenty Messerschmitt 110s going round in a circle, which they used to do – partly for defence and partly to be at the rear of any withdrawing bombers. So I – with cannon which I hadn't fired – climbed above them. And of course the 110's a fairly big aeroplane and when there's twenty of them I thought to myself, "Well, if I dive on them there's a chance of hitting something". I always think it was a bit of an Errol Flynn effort. Anyway, I dived firing away with my six seconds of ammunition, and used that up very quickly, as you can imagine. And then one of them broke away with an engine – I couldn't say it was on fire but it was smoking. It dived away and I went to follow it down but the others then attacked me so I carried straight on down. Didn't see what happened to the 110 and I only claimed it as a probable. But after the war, many years after the war, it was confirmed that it had crashed because the crew had baled out and were taken prisoner.

When he was himself shot down, he was in no doubt as to who were responsible, having gone to the help of a fellow pilot who was clearly in trouble:

I suddenly saw a Hurricane near Folkestone on his own. He was being attacked by four ME 109s. And before I could do any good he went down and he actually crashed near Sittingbourne and was killed. And the four 109s then devoted their attention to myself. They were no doubt experts because two got above me and two below me. And I was in a circle. I realized I was in a tight corner, did a lot of firing, which was I think more to boost my own morale and perhaps frighten them than any chance of hitting them. And then eventually there was a loud bang in my cockpit and I momentarily was sort of dazed. And when I came to the aircraft was going straight down and I thought, "Oh, this is it". Then decided suddenly it wasn't and grabbed the control column and shot straight up again. And as I slowed down I opened the hood, turned the aircraft over and baled out. It was very cold and obviously I was suffering from shock and then I suddenly noticed my right leg, that there was blood seeping through my flying boots. Subsequently it appeared that I had nine pieces of cannon shell in my right leg and I was taken to an emergency hospital near there. And that was the end of the Battle of Britain for me.

Sergeant Pilot Maurice Leng of 73 Squadron was also shot down; like Kingcome he never knew by whom. He refused to bale out, however, being determined if possible to bring his Hurricane home:

Suddenly there was a terrific crash in my back, which was the armour plating, shells hitting, shells and bullets and what have you. And I don't know what shot me down at that time, no idea. I think the official records say it was a 109 but I don't know. And it's rather like shooting a bird when its hit it sort of falls out of the sky. And this is what happened with my aeroplane, but it wasn't on fire, it didn't catch fire.

But I found that I could control it to a certain extent, that is I pulled the stick fully back and it went into a fairly steep glide. And obviously it was very dangerous to be wounded because you would be attacked again and finished off. But anyway I managed to get out of the action and I saw below me Gravesend. And it's rather strange what one's instincts, how your instincts, react. But I'd got a brand new aeroplane and I didn't want to jump out of it. I wasn't frightened to jump out in a parachute because it was semi-controllable. And I did the unwritten thing you should never do. I stayed with the aircraft, although I wasn't in complete control. And if I opened the throttle Glycol poured back and I couldn't see, so I closed the throttle. And the propeller was windmilling. And I saw Gravesend aerodrome and the Thames below me. So I did a big circle around it very high up – about ten thousand feet – circled down on to it and then did an approach and found that at thirty feet where you normally checked I couldn't check, it was still going down. So just before I slammed into the deck and killed myself, I slammed open the throttle and there were clouds of smoke and steam but it lifted the nose. And I shot across Gravesend aerodrome on the wheels and the engine caught fire, flames going everywhere, in front of me, so I stepped off the wing. Undid my straps and slid off the wing on to the grass – it was a grass airfield – and rolled over and over and I was completely unhurt and uninjured. And the aircraft went on and the fire engines came out and sprayed it and put out the flames. And I just ignored it, went to the mess and got myself a cup of tea or a drink – in those days the bar was very often open and you could have a drink. And the station wing commander engineer officer came into me and said, "That was stupid of you wasn't it?". I said, "Why? You've got an aeroplane down intact, a brand new aeroplane," I said, "It'll be repairable". He said, "Don't be silly, it's category 'A', it's a write off".

With so much happening, good and bad, Germans going down, friends failing to return, not to mention the mayhem of the Blitz, what was the attitude of the pilots to the progress of the battle and the war? Sergeant Pilot George Unwin had no doubts:

It never crossed our minds that we would ever be beaten, or that we could be beaten. Particularly the Spitfire pilot – why should we? He had the best aeroplane in the world – as far as he was concerned he was the best pilot in the world – and with the best aeroplane how could he be beaten? Oh no, we couldn't get in the air often enough in 12 Group, we really couldn't.

Asked, however, if there was any sense of making history, he replied:

None whatsoever. No. In fact, when Churchill said something about "Never in the field of human conflict has so much or something been owed to so few," my CO always reckoned he was referring to the unpaid mess bills.

CHAPTER EIGHT

When the Bomber Got Through

O NE OF THE VITAL QUESTIONS asked repeatedly in the pre-war years by people concerned about the nature of any future war was: "Would the bomber get through?". The widespread assumption was that if it did, the "rain" of terror thus unleashed would break the heart of any civilian population beneath it. Anyone who in the mid-1930s saw the film *Things To Come*, based on the alarming imaginings of the supreme prophet of the time, H.G. Wells, would never forget its impact. In particular, the vision of huge sinister aircraft emerging menacingly from clouds – as frightening in their way as the grim-grey Stealth bombers of today – accompanied by the brilliantly haunting music of Arthur Bliss, would have left an indelible impression of the awesome nature of hostile air power. What would happen if that celluloid fantasy became real?

In the skies over Britain in 1940, despite the superlative efforts of the nation's champions – not just the pilots, but all those vital others heavily engaged in the defence of the realm – the bomber could not be stopped from getting through. As the weeks of the summer slipped by and the Germans intensified their air campaign, Britain would become the test case that would prove or disprove the pessimistic assumptions of the theorists. Would the nerve of the populace hold or break? Would Britain be able to take it? These were not questions to which there were any easy answers.

Before the bombs there were the sirens. Anybody who lived through the war will never forget the chill at the heart when the air raid siren began its strange up-and-down wailing. From the second it began its first upward swoop it was unmistakable. It was a sound like no other, imperiously demanding attention. Listen, take action, or else! Some people likened it to the call of a *banshee*, that evil fairy of the Irish imagination which allegedly shrieks and wails before a death. But there was a whiff of almost benign tradition in such a comparison; this was a new invention, synthetic, soulless, an odious but necessary consequence of the new style of war.

Already, back in July, Philip Chignell of Hessle, near Hull, had conceived an utter loathing of that increasingly present phenomenon, the more so because the machine that produced it was installed rather too near his own dwelling for comfort:

> Last night the siren sounded, just as I had gone off to sleep, at 11 p.m. precisely. Katie had not given up her novel for she has a quiet hour at night whereas I get a quiet hour in the morning, a little arrangement that seems to work very well.

I never got out of bed for the darned row of the siren – a terrible shrieking row,
only a few doors away from us, a row that nobody could escape from, not even a
deaf man. I just stayed where I was and waited for the two minutes' yelling to cease
and then I turned over and pretended I should soon be asleep.

We have these alarms so frequently lately that one cannot keep count of them.
They come at all times of the day and night. Noon, midnight, dinner time, tea time
and in between times. I don't think there is one hour of the twenty four of the clock
that we have not had at least one alarm.

Chignell also noted the standard, equally memorable accompaniment to the
hated siren, the ominous unmistakable drone of enemy aircraft:

Last night it was dull and cloudy and for two or three hours Jerry was roaming and
humming very high up. We could hear the dull note of his aeroplane engine. The
sound came and went. Searchlights were after it from time to time, a dozen or
twelve of them, but they could not spot it, it was so high up and the clouds were
low. At 2 am., with the same time precision as before, the relief sounded and we
all made the best of the interrupted repose.

All this seemed to him, however, to be mere shadow-boxing. He reminded his sisters:

You know the story of Wolf, Wolf? Well, it is getting like that. One day perhaps he
will really get at us, so far it has been all noise and frightening.

Where there were the sirens, however, soon after there were the bombs. To begin
with, the visitations of the enemy's bombers were largely seen as being of nuisance
value only, and were borne with a patient shrug. Hence this report in *The Times*
of August 6 under the heading "People Unperturbed by Air Raids":

In East Anglia the hitherto limited use of the German air arm has fallen rather
more heavily inland than on the coast... One might therefore have expected
some of the inland towns, if any, to be the most upset by the course of the war thus
far. The truth is that everyday life continues in them much more normally than
along the coast. If some of the seaside resorts more or less resemble dead cities it
is because of the ban on summer visitors and voluntary evacuation, encouraged
by the government. The inland towns, on the contrary, are if anything fuller
than usual; and, unlike the holiday resorts, they can still make ends meet.

Their occupants take the occasional air raids sufficiently seriously to safe-
guard themselves, but without letting the danger prey on minds or nerves...

The civilian population has become hardened in a wonderfully short time. To avoid broken nights many people now sleep every night in their shelters, fitted with comfortable beds. A man whose wife and daughter occupy the family refuge nightly, while he continues to sleep in the house, told me how, after their most recent raid – it came at 6 a.m. – and the falling of bombs in the near neighbourhood "I made them a cup of tea and they went back to sleep". The British are the grand empiricists, the great exponents of trial and error…

Other early air-raid stories recorded a quirkish, even up-beat response to the current threat from the sky. Thus *The Times* of August 16, while also reporting an attack by twenty bombers on Croydon Airport, printed the following items under the heading "SANG-FROID" – that invaluable French word that better than any other term defines English, or British, coolness. The first, written two days earlier, was by a lady writing from an undisclosed coastal address:

Sir.
The village in which I am writing is on the edge of a harbour. In the first lull in a recent air raid after twenty minutes of steady gunfire and all the other noises, I went to see why my neighbour, an old-age pensioner of seventy, had not joined us. I found her enjoying a substantial dinner, which she was half way through. She said she had stayed to keep the canary company, as it seemed nervous.

The second, written the same day, was from a vicar's wife living in Sussex:

Sir.
Recently a friend of mine was woken in the early hours of the morning by the crash of bombs dropped by a German raider near her house. A minute or so after the explosion she heard the housemaid's knock on the bedroom door and a calm voice announcing "Bombs, please, madam!".

But already the bombing was becoming more than something that could be shrugged off with a laugh or a gesture of nonchalant resignation. On August 13, Frank Lockwood, a resident of Birmingham, a family man in his fifties who had served in the previous conflict, recorded in his diary what he called "our first real air-raid of the war":

We got up and went into shelter about 11 o'clock. Machines came over in about seven waves – they all seemed to come from the same direction – there was heavy

anti-aircraft fire [and] many bombs were dropped. No sirens sounded until the raid
had been going for some time. We could hear shrapnel dropping on roofs and in the
gardens. The children were splendid. It was 3.15 a.m. when the final all-clear went.

There was more serious matter to record on August 15:

We thought Tuesday's raid was pretty close to us but we had a worse experience
tonight. Dorothy had just got into bed and I was about to get in when we heard
airplane engines and…a salvo of bombs not too far away. We were soon up and
down stairs. I went and had a look round. We stayed up a while [but] all was quiet
so back we went to bed. About quarter to one or so we were awakened to a
terrific crash of bombs that fairly seemed to shake the house. We were soon up and
out in the shelter with the children. No siren sounded until 1.45. Bombers seemed
to come every quarter of an hour – same direction as the other night. About 2.30
there was a terrific fall of bombs – among them a "screaming bomb", which
almost seemed on top of us and fairly made the shelter quiver. The all-clear at 3.15.

Lockwood subsequently noted the night's "results":

11 people were killed in yesterday's raid. Don't know how many injured.

He would later comment that at this period there were numerous air attacks on
the London provinces while London slept peacefully. What he could not know was
that there was a definite reason why that was the case, a reason which lay deep in
the convoluted ever-changing thought processes of Herr Hitler.

Frank Lockwood's gratified comment that "the children were splendid" is a highly
significant one. Inevitably, there had been much concern in advance about the reaction of children to air-raids. Would they panic, be frightened out of their wits,
become impossible to console? Curious as it might seem, their response was often
not so much one of fear as of fascinated interest, even excitement.

Patricia Donald, whose thirteenth birthday was in August 1940, was a private
evacuee at Thornleigh Preparatory School and School Matrons' Training School
at Tunbridge Wells, Kent. The town was on what would come to be known as "Bomb
Alley", as it lay on a key German route to the capital. She would later describe the
diary she wrote throughout this period as an attempt to reveal "the personal
drama of people pitchforked into abnormal situations, trying to live a normal life".
Vivid, lively, precise as to details and timings, her account catches the mood of the
moment in a manner that makes remarkably light of the presence of danger:

Tuesday August 13

We had an air-raid today at 7 a.m. I woke up about a minute before the siren went off, then thought, "Oh goodness, it can't be another". I dressed quickly, putting on my usual over-vest, dressing-gown and shoes, and took two blankets, two small pillows, my gas mask, the wrong book and Tessie [her dog]. Adams [a trainee school matron] said sixty one planes were brought down yesterday and nine of ours. It was Peter's [an eight-year-old evacuee] birthday and I gave him six balloons and a jig-saw. The guests for Peter's party arrived in due course at about 4.30 p.m. and we played games until tea-time, and just as we were finishing, the siren went and we all went down to the ARP room and played games – "I Spy" and "Animal Noises". In some way Brian Farrance managed to push Rodney Bodkin over, and make him graze his cheek badly, and they didn't have any plaster so I went upstairs and got some Elastoplast and Miss Smith stuck it on. Then we played some more games and they left us thoroughly exausted [sic] at 6.30 p.m.

Friday August 23

I was woken up at about quarter to three by seven or eight bombs, about five miles [away]. I got out of bed and sat on the chair by Jeanie's bed. Then I began to hear German planes, machine-gun and anti-aircraft guns. It began to get so bad that we went down to the next landing and waited for the siren. It was about four o'clock by now. It got a bit quieter and Benge and Jeanie and I went upstairs to get into bed, when the siren went – after the raiders had gone. We stayed down there twenty minutes.

Friday August 30

We had a quiet time last night and we didn't have an air-raid till 11.35. We had been hearing guns and aeroplanes for quite a time, and we had got everything ready. We were playing with one ear and eye cocked, when Miss Howitt said "Oh! there it is!" and we all went indoors. About 11.45 we heard a terrific crash, which we guessed was a bomb falling about 100 yards away from the house. Only later we found it was an anti-aircraft gun. The all-clear went at 12.40. We had another one at two o'clock, just as I had settled down to have some glucose. We had tea down in the shelter, and the all-clear went at seven o'clock. We dashed out just as the all-clear was sounding, to look at a barrage balloon that had broken its moorings. Several aeroplanes swept up to it, and as the last one went past we heard the rat-tat-tat of machine-gun fire, and the balloon started to sink slowly. The siren went again at 7.20 and the all-clear went at eight o'clock. About ten o'clock Dotty, Jean, Benge, Tessie and I went and slept down in the shelter

Tuesday September 3

Today is the anniversary of the war, its first birthday. Bombs and cannons were heard at 12.30 a.m., and as they are not sounding the sirens in the night any more,

we thought we'd better go down so we went, and stayed down until 2.30. The next
siren went at 10.30 a.m. The all-clear went at 12.30 p.m.

Stephen Macfarlane was a twelve-year-old schoolboy at University College (Junior)
School at Holly Hill, Hampstead, London, in 1940. His family owned a house in
South Hill Park, Hampstead, and had a cottage at Chalfont St Peter,
Buckinghamshire, to which Stephen and his elder brother John frequently cycled
– a journey remarkably safe for young bicyclists then, even at a time of frequent air-
raids, that would surely seem impossibly dangerous now. The family were planning
to let the cottage in August 1940, and did so in mid-September to two young nurses.
Throughout the heady weeks of August and September, Stephen kept a detailed diary.
Lavishly illustrated with striking sketches, it contains a superb mixture of "normal"
small-boy pursuits and wartime dramas, all couched in idiosyncratic spelling which
is frequently bizarre but which always succeeds in conveying the intended meaning.
Singularly absent is any sense of fear. These are thrilling times and he is determined to record them. The diary begins at Buckinghamshire:

Tuesday August 20
This morning when I was cycling home from a searchlight unit near Jordans I
saw in a field four medium howitzers practicing. I raced home because I wanted
john to see them. When we both returned there were lots of wireless cars and
motor cycles. All the gun crews were lined up near the edge of the field. An RSM
shouted somthing thru a megaphone and the gun crews race to thier guns. And
loaded them with dummy shells. The RSM then shouted "unload, hitch up".
Then four heavy lorrys rumbled up. Then with lightning speed, men put net covers
on, and canvas covers on the sights. Some other gunners took up the wicker
mats (to stop gun sincking in mud) under each wheel. I scetched them, just
before they drove off. In the afternoon we saw a lot of lorrys going by and one had
an ariel lewis gun mounted.

Thursday August 22
Before breackfast this morning I went for a short cycle ride. Then wrote letter to
violet. She sent a letter yesterday, saying that she had seen a spitfier shoot down
a German bomber. Had a row with John. After dinner I polished floor in sitting
room. Had another row with john. After tea got paper and burnt rubbish, it
made tons of smoke.

Sunday August 25
Made tea for mother and father this morning. Mother said that in the night
there were warnings and she saw searchlights and heard a german plane about alot
and then some British fighters after it. Mummy is a pig she did not wake me.

His mother's failure to alert him seems to have made him determined not to miss any further such happenings, whether by night or day:

Monday August 26

Three raids last night but heard nothing. We got up very early because we wanted to get back to London before it got too hot. Me and John started on bike about 10. I was not half so tired on way home. On the road saw lots of army lorries and motor bikes. It was super when we got to North Holt. First we saw all the barbed wire and pillboxes. Outside one there was a vickers machine gun with a soldier cleaning it. In a field near by there was a batterie of two pounder anti air craft guns. They had so many fighters at Northholt that they had to make wind shields out of mounds of earth. Each wind shield had its own twin Lewis guns manned by soldiers. We saw twelve hurricanes taxi into position then, from the houses near-by, a rocket shot up, and when it hit the ground a thin colomb of smoke came up for wind direction. Then the twelve took off at once. Those hurricanes looked marvellous. You could see the pilots faces. Just after Northholt we came to what looked like two tea shops with nice verandas and painted jolly coulours at a roundabout. The windows were painted black but when you whent close you saw in the black windows slits and as the insides of the pill box was dark you could hardly see slits. A nasty surprise for German parachutists.

On way home, passed lots of factorys with soldiers garding and lots of road blocks. We passed a bren carrier tank as well. Did twenty five miles in two hours. Had dinner then went down to Hamlys toy shop with John. I brought a Hurricane, and John a Spitfire. Went home had tea then saw Jixes new kitten. She said that there were three raid alarms last night. Started making my hurricane, I then went to bed.

P.S. At Hamleys we got caught in an air raid. Very nice shelter, had a wireless and water and they sold chochlats.

Tuesday August 27

Last night there was a huge air raid but of course I slept through it. German bombers came over in relays. They bombed Hendon. I heard German bombers in my sleep. I woke up with a hell of a start at the all-clear. This morning went on with my model hurricane. In evening lisened to wireless then went to bed in Johns room. John finished his spitfire as well.

Wednesday August 28

There was another raid last night. The siren went exactly the same time as yester-day. Saw searchlights and heard German planes. This morning scetched Bren Carrier, then showed it to the soldiers, a lance corporal in charge crossed out the letters on it. I had put the exact letters on my drawing. Had dinner played with my plane, and soldiers.

This evening Mrs Bally said that an aerodrome had been bombed and no warning given. The man who was to give warning was found with bullet in back. fifth colomist at work.

Thursday August 29
More raids last night. Heard German aroeplanes, one went kind of chug chug. Bomb dropped about less than half a mile away it shook the house. Started making wooden model of messershmite. Had dinner then John went out to cinema. Me, Mummy and Daddy went out to see film called *My Son, My Son*. In the news afterwards we saw German planes so clearly that you could see the cross. Saw as well German planes crashing and a Hurricane diving with smoke pouring from tail.

Friday August 30
Went down to cottage on train. John went by bike. Air raid on way down. Gard at Northholt arodrome would not let John pass he had to go another way.

Saturday August 31
Air raid warning at breakfast. Went out, air raid warden told me to go home.

Sunday September 1
Air Raid last night. Two salvos of bombs dropped. Deladed action bombs dropped near. Read a bit this morning. Saw begginings of a road block outside our house. Air raid warning. Heard gunfire, saw fighters. Winsor and Slough bombed last night. There are lots of factorys at Slough. Had dinner early because Mother and Father wanted to go out for a bicycle ride. Mother and Daddy saw a camp for soldiers in a wood, the tents where so camoflaged that they could not hardly see them. John saw an ironside (armorrded car) on Friday. Mrs Welch the farmers wife said they watched a dog fight.

Monday September 2
Went up to London this morning by train. No raids last night. When got home had dinner, after that scrubbed my German helmet to bring up the real field gray.

Like Patricia Donald, on September 3 he recorded what he called "the annafersary of the war". He had no further comment on the occasion but on the following day there was much to record despite the, by then, unusual if brief lull in enemy activity:

Wednesday September 4
No air raids last night. Played with trains after breakfast. Were going to Hackny to see messerschmit 109 but had to wait for laundry. Air raid warning, heard fighters. Whent to see *Night Train To Munich*. After the film, at the entrance were

The Withdrawal from Dunkirk, June 1940. Oil Painting by Charles Cundall.

The man who would not contemplate defeat, Winston Churchill.

How to recognize the enemy in the event of invasion.

Dad's Army idealized: recruiting poster.

"West Country Manoeuvres: We are held up by ferocious Home guards" by Edward Ardizzone.

A reminder that 1940 was a year of many refugees abroad and of a second wave of evacuees in Britain.

Urging young women of the nation to "Go to it".

A necessary warning: many wartime casualties were the victims not of air raids but of street accidents.

What was it all about. A green and pleasant land worth fighting for.

"Sketch of an air raid on London", watercolour by Stephen Macfarlane, aged twelve.

The Battle of Britain, oil painting by veteran First World War artist, Paul Nash.

The classic poster of the Battle of Britain and the classic statement,
from Churchill's speech in the House of Commons, August 20.

Southwark Tunnel: women and children using a tunnel under the
Thames as an air raid shelter. Ink and wash drawing by Antony Gross

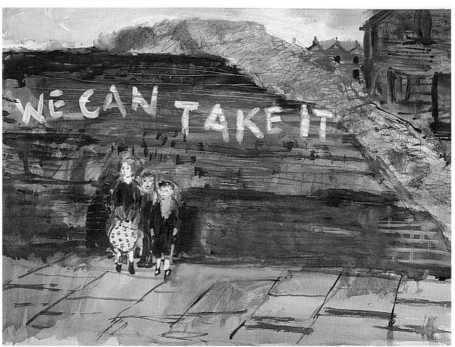

"We Can Take It": the spirit of the Blitz, as shown in a watercolour by Ruskin Spear.

German, French, Dutch and Belgian Army gas masks on show as well as bits of bombs, incendery bombs and casings of delaid action bombs. I gave a shilling towards a Hurricane.

Friday September 6
An air raid warning, heavy gunfire. We saw fighters going to chase off the raiders. Mother said bombs were dropped all night. Played trains went to get butter and margarine rations. John and I then cycled down to cottage, very hot. When we were by Northholt there was a warning and we saw fighters takeing off. The LDV have made barbed wire tressles and logs for road block outside our cottage.

Saturday September 7
Had warning last night, but nothing happened. And we had a quiet night. Went down to Chalfont St Peter we brought tons of food home. Then John, me and mother went blackberrying. Saw Spitfire, it was not low. A training aroeplane came very low and I waved to it, you could see the pilot. He waved back, you could see his arm stretched out waving. Went to meet Daddy, said that lots of bombs dropped all night.

Sunday September 8
Last night did not sleep well. An air raid, German planes came over, lots of searchlights. We kept on seeing funny red flares in the sky. All the evening we saw a bright red glare in the direction of London. We think it was a big fire. All last night LDV men garded the road block outside our house. They challenged every-body that went past. When one cyclist came past the LDV man said "advance to be recognized". The man then went on and the LDVs dragged him back. He said "I thought you said Pass Friend you are recognized".

His father's reference to the "lots of bombs dropped" on the night of September 7–8, and his own vivid sighting of "the bright red glare in the direction of London" were more than mere matters of detail. They signalled the long expected upward shift in the scale of the German attack on London, in effect the start of the Blitz.

The pace had been steadily quickening for fourteen days. Saturday August 24 was a fine day after a period of cloudy, showery weather. The *Jubilee History*'s chronology records "Violent increase in Luftwaffe activity", listing as the day's targets "Ramsgate, Dover, Portsmouth and airfields (Manston five times, Hornchurch, N. Weald)". Under the sub-heading "Night", it notes bombing in South Wales and on a Birmingham aircraft factory. It then adds, in italics, "unintentional bombs in central London". It is arguable to say that this was a key moment of the war.

Bombs on the British capital were not Hitler's intention, indeed he had issued emphatic orders to the contrary. However, the fact that bombs had fallen on London for the first time since 1918 produced an immediate response. On the night of August 25 RAF bombers flew to Berlin to launch a reprisal raid. Yet here again there was an unintentional error. Bombs struck not only legitimate military targets, but civilian areas as well. There were further raids on subsequent nights, and on the night of August 28 some Berliners were killed. The Nazi promise had been that no bombs would ever fall on the German capital. The unthinkable having happened, the stakes were instantly raised. Yielding to the ancient temptation of an eye for an eye and a tooth for a tooth, Hitler made his greatest strategic mistake in the prosecution of the Battle of Britain. He called off the attacks on airfields and launched a war against civilians, and in particular against the British capital. If Berlin bled, London would bleed too. This would produce much suffering among the Londoners, but it would leave Britain's defenders the bases from which to strike back. The Hurricanes and the Spitfires would not be trapped on cratered airfields. They would still be able to fly and therefore to fight. From that moment the Germans had effectively lost the battle.

As it happened, Liverpool not London was the first target of this new intensified phase. Over the four nights between August 28–31 an average of one hundred and fifty bombers attacked Merseyside. This was far from being precision bombing in that numerous other towns *en route* and around received a scatter of bombs. On the last night of the month, however, over a hundred and sixty fires were started in Liverpool's commercial centre. During the day, however, Hitler had given the go-ahead for the Luftwaffe to begin turning its attention to the prime target for his revenge. The capital's long ordeal was shortly to begin.

The accepted date for the start of the great attack on London is September 7. Up to 17.00 hours on that date, enemy activity, according to a Home Security Intelligence Summary issued later that same day, had been "extremely slight", with only a few bombs dropped on Bristol and on the RAF base at Hawkinge, Kent. But the relative peace of that fine summer Saturday was not to last. "Soon after 17.00 hours," the summary continued, "the enemy launched possibly his biggest air attack on this country so far." As many as a thousand German bombers crowded the skies over and around the capital. The focus was mainly on the East End, but many bombs fell elsewhere. Numerous fires were started, a train in Plumstead Station was hit resulting in some casualties and a blockage of the line, railway services out of Liverpool Street and Fenchurch Street were disrupted, Beckton gas works was damaged so that gas supplies to many parts of East London were greatly curtailed. Bombs also fell on Woolwich, Barking, Beckenham, Camberwell, Croydon, Putney and Kensington.

This was then followed by a heavy night raid. Stephen Macfarlane's diary had recorded this as seen from a distance. An ARP warden based in Chelsea, Miss Josephine "Jo" Oakman, who was in the middle of it, made the following almost staccato annotations of its progress in her diary, the bombers having fetched her out from what was meant to be a pleasant Saturday evening's relaxation:

20.40	Sirens. Was in the pictures.
20.50	One plane – two screamer bombs dropped, and seven others in rapid succession over Kensington way. Did a quick duck while out on patrol.
20.55	Another bomb very near – ducked again head first into trenches. Patrol work on bike and on foot.
21.00	Heavy AA gunfire.
22.01	Heavy thump – plane over.
22.20	Loads of Jerry planes – dogfights in dark.
23.47	Five awful thumps over Battersea – twelve fall in river, two in Battersea Park and one near Battersea Poly.

She continued her notes hour by hour into Sunday, ending with the following round-up:

5.10	Delayed action bomb went off and woke me up as I was sleeping at post. Electric lights failed in Chelsea for five minutes. No 22 Cadogan Sq has caught it – the front went in but the house was empty. Two more big fires were ignited at Docks. At 52 Pont Street, a bomb went through all floors and injured a lady. A Chelsea warden was hurt here. There is also a hole outside a garage in Pavilion Road. Smith Square Westminster also "copped it". Two planes came down at Clapham – one of which completely flattened two houses.

Two days later she had worse to report – the bombing of a shelter in Cadogan House.

September 10

4.00	God! What a day dawning! Peace after a night of hell but what a price! Over 41 poor dead things in that shelter including our own warden, Miss Darling, whose head was blown in.

Next day she added a further annotation:

Official number for the Cadogan House Shelter is fifty seven. Some were crushed beyond recognition and in pulp. Heaven help us all!

The night of September 7–8 is not only notable for the start of the Blitz; it also produced 1940's greatest invasion scare. The sudden surge in ferocity of the German air attacks at a time when, as it so happened, the tides were deemed to be especially favourable for a seaborne attack, created immediate ripples of alarm in high military circles. Could this be the prelude to the long-feared strike across the Channel? General Headquarters, Home Forces, wishing to take no chances, decided that the units of Eastern and Southern Commands should be brought to full alert – just in case. The only way to achieve this, even though the prospect of the enemy landing on British soil was at this stage merely a matter of hunch and guess-work, was to issue the agreed code-word for an actual invasion: "Cromwell". Other commands were hastily told of the situation and word was passed down the chain of command, not for action so much as for information.

Unfortunately, the Home Guard in certain areas was not let in on the secret. The result was inevitable: not quite Dad's Army's finest hour, but certainly one of its most valiant and determined, if also chaotic, ones.

The force had been taking itself increasingly seriously throughout the summer. Some 5000 of their number, for example, had been admitted for week-end training in the hallowed precincts of Bisley, while others had been undergoing instruction in techniques of guerrilla warfare in the grand setting of the Hurlingham Club. As a correspondent of *The Times* reported:

> One of the Hurlingham polo grounds – no one would recognize that austere sward now – has become the adopted home of the "Molotoff cocktail" and other lethal contrivances, its turf pitted with little tank traps of a type at once so simple and deadly that even the Irish Guards have been down to learn something about them... The pupils so far have been evenly balanced between veterans of the Great War and young men, and both attack their lessons with relish.

In addition, an area of run-down housing in one of the less fashionable parts of Chelsea had been given over to training in street-fighting. The same reporter noted of one mock-battle:

> For a few moments the showers of bricks and plaster provided a more than passing imitation of exploding grenades, while the "enemy" across the alley shinned up the drain pipes with an agility that sometimes belied their years, and did their best to make things hot with smoke bombs and any disturbing missile that lay to hand. It was a pity there were no real Germans there.

Now, suddenly, on the night of September 7–8, it seemed that the real Germans might be on their way. Thus when the code word "Cromwell" was received in areas where the the advice to wait for further instruction had not immediately followed, the Home Guard moved with a will. In some cases the mere fact that the emergency had been declared produced enemy sightings: they were expected, therefore they appeared. Hence the following entry in a report of events at the headquarters of a GPO battalion of the Home Guard based in Chester, which also included part of the North Wales coast in its area:

> 10.40 p.m. Postmaster, Conway, reported by telephone that he had made enquiries of the police who had informed him that an enemy aeroplane had passed over Conway and reports had been received that three parachutists had been seen to leave the plane near Tyngroes in the Conway Valley. The Conway Home Guard had been called out and had made a search.

In this case the emergency was soon found to have been based on a false alarm and the Conway men were recalled and sent home. But elsewhere the alarm spread with remarkable speed. In west Cornwall a key factor was the nervous reaction by the vicar of St Ives, who on seeing the local fishing fleet returning from the west instead of the east (the usual direction) mistook it for an enemy landing force and ordered the church bells to be rung. The reason for the choice of bells as the harbinger of invasion was at once apparent. There could be no better way of passing the message from one community to the next. Church towers and steeples instantly became the equivalent of the beacons of earlier times as they briskly passed the word through the shires. By late evening large sections of the country from Cornwall to the Western Isles were under the impression that the invasion had started. (It can only be hoped that John Betjeman's warning to wardens not to become too eager or too careless in the matter of bellringing saved some unnecessary casualties.) Home Guards were called out practically everywhere, nervously expecting parachutists to appear. "All one could hear," a columnist for the *Daily Herald* reported of the ensuing confusion, "was the echoing and re-echoing of the Home Guard challenge 'Who goes there?' with occasional rifle shots when the challenged party failed to stop."

In fact, invasion was on the verge of being struck off the German agenda. Hitler decided that he was going to make his decision as to whether or not to implement "Sealion" on September 14. On that date he postponed again, giving himself three more days in which to make up his mind. On September 17 he shelved the scheme indefinitely. But if invasion was no longer an option, the bombing campaign would continue, with London the prime target. The bomber would have its chance to prove its worth in what would become as much as anything a battle of wills. This would be the concluding phase of 1940's Spitfire Summer.

But before discussing the denouement of the battle of the air, it is important to turn to another aspect of 1940 all too easily overlooked: the war at sea.

CHAPTER NINE

"In Peril on the Sea"

T HE YEAR 1940 is so closely associated with the battle of the air, that it is all too easy to forget that there was another battle of Britain going on that summer – at sea. Here the danger was not of some major death-or-glory battle, in the style of a re-run of Jutland, but that the country's lifelines might be cut by one of the most chilling initiatives to emerge out of the First World War: the weapon that struck by stealth, invisibly, from under the water. In this context it is worth quoting Britain's apparently supremely confident wartime leader. In the volume of his Second World War memoirs rightly entitled *Their Finest Hour*, he wrote: "The only thing that ever really frightened me during the war was the U-boat peril".

As the German ground forces thrust far to the west of France, Hitler's U-boat supremo, Admiral Karl Doenitz, was poised to make his own dramatic move. On the day after the signing of the Armistice at Compiègne, a train already loaded with torpedoes, other vital *matériel*, and the men capable of using them, was despatched to the Biscay ports. Confined earlier to such outlets as the Baltic and the North Seas, the Germans now found themselves with access to the European coast from Norway's North Cape to the Spanish frontier.

The only problem was that Doenitz did not have enough enough U-boats to take advantage of his remarkable good fortune. His earlier pleas to Hitler to expand Germany's U-boat force had fallen on ears not so much deaf as listening to other priorities, and to other delusions: as already discussed, the Führer still harboured hopes that Britain's hostility might be assuaged with a mutually advantageous deal and that Britain would happily sit back while he did what he liked with the mainland of Europe. There was another obstacle. Nearer to Hitler's ear, and massaging his own outsize ego problem, was Reich Marshal Hermann Goering, head of the Luftwaffe: if anyone was capable of disadvantaging another suitor, however worthy, it was he.

So Doenitz did not have the force he had hoped for, but it was a formidable one nevertheless. He also had at his disposal some of the finest submariners (by consent of his enemies as well as his allies) that ever engaged in the undersea war. This period, relatively lean in terms of ship sinkings compared with later ones, was notable for the presence of a number of aces – "grey wolves" as they were called – who were to play a distinguished and, on the whole and given the hard rules of war, a not dishonourable part in the history of naval warfare.

But the targets were not always well chosen from the point of view of public relations. Gunther Prien, of the U-47, did not know what he had done when he sank the *Arandora Star*. He had killed many Germans and Italians as well as British. He returned to Kiel not to a triumphant welcome, as had been the case after his sinking of the *Royal Oak* in the previous year, but to a distinctly muted one. There were no headlines; instead, the fact that a German U-boat had been involved was deliberately obscured while the propaganda machine turned the story against the British for sending prisoners of war to sea in the first place. As for Prien, the British would have their revenge on him when the U-47 was sunk by British depth charges in the Atlantic in March 1941.

Merchant ships carrying cargo of use to an enemy were more legitimate targets in a conflict which was undeniably total. There would be a sustained culling of such vessels throughout most of the war, few of them making any impact on a public grieved by the loss of a ship bearing the White Ensign of the Royal Navy but inclined to dismiss the sinking of ships carrying the so-called "Red Duster" as almost routine. Yet every merchantman sunk was in its way as great a tragedy as the loss of a ship of war.

Jesse Vyse was eighteen years of age when he was engaged to serve as radio officer on the SS *Severn Leigh*. He had already seen some service in tankers and had enjoyed an exotic voyage across the Mediterranean but now in his new ship and his new appointment he was to have his first experience of the Atlantic. On August 14 he wrote to his family in Hull, at that time receiving sporadic visits from German bombers. He was in the most cheerful of moods:

Dear Mother, Vera and Dad,
It is with great pleasure that I have to tell you that we are leaving England in a northward direction. Our first call is Methyl – or some such name – up in Scotland. On arriving we pick up convoy for a trip to Canada which, I have been told, will last about six to eight weeks so all being well should not be long away.

I got my fags and tobacco and the postage was 1/1d, so if Vera would like to write a letter and stick half a dollar inside I think it will be OK, also a letter to Weymouth customs thanking them.

Tell Monty I think I've got everything I require but it has taken me all day to get settled in the room, which was in rather an untidy state when I arrived and the same attention is not to be had here as was the case in the tankers. However, am OK now and have already had one two-hour sleep in the bunk but I found it rather lumpy.

At the moment we're anchored at Spurn but we're due to sail in an hour's time (that's at 3 o'clock a.m.).

Well, I guess that's the lot just now so will say cheerio, hoping you're not troubled with a lot of air raids, so cheerio again and will be back soon.
  Jess.   XX

On August 23, the *Severn Leigh* was torpedoed in mid-Atlantic by the U-37, which was
commanded by one of Doenitz's grey wolves, if not quite of the front rank, *Kapitan
sur Zee* Victor Oehrn. The ship did not sink under the impact of the torpedo, so it was
despatched by the U-boat's gun. Meanwhile, *Severn Leigh's* crew of forty-two had got
into two boats, one on the port and the other on the starboard side. The port side boat
was hit by a shell, resulting in several horrendous casualties and some deaths, though
whether this was by design or accident was not clear. The authors of a recent book on
survival at sea in the Second World War offer the following comment:

> Were incidents of this kind the inevitable outcome of Admiral Doenitz's order No.
> 154 of late November/early December 1939, which stressed that one must be hard
> in war, and instructed the U-boats to rescue no one and not to concern themselves
> with lifeboats? Were they, perhaps, the result of over-zealous officers trying to prove
> just how hard they could be? Can some be explained as tragic accidents where, in
> pressing home their attacks, aircraft, E-boats, surface raiders or U-boats failed to
> notice men who were abandoning ship or were already in the water? Can others
> be explained as simply cases of distraught survivors assuming that ricochets or
> poorly aimed shots were being fired at them deliberately?

The authors offer no conclusion themselves but record the view of an American
historian reported to have studied an unpublished autobiography by Victor Oehrn
and who gives the U-boat commander the benefit of the doubt. Oehrn's version
suggests that the killing and maiming of members of the crew was caused by a stray
shell, and that he was so concerned about the likely effect on world opinion of what
would appear to be an atrocity that he seriously thought of ensuring that none of
the other survivors should live to tell the tale.

Oehrn, having refrained from so doing, left the survivors of the *Severn Leigh* to
make what best progress they could, with one lifeboat and two rafts. The rafts were
tied together and five seriously wounded men were placed on them with eight fit
men to look after them. But towing the rafts proved extremely difficult; the rope
kept breaking and the tiny convoy was making hardly any speed at all. The sight
of a ship passing by five miles off but offering no response to their desperate signals
only added to the general gloom. The Captain was left with an appalling choice:
if they carried on as they had begun they would never reach land; if they all
crowded into the boat there would be no room to lay out the remaining wounded
men, even though their number was now reduced to three, two having died
during the first night. In the words of the Captain's own account:

It was a case of sacrificing twenty-nine men for the three injured men, or sacrificing the three injured men for the twenty-nine able men. I therefore consulted my second officer, chief engineer and the sound and able men, pointing out the bare hope that it was possible – without the rafts – to reach land in ten days, but the longer action was delayed, the lesser would the hope be, and so it was decided to abandon the rafts with the three injured men left on. Although it was to me a terrible action, yet, my duty lay in the fact of my endeavour to save as many as possible.

Jesse Vyse was among the twenty-nine survivors who then set off in the *Severn Leigh*'s lifeboat hoping either to catch the attention of another ship or to make a landfall. They had some whisky and food on board but only twenty gallons of fresh water. Thirst became the real enemy as the clamour for water wracked the crew and they suffered a major blow when, one keg having been emptied, a second, opened on the morning of August 31, was found to have been, as the Captain described it, "pillaged" during the previous night.

Four days earlier, on the August 27, Jesse Vyse's mother, having heard of German claims to have sunk the *Severn Leigh*, wrote to her son, desperately hoping that the claim was false. Assuming that was the case, she filled the letter with details of Hull's and the family's recent experience of the attentions of the Luftwaffe:

Dear Jesse,

The Germans claim to have sunk the *Severn Leigh* but we are trying to beleave[sic] it is one of their tall yarns, that is of course we want to think so. God knows what we are going through wondering where you are and how you are faring. I have been putting this letter off thinking there may be news, but if it does not find you it will perhaps come back. I hope it finds you quite well. We are all feeling washed out this morning, we all went in the hide hole at nine o'clock last night and came out 4.30 this morning. I had to crawl out and have my supper though I cannot sleep with little Mary calling. Vera had to have her wash. What she has to get washed to go and sleep in an air rade [sic] shelter for beets [sic] me. We had a good time on our holidays but Jerry paid us a visit even there, the last night we were there he nearly dropped his last bomb in the back yard, or it sounded there – the whole house rocked. I never got out of bed so sharp in my life but we are all in a piece yet and praying for you darling. God keep you safe. I have given your address to all your pals, except Bill. I have not seen him, I have not got Ken's address yet and perhaps I had better wait whilst I get some definate news of you before I send it. I should hate to help Hitler. This letter must be short because I want to get it off. Vera and Dad send all their love to you. We are all anxious about you. All my love Sweetheart and take care of yourself, if you can. Write soon.

Mother XXXX

P.S. This sounds a doleful letter. I would like to make you smile. If the fact that your sister fell out of the middle bunk in the air raid shelter the other night sounds funny, here goes. We were all asleep, I think she must have tried to turn over at any rate but for the fact my knees were sticking out a bit and there is not so much space room as you know she might have got a nasty bump, as it was when we sorted the arms knees and legs and things out and found we were all still in a piece we had a good laugh. She might describe it herself when she writes to you. She will do it much better than I can. I personally thought ould nick had come for a minute or two. This is really all for now.

So cheerio   Mam   Keep smiling

On September 5, at the end of a voyage of 850 miles, ten survivors of the *Severn Leigh* having been taken far from their hoped-for landfall in Ireland arrived at Northton, on the Hebridean island of Lewis. After being cared for by local people they were transferred to hospital in Stornoway, one more of their number dying on the way. As it happened, on the day their boat reached land, one of the injured men who had been abandoned on the raft was landed at Halifax, Nova Scotia, by a British warship which had come across the raft by chance in mid-Atlantic.

Jesse Vyse, however, was not among those who came home. Desperate for information his parents wrote to a fellow Hull seaman who had been one of the *Severn Leigh*'s crew. They received this letter by return:

Dear Mam,
I have received your note to hand yesterday asking me if I knew anything about your dear son. Well Mam, I regret to say your son was in the only surviving boat and he passed away peacefully in his sleep on September 5. When we left the ship there was twenty nine of us in the boat but only nine of us survived and we done all we could for those who passed away. As each person died he had a sea burial by the Master of the Ship saying prayers for them. There was nothing more we could do for them, and I sympathise with you in your grief.

Yours Respectfully,
W.J. Garvey

In fact the official death certificate gives "4.9.40" as the date of Jesse Vyse's death. The eager 18-year-old Radio Officer died just one day away from safety.

Meanwhile the Children's Overseas Reception Board – CORB – had been continuing its work of exporting "seavacuees", or "seavacs", as they had come to be known, to various overseas destinations. Its organizers experienced a serious jolt in late August when one of the ships involved in the scheme, the Dutch vessel SS *Volendam*, was struck by a German torpedo. Fortunately, the ship did not sink and though the children had to be got off into open boats there were no fatalities. CORB's Chairman, Geoffrey Shakespeare, was able to send cheerful telegrams to all the parents concerned:

> Glad to inform you your child safe and landed at northern port, ship damaged but all children well and happy. Children returning home within few days.

Four children from Grangemouth, Scotland, had been of the party: Sylvia and Alex Winton, aged seven and six respectively, and Jessie and Shiela Mackay, aged nine and thirteen. Shiela wrote a lively account of their adventures and of their fortunate rescue shortly after her happy return under the title "True Story". To begin with the voyage was hugely enjoyable. After their first night at sea she and her friends made their way excitedly to the upper decks:

> The next day was spent mostly going to the end of the boat and watching the large convoy behind us. It was a beautiful day. The Sun was warm and shone all its brilliant rays on us. From the back of the boat it was simply marvellous to watch all the ships in the convoy. The water was a mass of calm blue. And we could see our reflections as we bent over the side. There wasn't a cloud in the beautiful blue sky.
>
> After tea I came out to the back of the boat myself. I was never more thrilled at the sight before my eyes. It was wonderful, honestly! It was quite dark until the bright Moon came peeping out from behind the clouds. The sea was beautiful and calm. You could see the reflection of the Moon in the shimmering water. As I walked away I never imagined what would be in store for us that night. I fell sound asleep as soon as my head touched the pillow.
>
> It was about half past ten that same night that I woke to find someone shaking me violently. When I sat up Jessie and the two Robertsons were up and fully dressed. Then I heard the alarm ringing. I got up and before I was half dressed Jessie and the Robertsons were away. I wasn't properly awake either. I just drifted along the crowded passage the way the rest were going. Then a big black sailor came up to me and asked me my boat station. I told him and I can remember he just hoisted me over his shoulders and took me safely to my boat station. By this time I was wide awake. I thanked the sailor and then got hold of Jessie. I bet you I gave her a right good row for leaving me.
>
> I thought it was another practice alarm at first. Then when we had to climb into the lifeboats I realized with a shiver it was no practice. I've never seen the sea as rough in my life as it was that night. It was also pitch black. We got into the lifeboats. Then a man at each end began lowering it into the water. It seemed a long

way down to the water and the boats kept swinging back and forward and crashing against the sides of the ship. But at last we reached near the water. The man cut one end of the rope and the one end of the boat fell with a splash into the water leaving the other end in mid-air. But the man at the other end cut the other rope and then we were rocking up and down in the very stormy seas.

Then I discerned a man coming down the rope ladder into our boat. The iron thing that had held the rope was swinging about, it went towards the man and crashed against his head. He was knocked unconscious and fell into the water and got drowned. I didn't realize how horrible it was at the time. I was just wondering if I would go the same way as him! Wondering if I would ever see dry land again. Wondering if I would ever come out alive.

I was hanging onto Jessie like grim death. We were all squashed on top of one another. And what was worse, I was sitting near the edge. I kept looking at the deep water and shivering thinking how cold it would be to be pitched in there. We tossed and pitched about for about a quarter of an hour. I gave Jessie my gloves to keep her hands warm and she let them fall in the water.

We could see our ship going down-down-down-down-down. But it never went right down. We could see the outline of other lifeboats pitching up and down and all you could hear was "heave! help! help! heave!". In the midst of all this wee Sylvia Winton, whose wee brother was in a different boat, happened to see a small cap come floating along the water. She picked it up and said it looked like Alex's. She said she would have to give it to him when she got home. There was only one girl crying on the whole boat and that was because she had lost her little sister. But she found her later on.

Suddenly we saw a black shape looming up in front of us. We suddenly crashed into it, and nearly got jerked into the water. However, we came round to the side to find it was an oil tanker. I was nearest the railings and I had to put my hands out and catch hold of the railings and try and keep the boat in then it would slide away again. I was very nearly in tears. But at last the captain just took hold of me and lifted me right out of the lifeboat on to the tanker. Then I put out my arms and hauled Jessie up. I felt glad to be walking on something firm again. I went along deck and up the steps. Just as I went up the steps the oil tanker dipped down and a huge wave came right over the top of me and I just stood clinging on to the railings. I was drenched but I soon got some hot tea along with the rest. The men were very kind in letting us sleep in their bunks while they slept in the passages. It was when I was talking to a nice cheery man with a smiling face that I suddenly felt terribly homesick .

Sickness of a different kind struck all of them because of the oil fumes and the rocking of the boat. By the time they recovered they were within sight of home:

Next day, after a bit, we came out again. And the sight before our eyes was swell. We saw all the hills of Scotland. Good old Scotland! Were we glad to see dry land once again. We were all saying, "this is the last time I'll set foot on a boat ever again".

We reached Gourock and were driven in cars to the Queen's Hotel. We were all glad to get our feet planted on firm ground once more. We went into the hotel to find beds made on the floor for us. When we stood still we were saying, "I wish this hotel would stop rocking about".

They were then taken to a school in Glasgow, where they stayed for about a week while parents were notified. By the time they returned home their antipathy to the thought of a sea voyage had clearly faded:

> My mother was at the station to meet Jessie and I. The first thing I said when I got off the train was, "Could I go back?".

The fact that not one "seavac" had been lost was an enormous relief to the scheme's organizers. Among Shiela Mackay's papers is a CORB luggage label from the committee's chairman with a piece of tartan attached to it bearing the message: "WARMEST CONGRATULATIONS. We are all proud of your bravery. GOOD LUCK".

Sadly, CORB's good fortune was not to continue for much longer. Beryl Myatt, aged nine, born in Newcastle but, in 1940, living in Hillingdon, Middlesex, sailed for Canada under the auspices of the CORB scheme in mid-September. The ship on which she embarked was the SS *City of Benares*. On September 21 her parents wrote her a cheerful letter, embellished on the front page by the "signature" of her much loved pet dog, captioned: "Chummy sends his love. This is his paw mark." They assumed that by the time the letter reached her she would be safe with her aunt in Winnipeg:

> Our Dearest Beryl,
>
> This is our second letter to you, since you set out on your big adventure, dear, and we suppose you were very surprised when you arrived at Auntie Emmies to find a letter and your *Dandy* and *Sunny Stories* waiting there for you. We will send them each week.
>
> We expect that you enjoyed your voyage on the boat across the wide Atlantic Ocean, and your long journey on the train to Winnipeg. We don't suppose you saw any icebergs during your voyage across, as it would hardly be quite cold enough at this time of the year. How would you like to be a nurse on a big ocean liner when you grow up, dear?

Now, sweetheart, don't forget what we told you. We want you to let auntie and uncle see that you can be a great help to them about the house by helping to the best of your ability, such as running errands, and helping auntie with her house-work and her baking and, above all dear, keep your bedroom tidy and always hang your clothes up in their right place, and this will show auntie and uncle that you really appreciate the opportunity they have given you to have a grand holiday in one of the most interesting countries in the World: Canada – the home of the maple leaf. You haven't forgotten, have you, "The maple leaf for Canada, the rose for England, the leek for Wales, the thistle for Scotland, and the shamrock for Ireland"?

You remember the photograph you had taken at Christchurch School, Kilburn – well, Mummy wants to know if you would like us to send it on to you. Let us know, dear, will you?

How are Pat and Sue. We hope they are OK and that they were not seasick or in any way upset by their journey. The weather here is still fairly nice. What kind of weather are you having?

Well dear, please give our love to auntie and uncle, and when you write you must tell us all about what you are doing. Everybody at home sends their love. Must close now with tons of love and heaps of kisses. God bless you.

Mummy and Daddy.   XXXXXXXXXXXXXXXXXXXXXXXXXX

Unknown to Mr and Mrs Myatt, their daughter's ship had been sunk four days earlier and Beryl was not among the handful of survivors. The *City of Benares* had been torpedoed by the U-48 far out in the Atlantic, during a storm. The ship had 400 passengers, of whom ninety were "seavacuees", most of whom perished. The newspapers raged at an atrocity which had resulted in the loss of so many young children. The Myatt family bought and retained a copy of the *Sunday Express*, with its typically angry headline:

CHILDREN'S LINER SUNK WITHOUT WARNING IN GALE
Outrage in Atlantic
Boats Swamped by Terrific Seas 600 Miles From Land

At the very top of the page immediately below the newspaper title ran a small print line of bitter accusation: "Sent to escape the bombers, 89 English children are murdered by a U-boat".

In fact, the final figure was not so high, seventy-seven being the actual number; thirteen were saved. Five escorts were lost; four survived. Some lifeboats managed to get away from the ship, but over 300 passengers died either on the ship or while waiting for rescue in the boats. Most of the boats were picked up by the destroyer HMS *Hurricane* on the day after the sinking, but one boat, carrying among others six boys and two of their adult escorts, was adrift for eight days before it was spotted by a Sunderland flying boat which directed the destroyer HMS *Anthony* to the rescue. It has been claimed that this sinking made an even bigger impression on British public opinion than the loss of the *Athenia* right at the beginning of the war, a year earlier. Certainly there was a shocked and angry reaction to yet another example of what can so often happen in time of war, a tragic killing of innocents, whose only crime in this case had been that their families had wanted to send them to a safe haven away from bombs and the threat of invasion.

Vera Brittain wrote movingly about the disaster in her book *England's Hour*, paying special tribute to the young music teacher Mary Cornish who had so impressed the CORB selection committee when she applied to join the scheme some weeks earlier. She and a priest, Father O'Sullivan, had been the escorts in the boat that had had to wait eight long days for rescue, doing their best throughout to sustain the courage and morale of the half a dozen lads in their care. *The Absurd and the Brave*, a remarkable book about CORB by one of the scheme's own "seavacs", describes how when the boys had been hoisted on board the destroyer, a sailor told Miss Cornish kindly, "You've handed over to the Navy now!" Only when her charges were safe in their assigned bunks did she consent to take some refreshment herself, but before she could do so, she collapsed. A few weeks later she was awarded the British Empire Medal in recognition of her steadfastness and courage.

The report in the newspaper retained by the Myatt family ended with the brave statement: "The loss of the children will not affect the board's plans for evacuation from this country". In fact that was not the case. After the sinking of the *City of Benares* there was no heart or will to continue. The scheme was rapidly wound up.

As it happened a successful voyage to another destination was taking place without problem or difficulty at the same time. Even as the *City of Benares* was heading for Canada, the SS *Lanstephan Castle* was steaming through the tropics to Cape Town. It was a happy voyage ending in a splendid and enthusiastic welcome. The *Cape Argus* reported the event with appropriate photographs and breezy headlines:

308 'GUEST CHILDREN' ARRIVE
Lusty Cheers on Arrival in Table Bay
Warm Welcome to the Union

The only casualty, the newspaper noted, was "seven-year-old Robin Wilson, of Surrey, who fell off his bunk a couple of days ago and fractured his arm". There were also ten mild cases of measles, who were removed from the ship's hospital immediately the ship docked and taken by ambulance to an isolation ward in a nearby town, the saddest case being six-year-old Patricia Kneale, who had been found to have the disease that very morning. The High Commissioner for the United Kingdom came on board, as did, among a select number of dignitaries, the Minister of Social Welfare, Mr W.D. Madeley, who at an assembly on deck before the new guests went ashore greeted them with the message: "We welcome you to our arms and our hearts, you children of Great Britain!".

Freda Troup was an escort on the voyage, fulfiling the same role as Mary Cornish on the *City of Benares*. Born in Pretoria but with an Oxford degree in geography, she had been teaching in Cambridge when a change in family circumstances made her decide to return to South Africa to spend some time with her parents. A friend had suggested the idea of doing so gratis as an escort under the CORB scheme. She had applied and been accepted, becoming one of twenty escorts appointed to the *Llanstephan Castle*. The voyage had turned out to be a rewarding and enjoyable experience. There was obviously a threat from enemy torpedoes but there had been no alarms. Once they had survived the miseries of seasickness both the cared for and the carers had settled to what had become virtually a peacetime cruise. There was a swimming pool to romp in, table-tennis could be played if the sea was sufficiently calm, on the Saturday night before they landed there was what one thirteen-year-old, Ken Humphrey, described in a diary note as "a super concert given by the escorts and the officers", a ship's choir contributed an anthem to a church service on the Sunday morning. Albatrosses rather than U-boats followed in the ship's wake. On the day before they sighted Cape Town there was a final happy occasion, of which the youngster already quoted wrote: "Had prize-giving in the afternoon and had a super tea-party in which we had crackers and streamers". Next day: "Had breakfast and looked over the side till we docked. When we docked we were singing. We had many photos taken and after dinner I spoke into a 'mike' and had a photo taken with a few others on all fours." Re-reading the diary years later its author wondered: "Why no mention of the *Benares* when we were told about it?".

Perhaps the thoughtful comment of Freda Troup, by then Mrs Freda Levson, written in 1995, provides an answer to that question. Recalling, and still much moved by, the unforgettable events of 1940, she wrote:

> We were sailing south in lovely cruising weather when we were appalled to hear of the wicked attack on the *City of Benares*, well known to be a children's ship, though it would have been blacked out – and on the vilest of nights... The ship and its tragic passengers haunted us then and have come often to my thoughts in the half century since.
>
>   Our worry at the time was whether to tell our children but decided they were most likely to hear of it somehow and it would be best to speak of it as normally as possible. However, they, from Cardiff, Sheffield, Coventry, had pockets full of samples of shrapnel and bomber mementoes and seemed to take everything in their stride.

CHAPTER TEN

Blitz: and Closedown

S TRICTLY, THE GERMAN WORD *BLITZ* MEANS "LIGHTNING". Its first appearance in the vocabulary of 1939–45 was as part of the portmanteau phrase *Blitzkrieg*, meaning "lightning war". It was *Blitzkrieg* that did for Poland, the Low Countries and France. Later events in 1940 led to its adoption in Britain, though for British domestic purposes it was swiftly stripped of the syllable which actually made sense of it. Thus *Blitzkrieg* remained a foreign word but "blitz" became part of the language. Effectively, it is an English colloquial word now. It has numerous uses. A recent Oxford dictionary even records such humdrum applications as "must have a blitz on this room". Beginning with a capital letter, however, it is indissolubly linked to 1940: in this context it is "The Blitz". The Blitz even spawned a dispiriting successor, in that the German night attacks of January–May 1944 became known as the "Baby Blitz" or "Little Blitz". But the classic Blitz period began in September 1940, overlapping into May 1941 – continuing well beyond the closedown of the Battle of Britain. It has been estimated that during those eight months there were one hundred and twenty seven large-scale night raids ("large-scale" meaning raids in which over a hundred tons of bombs were dropped), of which seventy-two were on London. More than two million homes, sixty per cent of them in London, were destroyed by 46,000 tons of high explosive and 110,000 incendiary bombs. Numerous other cities were targeted. *The Macmillan Dictionary of the Second World War* names the following: Belfast, Birkenhead, Birmingham, Bristol, Cardiff, Coventry, Glasgow-Clydeside, Hull, Liverpool, Manchester, Newcastle-Tyneside, Nottingham, Plymouth, Portsmouth, Sheffield and Southampton. So this was to a large extent a nationwide ordeal, though inevitably the capital, Hitler's special object of revenge because of the now undeniable vulnerability of his own capital, Berlin, took the brunt.

Monica Robinson, aged sixteen, joined the well-known firm of Debenham & Freebody, in Wigmore Street, London, shortly before the start of the Blitz on London. Her ambition had been to study textile design, but this was not possible in the straitened circumstances of 1940, so she had opted for the next best thing: a post in the silk fabric department of a major West End store. That she was allowed in at all, as it happened, was due to the national emergency and the absence of so many men in the forces: this was normally an exclusive all-male preserve. Nevertheless, she found herself in an ambience that seemed marvellously to have survived the impact of war; it was also one in which she and her fellow new arrivals clearly had to know their place:

> How tamed and polite you had to be in this new and rather austere world. Exuberant teenage behaviour (a term not invented then) had to be severely curbed to meet the genteel requirements of this old-fashioned and prestigious store.
>
> As a junior, it was my job to run errands, tidy the department, dust counters, and dress and drape the stands each morning so that the fabrics were displayed to their best. Occasionally, a customer would request a length of silk to be delivered to their dressmaker. And once, Ivor Novello asked for an immediate delivery of beautiful pale blue embroidered taffeta for one of his romantic musicals about to be performed. That was the pinnacle of outside visits – to glimpse the famous man himself.

At first life proceeded at almost a peace-time pace and with little obvious cause for anxiety, though regulations required that she and her fellow shop assistants should always be prepared for emergencies:

> We carried our gas masks wherever we went, and when possible chose a case to match an outfit. In the store, a navy blue dress or "costume" had to be worn. We brought our own packed lunch, and on good sunny days several of us would eat sitting on the roof of the building. From there we had a vantage-point, so that if we were lucky enough to have an orange, we could spit pips down on to unsuspecting passers-by in Wigmore Street. Remuneration was low for retail workers – for juniors 14/- gross, with 1/2d then deducted, it had to be stretched for buying clothes, fares to work and a contribution towards housekeeping expenses at home. For a treat we splashed out on morning coffee and a freshly made currant bun at the Ambrosia cafe opposite the staff entrance in Welbeck Street, perching on bar stools, showing off and discussing boy-friends, the straight-laced fogeys with whom we worked, whose relative or friend had recently joined the services and, once the Blitz started, who had been near to the previous night's bombing. We saved for a trip to the "pictures", and Laurence Olivier and Greer Garson in *Pride And Prejudice* was not to be missed. Such innocent forays were our adventures amid the confines of restricted opportunities for leisure and pleasure.

The beginning of the heavy bombing raids in early September brought about a sharp change of style; emergency procedures were sharpened up, but there were also curious compensations, such as that of being introduced to a fascinating part of the store of which previously the new arrivals had hardly been aware:

If the sirens sounded during the daytime, we all trooped down to the bowels of the building. This was a vast area lined down one side with wide benches, which in normal times would have housed spare stock. It formed part of a long underground passageway which extended all the way from underneath the shop in Wigmore Street and the connecting roads above ground, to emerge in Marshall & Snelgrove, our "sister" store in Oxford Street. It was a tremendous place in which to lose a few minutes away from the department and the boring old grandfathers. We didn't mind the interruption of an emergency – we hoped we wouldn't be bombed of course – but the thought of spending some time in the "dungeons" didn't worry the younger ones. Sitting on the benches we sang *Begin The Beguine* and *A Nightingale Sang In Berkeley Square* and talked our way through the enforced spell, sewing on hooks and threading the while.

At this time she was living in North London. What did change markedly from now forward was the nature of what had been a routine journey to work:

This occasionally took on a hazardous tinge, depending upon the Luftwaffe's activities. The journey consisted of a walk to East Finchley station (a most modern building and a good example of 1930's architecture) to travel on the Northern Line to Tottenham Court Road, changing on to the Central Line, to exit at Bond Street tube station.

At all the underground stations you had to negotiate your way around those who were taking shelter from air raids. There were rows of tiered bunks and spaces to lie fully outstretched. Children screamed, played and cried, while tired parents, aunts, uncles, grandparents, etc., made the best of it, huddled within these dismal surroundings, though many lives must have been saved by this provision. As the train entered the station, the stench from the lavatories even now can fill the nostrils.

There were also obvious hazards from the raids themselves, considerably emphasized when another store, barely a quarter of a mile away, was virtually destroyed during a night attack:

On the morning after John Lewis's had been hit, we had to tread a path to Debenham's from Bond Street, along Oxford Street, picking our way through burnt and sodden fabrics, broken glassware, china and the fire-damaged contents of the store – a double suffering from the bombing and the firemen's rescue work.

Meanwhile, the war was beginning to make its presence felt round the clock, so that as well as the increasing tensions by day "so many sleepless nights were had listening to the planes coming over, inwardly cheered by hearing the boom, boom of the Hampstead Heath heavy Ack Ack guns accompanied by dazzling searchlights scanning the sky for raiders". For the young Monica Robinson 1940 was, as she would later describe it, "quite an eventful year".

Earlier that summer, partly deliberately, as a kind of defiant choice, partly because it seemed entirely natural to do, the capital had played the game of "business as usual". That had certainly been the case in the commercial world which Monica Robinson had entered that summer. Yet the ratcheting up of the level of hostilities with the start of the Blitz necessarily enforced certain compromises.

The Promenade Concerts had started bravely enough but early September saw them abruptly abandoned, the last performance having been on that dramatic Saturday September 7. To quote a letter by Ernest Chapman, a young employee of the well-known London music publisher Boosey & Hawkes, this was "not because of small audiences, but because of the danger of having such a huge audience in so small a place during air raids. As far as it went, the season was a great success and the audiences on some nights were of a record size."

If the "Proms" had to concede, the by then traditional lunchtime concerts at the National Gallery did not. "Business as usual" was not quite how their organizers would have expressed their philosophy but it was that nevertheless. The concerts had started back in 1939, with the pianist Myra Hess originally as the sole and later as the principal (and certainly the best remembered) performer. Sir Kenneth Clark, Director of the National Gallery, who had leapt at the idea of providing such concerts at a time of cultural as well as literal black-out, wrote a moving description of the effect Myra Hess had on those who gathered in a setting which had necessarily been deprived of its pictures, and which desperately needed something positive to counter its dingy wartime gloom:

> I stood behind one of the curtains and looked at the packed audience. They had come with anxious, hungry faces, but as they listened to the music and looked at Myra's rapt expression, they lost the thought of their private worries. I had never seen faces so transformed...

What produced this effect even more than the quality of musical performance was what Clark described as "Myra's sublime optimism":

> I do not mean optimism about the outcome of the war, on which subject she probably felt as doubtful as any other reasonable person. I am thinking of her belief that a majority of human beings could share the emotions of love, pity, brotherhood and resignation that the great composers have expressed in their music.

The advent of the Blitz did eventually force a concession, but only one of place, not of principle. A newspaper report of September 16 noted, laconically:

> The National Gallery concerts are now being carried on in a room downstairs, set apart as a shelter since the beginning of the war, in order to avoid interruption of the programme if and when the sirens are sounded. Arrangements for increased accommodation below are being made.

The concerts would shortly, almost inevitably, have their own special "Blitz" experience. On October 15 a time bomb fell on the National Gallery, ruling out any performance there that day. Immediately, the High Commissioner for South Africa offered the use of the library in nearby South Africa House and the concert went ahead – the only time a concert took place outside the Gallery. Subsequently, a second time-bomb was found in the Gallery itself, so the concerts were moved to a room in the farthest part of the building. Two days later the bomb exploded. On this occasion the work being played was a Beethoven string quartet. The bomb went off during the trio of the minuet. Present that day was the poet Stephen Spender:

> The musicians did not lift the bows from the strings. A few of the audience, who had been listening with heads bowed, straightened themselves for an instant and then resumed their posture.

London's cinemas also gallantly stayed open. In particular, the East End had suffered heavily in the attack on September 7 and continued to do so. In the period September 7 to October 5 there were thirty-eight major attacks, but there were always customers for every house. If the sirens sounded before the end of the programme, as they invariably did, the cinemas offered shelter to their patrons, and entertainment as well. The advertised programme would be re-run, stand-by features would be shown, the theatre organist would play his heart out, and there would often be impromptu song and dance routines on the stage. Meanwhile, the café staff offered tea and soft drinks until the small hours. When the bombing started people simply moved back for safety under the overhang of the circle, though apparently some courting couples preferred to take their chances and remained upstairs. The philosophy of "Business as usual" clearly offered fine opportunities for the usual business.

By this time the Blitz was well under way, and though there was much *sangfroid*, there was also much anxiety, fear, even terror– justifiably because the bombs raining down from the aircraft overhead were no joke; they maimed, killed and destroyed.

The remarkably frank and vivid diary of the Chelsea ARP Warden, Miss Jo Oakman, makes this abundantly clear. This is her entry for September 14 ("H.E." means a high explosive bomb):

18.27. Bomb on church of the Holy Redeemer. Got sent off by Bert Thorpe on bike patrol in Glebe Place and hardly got away when an H.E. sailed through church window, through crypt floor to cellar, where it exploded against some strutting among 80-odd people. I got knocked off the bike. A second bomb knocked me down again and the third sent a brick on to my tin hat. I went to Holy Redeemer and Browning and I set to work on stirrup pumps as the coke had caught alight. Smoke from the coke was coming through the broken church window. The cries and groans were awful. God help them all. A 20-stone woman blocked the doorway and we couldn't get her up the stairs. Later we got her up with help from the police but she died. Some had got out via the back entrance and the window. Thorpe was under the arch – I rolled him over and saw his face. God! he had none and what he had was a mess. All his limbs were broken and lay at horrible angles. I recognised him by his hair, uniform and ring on his hand. Did a bit of first aid and heaps of odd jobs, everybody was wonderful – accompanied and helped the dying.

Numerous other places had been badly hit: Upper Cheyne Row ("5-7 dead under wreckage"), Lawrence Street ("a man and woman were both severely injured in the basement of a house"), Moore's Gardens ("a bomb fell near the train bridge and caused some casualties in the street"). Miss Oakman continues:

The injured seemed endless. I thought the fire brigade would never come – I think the fire brigade went to the wrong place… There was a shortage of ambulances (the wounded were lying in Upper Cheyne Row in stretchers), first aid stuff at the Post but no iodine, only dry dressings – and they were not big enough. Later in the night the dead were moved in cars.

I think my heart broke this night over the sights I have seen today. The Goulding family: father and daughter, finding their lost son Gerald whom I put in an Anderson shelter down the road and dressed his foot. He was hysterical and wanted to get away and let his family know he was alive. One must have a heart somehow and somewhere – and mine, I think, broke. The love of that family for one another is a great thing and an everlasting. It made me cry; I cannot forget it. We still worked at the Holy Redeemer.

They carried on into the early hours of Sunday September 15:

Some of the dead (about thirteen) spent the night beside Holy Redeemer, as we had no time to remove them owing to the coming of the next raid. They were moved early in the dawn. Some of them were in a shocking state. Harrods' vans were used to remove the poor things. Some had precious little clothes left on them. The big room in Cook's School was full of wounded – saw most shocking sights in way of face injuries. I got home at 10 hours to find my home gone, an oil bomb took the back off the house so I rescued some stuff and turned in with Browning.

Even this unhappy discovery allowed her no let-up. This on Wednesday September 18:

23.30. Incendiary bombs – all over the place – put them out with earth, behind Mulberry Close, Embankment, shelters in Embankment, Upper Cheyne Row, heaven only knows where else; they seemed never ending. Climbed all over the place in gardens putting out fires, nuisance – in my new suit. Some of the fires burnt in the river, a launch was hit, etc. Oh boy! Some night! All ablaze – Chelsea Park Gardens and 20 Bramerton St caught a great fire each, and made some flare. Some H.E. bombs also fell. I was out in Old Church St when first two bombs fell on bike patrol. I dropped the bike and flew for an archway.

The following day brought an unexpected if gratifying occasion:

Got kept at post to be introduced to queen at 10.35. Was introduced as a "gallant warden", but also managed to introduce Landsell (Deputy Chief Warden) as the "fellow who did all the work". Cheers – got a word in for him at last. He's a grand fellow. He said to the queen "she's good too!". The queen thanked him for "doing all he had done for her people". She was very sweet – and so genuine and natural. The queen shook my hand also and said something about "you gallant women". It sure was a thrill – we're all right and so is HM the Queen.

As it happened, Queen Elizabeth must have felt considerably more at ease and much more part of the scene than she had done earlier. On September 13 Buckingham Palace had been bombed, thus offering the royal family a greatly valued solidarity with the people of the capital, and that of the country.

Though it might have seemed quite otherwise to Jo Oakman, the week through which she had just struggled saw the turning point in the Battle of Britain. Sunday September 15 would in fact be formally named as "Battle of Britain Day". It was the day of the largest ever German formations over London; no fewer than twenty-four Fighter Command squadrons met them and broke them up. "An undisputed victory" was how it would be described in the *Jubilee History*. This was the time when the figures of aeroplane losses became akin to cricket scores. In its enthusiasm the RAF claimed 185 aircraft shot down; the actual number was 53, with 16 damaged. The RAF lost 26 planes and 13 pilots. But the exaggerated figures, given out on the BBC, headlined in the newspapers, were themselves a weapon. The boost to morale was immense. On Tuesday September 17 the *News Chronicle* came out with a typically exultant leading article:

DOWN LIKE FLIES

If there must be talk about a blitzkrieg let it now be said that it is we who wage it: for it is the Royal Air Force that strikes like lightning and it is the Luftwaffe that is stricken. Our planes race out above the Channel – whose waters are as much ours as they have ever been – and rip Goering's bombers out of the skies so that they fall like flies before the onslaught of any antiseptic syringe.

On Sunday, 185 of the winged pirates crashed down to earth. Day after day the Germans have attempted to drive the RAF back so that they have a better opportunity to launch their planned invasion. And day after day the RAF has been waiting for them, shooting Hitler's dreams away at a rate that – if he is allowed to know the number – must soon call a halt to even his personal frenzy.

Yet though from the point of view of morale the battle was going Britain's way, this by no means meant that the bombers were not "getting through" or that those on the ground could start to relax. The bombs, to quote a poem of the time by W.H. Auden, were still "real and dangerous" and people still had to steel their courage to face them. Harold Nicolson, writing in his diary in his London flat on September 19, tried to analyse his complex reactions:

I turn out the lights and listen to the bombardment. It is continuous, and the back of the museum opposite flashes with lights the whole time. There are scudding low clouds, but above them the insistent drone of the German planes and the occasional crump of a bomb. Night after night, night after night, the bombardment of London continues. It is like the Conciergerie [*a notorious Paris prison in which opponents of the French Revolution were held prior to their almost certain visit to the Place de la Guillotine*] since every morning one is pleased to see one's friends appearing again. I am nerveless, and yet I am conscious that when I hear a motor in the empty streets I tauten myself lest it be a bomb screaming towards me. Underneath, the fibres of one's nerve resistance must be sapped. There is a lull now. The guns die down towards the horizon like a thunderstorm passing to the south. But they will come back again in fifteen minutes. We are conscious all the time that this is a moment in history. But it is very like falling down a mountain. One is aware of death and fate, but thinks mainly of catching hold of some jutting piece of rock. I have a sense of strain and unhappiness, but none of fear.

One feels so proud.

But neither he nor anyone else could be quite free of the fear of personal injury, for many if not most an anxiety substantially greater than the fear of sudden extinction. On September 24 he wrote:

I detect in myself a certain area of claustrophobia. I do not mind being blown up. What I dread is being buried under huge piles of masonry and hearing the water drip slowly, smelling the gas creeping towards me and hearing the faint cries of colleagues condemned to a slow and ungainly death.

This was a drama with many weeks, indeed many months, to run.

Though London was the prime focus at this time the Blitz took in numerous other areas as well. The famous September 15 also saw raids on Portland, Southampton and the Midlands. Over the following days there were attacks on Merseyside (a serious assault, with raids on eight nights out of nine), while East Anglia, Kent and the southeast generally were given occasional visits. On September 17, the RAF struck back sharply, sinking eighty four barges that were being prepared for possible invasion at Dunkirk. This was not the only such attack. *The Times* carried the following item on September 16:

HAVOC IN ANTWERP DOCKS
DEVASTATION AMONG BARGES

Flying through appalling weather – aircraft were struck by lightning, wireless aerials were burned off in violent electric storms, and machines were "iced up" – [our] raiders struck heavily at the invasion's front line…

One of the night's most devastating onslaughts was made on Antwerp, which an earlier would-be invader of this country described as "a pistol pointed at the heart of England". Havoc was caused in the vast network of docks, warehouses and petrol sheds on the banks of the Scheldt and the shipping lying in the stream… The general report of the raid states: "Barges at the mouth of the docks and shipping alongside the basins was successfully bombed. One ship was seen to be on fire, and a big blaze was started on the north side of the basin. Another fire on the south side of the basin was believed from its appearance to be an oil fire."

It was a raid that took place about this time on the peripheries of London that produced the finest hour in the early military career of Tony Stiebel. He had

joined the LDV/Home Guard from his school at Beaumont near Windsor, becom-
ing a member of the prestigious Crown Lands Battalion – proud of its link to the
Grenadier Guards – and had been somewhat contemptuous of the
Buckinghamshire Battalion, to which volunteers from nearby Eton were assigned.
Since, however, his mother lived in Datchet, in the holidays he transferred to the
Datchet platoon, which was part of the Buckinghamshire Battalion. The switch was,
however, to give him a moment of considerable glory, and to produce a feather in
the cap of the Home Guard. The start of the Blitz had given him and his comrades
what he called "a ringside view of the bombing of London", which was only
twenty miles to the East. At times the bombs and flashes were continuous and could
be heard clearly when the wind blew in the right direction. But then the bombers
suddenly moved nearer:

> I and another young volunteer, Blundell, whom I did not really know except as a
> member of the Datchet Platoon, were told to go to an observation post on guard
> duty. We cycled out on the road to Wraysbury – there was an air-raid on at the
> time.
>
> As we got to the OP, we heard a terrible screaming sound – a very large bomb
> had come down about thirty yards away – we went to ground, but there was no
> explosion. So it was either a dud or a time bomb – but which? We phoned our HQ
> and started to clear the people out of the houses in the area. Most had no trans-
> port and at midnight were not too keen on going out into the night without all
> their belongings, dogs, birds, etc. The police and ARP arrived and took over the
> evacuation and Blundell and I controlled traffic. It was amazing how many cars
> were drawn to the scene for one reason or another – voluntary helpers with
> comforts and food, civic services such as gas, electricity or water-supply people –
> all wanted a share of the action in spite of our telling them that there was an unex-
> ploded bomb. They simply would not understand that all their particular jobs had
> to wait until at least the bomb disposal unit arrived to assess the situation.
> We managed to clear the area for about three hundred yards around the site in a
> couple of hours. Blundell and I remained at the OP – an uncompleted pill-box –
> and when all was apparently quiet, we heard a loud hissing and dropped to
> ground speedily as the bomb exploded. As the dust settled, we saw a crater about
> ten feet deep and thirty feet across – no more than thirty yards from our OP. We
> had no damage except dust and dirt. However, ten or twelve houses were demol-
> ished and windows were broken over a large area. The experts later said that it was
> a 500 kg bomb.

This episode resulted in the battalion commander issuing the following statement
in his orders on 23/9/40:

ACTS OF GALLANTRY

The action of two members of the Datchet Bn. D Coy. during an air-raid has been brought to notice.

At a time when bombs were actually falling in the vicinity of Datchet village, J.M. Blundell, aged 18, and H.A.J. Stiebel, aged 17, were on duty at an OP. A bomb fell close to the OP and while police and ARP evacuated all the inhabitants from houses within three hundred yards, these two did all police work, stopping cars, diverting traffic, etc., and they remained at their post when the bomb burst; they managed to take shelter in a partly built block-house when the first slight hissing noise preceded the explosion of the bomb.

The action of these two young members of the Home Guard deserves the highest commendation; they have set a fine example of courage and devotion to duty to the whole battalion.

The two teenagers were the subject of two further letters of commendation, one from Lord Wigram of the Grenadier Guards, Commanding Officer of the Crown Lands Battalion, and a second from Headquarters, Southern Command, on behalf of its General Officer Commanding, to HQ South Midland Area, which concluded:

I am to ask you to convey the Army Commander's congratulations to these two volunteers and to say how greatly he appreciates such evidence of coolness and bravery, more especially on account of their comparative youth. The Army Commander wishes this letter to be read aloud at a parade. A copy is enclosed for each volunteer.

Stiebel would later join the Army as a professional and ultimately become an officer of the prestigious armoured regiment, the 17th/21st Lancers. He would not forget, however, his and his fellow volunteer's minor yet effective, and highly professional, contribution to the Battle of Britain.

Throughout the Blitz Dr Charles Forbes Maclean reported regularly to his daughter in Glasgow from his home in Balham, South London. A native of Inverness who had served as a doctor in the Boer War and worked as a General Practitioner in Balham since 1916, he was a man with a ready compassion but he was also an acute and critical observer, questioning much and taken in by little. He was not inclined to join in the general chorus of easy praise for the capital's anti-aircraft defences, as expressed, for example, in a letter from a lady in Stoke Newington which appeared in the *News Chronicle* of September 17 under the heading "Thanks Gunners":

Our new defences of Wednesday night gave everyone in our locality both courage and confidence. We want our gunners to be thanked over and over again for their fine work.

On September 16, as it happened the day on which, presumably, the above letter was selected for publication, Dr Maclean told his daughter:

About this barrage you hear and read about. Don't get an exaggerated idea about it. You would think that a close wall of shells surrounds us. It isn't so, nor indeed anything like that. All that happens is that when a plane is spotted a few long-range guns fire shrapnel into that area far up in the sky, and when the plane comes lower the small A.A. guns join in. To call it a barrage such as was used in the land fighting of the last war is simply not true. The authorities say it is successful but the Germans seem to get through it just the same… Why is it that our Spitfires do not attack the enemy over London?   I cannot guess but there must be some good reason for it, for the same freedom is afforded our bombers over Berlin…

But where he felt praise was due he was ready to offer it. Thus in the middle of an earlier letter written on the same day he interrupted his own train of thought on other matters to write with a sudden burst of enthusiasm:

And here I must stop to utter my three cheers – Hip-hip, Hip-hip, Hip-hip – St. Paul's has been saved. No deed of courage as great as these men did has been performed in this or any war. To dig up and remove that time bomb from Dean's Yard, weighing, I hear, a ton, which took more than a day to do, was such cold-blooded courage that I stand amazed. A nation with people like that is bound to win.

Two nights later he wrote to his daughter at length during an actual raid:

Wednesday night, September 18
There is a bomber very low just now, and the guns are unaccountably silent though they were banging away good-o just before. There must have been some of the swine over Croydon way for the gun flashes from there light up the sky like summer lightning. Blast this bomber overhead. I shall have to retreat. By the way, the topical swear word for this time must surely be "blast". Well blast him, I'm off…

Clearly he emerged shortly afterwardss to continue:

I do not think I have told you what my routine is now every night. After listening for some time to the affray till it has sorted itself out, leaving my solitary

bomber on his tiresome sentry-go over this house which will go on all through the
night, I prepare to go into the basement. I take off the clothing I have been wearing in the daytime, put on pyjamas and an old suit of clothes, the dressing gown
and a cloth cap. (My word he is close tonight.) In the basement, where I have a
reading lamp behind my shoulder, I read and smoke and eat a biscuit or two till
11.30 or 12 when, if there is nothing of interest outside, I wrap myself in the large
skin rug and with two cushions conveniently placed on the low sloping deck-chair
I prepare to sleep after turning out the light. Sometimes I get to sleep at once, but
sometimes the sleep is very fitful. But however the sleep may be during the first
part of the morning, it is most usual to be asleep when the "all clear" sounds and
not to waken. There is nothing very surprising in this because the "all clear" has
to be preceded by an interval of silence as much as twenty minutes while the
Germans are on their way home and we are making sure that the bombers have
gone to roost.

Recent direct hits on nearby streets dominated his thoughts as he carried on
writing into the night:

I learnt the facts later in the morning. There must have been three bombs, which
made the great explosion about 12 o'clock... The third bomb fell on the house
which forms the left-hand corner of Streathbourne and Elmbourne Roads –
looking towards the common. It didn't fall directly on the house, but in the
narrow front garden and touching the house and when it burst it took the legs
away from the house and the upper floors simply sank down all askew on the
wreckage of the ground floor. Indeed, the floor of an upper room didn't break up
but slid sideways all in one piece. Pictures on the bedroom walls were still there,
and a large round mirror still hung on the wall above the fireplace from which the
gas fire had been wrenched. On the top of all was a doll's pram.

On Friday evening, September 20, he was writing again, once more about a recent
nearby tragedy and once more to the sound of the constant hostile presence up
above:

He – the irritating one – is overhead again and flying low. This is the third night
that the bomber has flown very low – much below our balloon level. It is clear
therefore that he knows where the balloons are and, when he wants to, he can come
lower than the guns care to fire...

I heard of the havoc [at Mitcham] and went to see it this afternoon. The first
terrible bomb fell on a large imposing church near the clock tower. Of it the arch
of the main entrance still remains upright but that is all. Of fifty dwelling houses
of two storeys there remains to be seen only laths and mortar and thirty or forty

more are uninhabitable. But that isn't all, for less than ¼ of a mile away there was another large imposing brick church and of it the front still stands but that is all. Of the really nice two-storey houses near at least forty are now so broken up and tossed together that it is impossible to say which broken pieces of furniture is whose. At least another thirty dwelling houses are permanently or temporarily uninhabitable. Two extraordinary bombs did all this. It was a most moving sight and I could not restrain my tears. Is it possible for the Germans ever to apologize for this and would they if they knew? The place was far from any conceivable military objective. The gas works must be more than a mile away. When I think of the bombs on Balham compared to this cataclysmic affair I feel grateful that we have been let off so lightly… If a bomb of the character of either of those on Mitcham had fallen on Wontner Road there would have been little of this house left. This awesome sight, and the dolly's pram, have moved me very much.

Resentment at what the Luftwaffe was doing to London was not confined to Londoners. The intensely patriotic teenager from Cheshire, Brian Poole, now an ardent member of the Home Guard, wrote to his American pen friend on September 20 in high temper:

All's well. Still alive and kicking. But greatly annoyed at the brutal bombing by our swinish enemy of London. It's terrible to think of this beautiful city. I shall kill every Hun I can lay my hands on if they destroy the Tower of London, the Houses of Parliament or any building like that. I shall go raving mad. Just think of the Tower of London, built in 1088, nearly 900 years old. If it was destroyed, it would be terrible. It's buildings like these that the greatness of our Empire has grown round. But the people of London will hold fast. It is their destiny to lead Britain to victory. The result of their endurance now will be glorious. If London holds fast, not only Britain and the peoples of the British Empire are saved, but all the civilised peoples of the world.

Then the dastardly attempts on the lives of our great king and queen. They have proved themselves great and inspiring in our hour of trouble.

The monarchy had a further inspiration to offer just three days after Poole wrote his letter. On September 23, the King announced the creation of a new decoration: the George Cross, an award for heroism on the home front to be equal to in value to the Victoria Cross, instituted by his grandmother for heroism in the field. In practice, soldiers rather than civilians took most of the awards, bomb disposal squads being particularly honoured. It was the King's own idea and he announced it in a memorable broadcast which included the resonant statement: "Tonight we are a Nation on guard and in the line."

What were they like, the men of the Luftwaffe in the aircraft above Britain, so irritating to Dr Maclean, so loathed by Brian Poole, and against whom the nation was now "on guard"? To those on the ground they were the villains of the piece, devilmen bent on mindless destruction at the behest of a cruel and corrupt leadership, worthy only of hatred and contempt.

The conflict of 1940 – indeed the whole of the 1939–1945 war – has been seen for so long as a battle simply of good people against evil ones that it is almost impossible to imagine that those who fought for Germany were anything other than ruthless monsters without any redeeming feature. But time has moved on, we now find ourselves in a different Europe and a different century, and it is therefore perhaps timely to put a human face to the young men who fought on the other side.

Ulrich Steinhilper was a Messerschmitt pilot in 1940. In a book entitled *Spitfire On My Tail* published in 1989, based on his wartime letters and co-written with an English author, he offered an alternative view of the air war over Britain without bombast and without making untenable claims. Thus he could state unequivocally:

> There is no doubt in my mind that the RAF broke the back and the spirit of the
> Luftwaffe during the Battle of Britain. The losses of aircraft could be made up but
> the experienced men who had formed the cadre of the Luftwaffe could not be
> replaced.

He was heavily engaged in the earlier phase of the air war, when the Luftwaffe paid special attention to the front line airfields. From his account of the attack on RAF Manston, Kent, on August 19, it is evident that he shared the same chilling awareness as that experienced by Richard Hillary – that while his basic task was to destroy aircraft this would also involve the killing of men:

> Flying practically due south we roared over the coast just east of Margate and
> within seconds were approaching Manston over a small group of buildings. I spot-
> ted the tanker refuelling a Spitfire quite close to the boundary of the airfield and
> moved position to line up. Dropping height to about three or four metres to
> minimise the height deflection on the shot, I saw the tanker rapidly filling the red
> illuminated ring. Increasing the pressure on the trigger and the button, I felt all
> four machine-guns begin to fire with a light vibration in the airframe. Grey lines
> of tracer streaked forward and began to focus on the vehicle. I saw the strikes and
> flashes as the bullets began to hit home and the tanker began to burn. In seconds
> I had hurtled over it and I turned my attention to two Spitfires, which had been
> placed out at dispersal, awaiting attention. Again the grey lines streaked out, first

tearing up the ground and then concentrating on the aircraft. They both began to burn as the tanker erupted into a ball of fire behind me. Banking left, we hedge-hopped out of Manston and moments later were crossing the Bay of Manston (Pegwell Bay) with its distinctive little river.

Again I was assailed by the conflict of feelings. Firstly, I had, at last, done what I had been trained to do and done it well. It was a victory for me and a victory for Germany. I had set thousands of litres of precious fuel on fire and left three Spitfires in ruins. That could save the lives of many of my colleagues. But I had also seen that my attack had cost the life of at least one man and that was, and still is, hard to take.

The attitude of Steinhilper and his fellow flyers to the pilots pitted against them seems to have been remarkably friendly, more that of participants in a strenuous sporting contest than in a life-or-death struggle:

At the end of August a lone Spitfire was bold enough to detach itself from a larger formation and make a low-level approach on our field. Unfortunately, he was hit and the pilot had to take to his parachute. He turned out to be a sergeant pilot and was taken prisoner and brought to see us. Naturally, he was treated like a hero and was offered the best of everything we had to eat and drink and we all had a fine time. One thing I distinctly remember about him was that if any of us made any funny remarks about Churchill, he'd correct us by saying, "Mister Churchill if you please!".

Towards the end of September/beginning of October we again had contact with an enemy pilot. Just about dawn a light bomber was hit by our flak and tore into the ground just 200 metres from our tents. Naturally, we all ran out to see it... We couldn't identify the type, it was such a wreck. It looked as though all of the crew were dead, but then someone spotted that the pilot was still moving, though trapped in the wreckage. From within the tangle we heard the ominous crackling of fire and soon saw the black smoke begin to curl up as fire took hold. We began to try to pull him from the wreck but it was no use. Then Dr Greiling appeared and told us to use what extinguishers we had to keep the fire away from the trapped man, whilst the rescue crew began to cut through the mass of wires and wood. The poor man wasn't even unconscious and knew that the fire was spreading, but he kept calm. I wanted to walk away from the hideous mess; I didn't want to be there if the fire got to him. But then he asked for a cigarette and I was the only one with any to hand. With his arm free he smoked the cigarette and cursed vehemently about his mission. Soon the pain of his injuries began to overwhelm him and Dr Greiling gave him a large shot of morphine, which knocked him out. Through diligent and skilled work our rescue crew got him out and he was whisked off to hospital where, unfortunately, despite the very best medical care he died after about three days.

Soon after this another sergeant pilot was brought down near us and he gave me his mother's address so that if we were successful in our invasion, I could pop around and give her the news that he was OK.

As the battle over London intensified the going got notably tougher. Of a raid on September 8 he wrote:

Now we really came up against the full force of the RAF. If the calculations of our High Command had been correct there should have been minimal fighter opposition to us now. But whilst we saw numerous head-on and flank attacks on the bombers below we were often too busy with our own defence to intervene. There were constant dog-fights with aircraft wheeling and diving, pursuing each other, sometimes with success, sometimes not. There were stark black lines diving down, showing the path of a stricken aircraft and parachutes floating in the thin, cold air. There was tragedy too as I watched one parachute begin to burn, its helpless charge falling faster and faster. Hard to take too were the accidents of identification. I sat helpless with the hard lump of frustration boiling in my chest as I saw below me a 109 latch on to the tail of another of our fighters and then to see them suddenly linked by four straight grey lines as the guns were fired. Quickly the yellow tail of the leading fighter ignited and it rolled out to dive towards the ground. In such tense and charged surroundings such mistakes were inevitable.

The whole aim of the air assault was to bring about appropriate conditions for the promised invasion. As the raids went on with increasing casualties the question began to be raised as to whether this massive and sustained effort would in the end come to nothing. The following is from Steinhilper's contemporary diary:

September 22, 1940
The British are slowly getting on our nerves at night, because of their persistent activity. Their AA guns are in virtually continuous use and so we can hardly close our eyes. But there is nothing else we can do about that other than curse. I am anxious to learn whether, after all we've done, invasion will really get started this year.

The deaths and shootings down continued and there was no invasion. Steinhilper would later write of the losses in his fighter group up to September 30: "Of the original thirty six pilots there were precious few left". Writing to his family at that time he commented: "If anybody at home asks about us, of course we are happy and proud of our deeds". He added, however, "If the war continues like this I can't imagine how it will go on".

Peter Stahl was an NCO pilot of a Junkers 88 bomber, his official rank being

Unteroffizier. His wartime diary, published in English under the title of *The Diving Eagle*, shows an increasing frustration as the bombing campaign dragged on into October, with many raids mounted for little purpose other than to maintain psychological pressure, while all signs of an impending invasion were rapidly disappearing. Mostly these attacks were by night, but not always:

October 14, 1940

Unusual – a daytime harassment raid on London. We take off in beautiful sunny weather at 15.30 hrs, our orders being to cause an air-raid alarm in London at the very least. Naturally, I am also given specific orders to attack a target of some importance, some locks in the dock area. Nevertheless, it must be evident even to the higher Luftwaffe command that a single bomber could not carry out this task with any real hope of success. The idea is simply to have air raid sirens howling in London twenty-four hours a day. It may sound good in theory but we have no doubt that this will cause us operational crews a lot of hardship and casualties.

October 15, 1940

Another night raid on London. Take-off time 19.25 hrs, landing back at the base 2220 hrs.

By now all the bearings, radio and light beacons, anti-aircraft zones and peaceful sections along the whole route are well known to us. After the pre-flight briefing Oberleutnant Wolf sums it up in a few words: "It is the same old tour today. We have been allocated the target area A, and all take-off times are on the flight plan. Before that there's coffee, afterwards a good stew. Have a good trip!".

The weather on the way out is fine. We climb steadily while crossing the North Sea and arrive over the British Isles at 5,000 metres. We continue gaining altitude while flying towards the target, which is easily recognisable due to the massed anti-aircraft fire in the sky. All the signs are that this is going to be a hard night, right from the start. The number of searchlights that greet us on the coast is immense: we have never seen anything like it before. There seem to be hundreds of anti-aircraft guns along our route, and we do not have any peace for one minute. I try every trick in my book, every anti-aircraft evasion manoeuvre I know, but in vain: the explosions are the closest I have ever experienced. Even Hans becomes restless, which is most unusual.

October 16, 1940

During our approach flight to London it becomes almost spooky in our glazed housing. The searchlights have lit up the clouds so we are flying blind, and we feel as if we are hanging in our fuzzy surroundings, sitting inside a white cotton-wool ball, with no idea what is happening above and below us. I have flown blind a lot in my time, but I have never been exposed to this kind of situation. I have to concentrate really hard "to pull together my whole brain", as we used to say, to avoid making any errors. And that takes nerve! My sole wish is to be out of here, and quick.

Curiously as it might seem, the old First-World-War name for the British infantry-man was still in vogue in this entirely different kind of warfare:

In this night the Tommies have made what I consider to be a mistake by firing their AA guns in addition to using searchlights. The explosions of AA shells in the clouds around us provide welcome points of reference to my eyes and my brain: the grad-ual crescendo of AA shell explosions shows clearly that we are near our target area. Without any sight of the ground we can only drop our bombs according to this indication and our own navigational calculations.

Our task completed, we turn back on a home course. There are no problems and our flight over the British coastline is clearly indicated by the farewell of the search-lights. When passing through the temperature line around zero degrees we experi-ence very heavy icing-up, so intense that we lose our aerial mast while the fuselage is drummed by pieces of ice shed by the propeller blades. I start losing altitude as quickly and steeply as I dare to get into some warmer air. We level off at just 100 metres over the Channel, still without sight of the water, but at least the external temperature is now +5°C. Gradually, the ice thaws out and I can breathe more easily.

I have to approach our base blind, and land safely in foggy haze in the pitch-black night. Most of the other crews had to be diverted to various alternate airfields. Our losses amount to four Ju 88s with their crews, including Hauptmann Hass. This is a heavy blow, because to me this officer was an example in every way. He had it in him to do great things and was a wonderful human being. He possessed modesty, intelligence, discretion and bearing in a measure one seldom comes across in a person. We assume he has fallen victim to the treacherous icing-up, which is seldom encountered in such density as last night.

There are two crashes on the airfield during landing operations, although the crews are fortunate to escape without serious injury. In addition, Oberleutnant Baumbach and Feldwebel Timm literally fell out of the clouds on to the bleak land-scape while flying blind, but Fate was kind to them: both machines were totally destroyed but the crews survived.

While on the way by bus to our quarters we discuss the question, in view of the known unfavourable conditions, of how daft it is to send out hundreds of aircrews by night without any hope of reasonable results, and run the risk of having heavy losses simply on account of the bad weather.

One of us comes up with what is probably the correct reason: "What do you think, how many new generals does the Luftwaffe add to its ranks after each such shit operation?"

"You mean shit generals, not shit operations!" somebody else adds, and we fall silent. It does make one think.

And tomorrow, the communiqué of the armed forces high command will state that our brave aircrews have flown another major operation and despite bad weather conditions have inflicted devastating blows on various vital targets. Our own losses were only "minimal"!

In fact, by this time the battle was developing into what Oberleutnant Ulrich Steinhilper would later describe as "a war of attrition, an airborne version of the dreadful trench warfare of 1917–18":

Sooner or later one side had to run out of aircraft and the young men to fly them. Given that we spent sixty per cent of our time flying over hostile territory, and that London was invariably the target, requiring maximum range penetrations, the odds were well and truly stacked against us. Time was now against us and time was running out.

On October 27 Steinhilper was shot down near Canterbury, Kent. His Messerschmitt 109 embedded itself at terrifying speed into the ground. He managed to bale out. His future thereafter lay in the considerable rigours of an interrogation camp, transportation to Canada (happily avoiding the fate of those who had sailed on the *Arandora Star*) and six years of captivity. It was the end of his fighting war. His departure from the scene virtually coincided with the closedown of the Battle of Britain.

Almost, but not quite. One British pilot who played a part in the very last phase of the battle was Pilot Officer John Carpenter, aged 19. He had joined 222 Squadron at Hornchurch in late June following service earlier in the Norway campaign. A Hurricane pilot, he had accounted for three German aircraft and claimed a probable fourth before being shot down in early September. The following is from a letter dated September 7 to his parents, describing what had happened:

The bad penny has turned up again, but this time in hospital. You know I always hate hospitals, but I must confess I am enjoying myself in this one.

I suppose I had better tell you how I got in here in the first place. I had just attacked an Me 109 and was breaking away at some pretty speed when (I did not know at the time) I was hit by one of our own 3.7 anti-aircraft shells.

I am not shooting a line when I say that the machine just disappeared from under me in one big BANG! And, with a bit of good luck that must go with that watch of yours, I found myself propelled clear of the aeroplane. I pulled the ripcord and started my graceful descent to earth. I must have got a hit over the head somewhere because I could not see coming down. I knew I was nearing the earth but my eyes just would not function.

Considering all the good luck I have had it was not surprising that it had to change, for I landed in the hardest, nobbliest and most spiteful tree you could find; it was a kind of nut tree. Needless to say, I was carted off to hospital with many scratches and cuts, where they chloroformed me and did a lot of needlework. But now I am glad to say [that] having recovered from the effects of chloroform, which made me sick as a dog, I hope to be able to get up soon.

He was back flying shortly before the Battle of Britain officially ended on October 31. Having cheerfully survived one drama he managed a second just in time. On October 30 he was once again shot down – on this occasion not by his own side. Falling on his own ground he was spared the grim ordeals facing such as Oberleutnant Steinhilper. The episode produced another lively account for his parents:

More exciting events to report, yesterday morning while patrolling over Maidstone at 30,000 feet we ran into about eighty ME 109s, which turned to give fight. I dived down and had a good old burst at one of them, but before I had finished I was myself attacked by two 109s and I was absolutely peppered with cannon shells and machine gun fire.

My instrument panel broke up in front of me for the fire came from over my shoulder. The engine started thumping and vibrating so much that I thought it might shake the wings off. But I found that by putting it into fine pitch the vibration was not so bad. Luckily the engine did not seize up for I managed to struggle back over the aerodrome.

This was the point I was dreading most for I had to come down through 3,000 feet of thick cloud without any instruments. This I managed to do with a bit of luck and I came out over the aerodrome. I put the undercarriage and flaps down and prayed that nothing would break before I was on the deck. I made an ordinary landing but at the end of the run one wheel slowly collapsed so that I was stuck in the middle of the aerodrome with one wheel up.

When I got out and inspected the aeroplane, the flight sergeant counted over 300 holes in the fuselage, a piece of the propeller had been shot away, my wireless mast had been carried away by a cannon shell, in fact it looked something like a sieve. I was congratulated for bringing it back as it was and landing it without further damage on the aerodrome. I am claiming one 109 as a probable, which makes up a bit.

Carpenter survived 1940 and subsequently served in the Mediterranean theatre and in Italy. He was awarded a Distinguished Flying Cross in 1942 and a bar in 1944. In January of that year he was given his own command, of 72 Squadron. After the war he served as a test pilot with Hawkers and retired from the RAF in 1959, retaining the rank of squadron leader.

Unteroffizier Peter Stahl also survived the war, after serving on the Russian Front, in the Mediterranean and Middle Eastern campaigns (being finally commissioned at this stage), and last of all in the *Kampfgeschwader* (Bomber Wing) 200, an élite force under the direct command of Adolf Hitler. He edited and published his remarkable diary in 1978 and it was issued in an English translation in 1984.

Ulrich Steinhilper returned to Germany in 1946 to build a distinguished career with IBM, being later credited as the man who formulated the initial concept of word processing. His Messerschmitt was disinterred in 1980 by members of the Kent Battle of Britain Museum Recovery Group and is now on permanent display at their museum on the site of the former airfield known to students of 1940 as RAF Hawkinge.

So ended the Battle of Britain. It was an undoubted victory but it was one with a high cost. While celebrating a success in war, no one should overlook the human price. Above all the "few" should not be forgotten. The following is the comment of one of them, looking back:

> From an hour before dawn until dusk we lived at our dispersal point on the airfield, and fought until we ran out of ammunition. At night we drank and played and made love like there was no hereafter. I can't remember all the pilots who flew with us. Some came in the morning and were dead by nightfall. The Biggin Hill Chapel keeps the record. I swore never to hate anyone again after I'd seen one of our team I loathed blow up beside me when caught by a 109. First, Norman Hargreaves had gone, then Sergeant Eyles. Gus Edwards was found dead a week after he went missing, in the middle of a forest. Similarly, Howard Hill, after three weeks, lodged in the top of a tall tree, decomposing in his cockpit, his hands on the controls and the top of his head blown off by a cannon shell. Pat Patterson, though badly burned in a previous escape, refused to be grounded. I saw him spin down quite close to me, having been hit and struggling to get out of his blazing cockpit. A burned offering to the God of War*.

But as well as the cost, the "results" also matter because they show that the cost was not in vain. By the end of October the Luftwaffe had lost about 1,800 aircraft and over 2,500 aircrew. The figures for Fighter Command were 1,100 aircraft lost and about 550 pilots killed. Meanwhile, on the ground, contrary to pre-war theories, British society had shown few signs of disintegrating under the onslaught of the greatly feared bomber (though it should be said that this was far from being the

(*Tony Bartley, *Smoke Trails in the Sky*)

end of the nation's ordeal, there being many more raids to come). There had been fear, distress and anger, but there had also been much courage, determination and a widespread feeling of breezy defiance. More countless civilians had shown they could cope with living two lives; engaged in their own jobs by day, aiding the war effort by night. The front line had come to them and by and large they had proved equal to the challenge. "The citizens are getting less sleep than usual," a *Times* report stated as the London bombing moved into its most intensive phase in September, "especially those who after the day's work do a Home Guard patrol, a turn at a warden's post, or man a fire pump; but morning finds them streaming into factory and office much as usual, and certainly still cheerful".

The same report described a visit paid by Mr Herbert Morrison, Minister of Supply and founder of the "Go to it" campaign, to a bombed area in northeast London. He spoke repeatedly of the magnificent gallantry of ARP Wardens and of those many others who had shown fine courage in the face of the enemy's efforts to break the nation's spirit. He was enthusiastically received. Cries of "Go to it, Herbert" greeted the Minister as he walked around, and when he urged people in one street to keep their chins up they chorused in reply: "We are keeping at it".

There was no doubt which side would emerge with greater credit from the long ordeal of 1940.

Ottawa, Winter 1941

W INSTON CHURCHILL'S BEST UTTERANCE ON 1940 was delivered in the following year, in another season and on the far side of the Atlantic. On December 7, 1941, the Japanese attacked Pearl Harbor. This brought the United States into the conflict and, in the view of the Prime Minister, guaranteed Nazi Germany's defeat. Now Britain had a companion-in-arms of world stature at her side. Churchill sailed to America to seal the new alliance.

President Roosevelt granted his honoured guest the hospitality of the White House. His room proved so hot that he decided to open the bedroom window. He told his doctor the following morning: "It was very stiff. I had to use considerable force and I noticed all at once that I was short of breath. I had a dull pain over my heart. It went down my left arm. It didn't last very long, but it has never happened before. What is it? Is my heart all right?"

In fact, it was not all right. He was suffering from *angina pectoris*, a fact that remained a secret until after his death twenty-four years later. The proper course of treatment was sustained rest. But his doctor, Sir Charles Wilson, knew that that was not possible for such a man at such a time. Nor was it necessary for him to know. Wilson told him: "Your circulation was a bit sluggish. It is nothing serious. You needn't rest in the sense of lying up, but you mustn't do more than you can help in the way of exertion for a little while."

Undeterred Churchill proceeded much as before. After several rigorous meetings in Washington and a speech to Congress, he left for Ottawa, travelling in Roosevelt's private railroad car. Winters are severe in Canada and the Prime Minister and his doctor drove to Government House through streets banked with snow. It was a far cry from the long summer days of the previous year. On the following day, December 30, Churchill addressed the Canadian Parliament. He was in splendid form, surveying the war in all its aspects. Having paid tribute to what the Canadians had achieved and the contributions they had made to the Empire's cause, he continued:

> I should like to point out to you that we have not at any time asked for any mitigation in the fury or malice of the enemy. The peoples of the British Empire may love peace. They do not seek the lands or wealth of any country. But they are a tough and hardy lot. We have not journeyed across the centuries, across the oceans, across the mountains, across the prairies, because we are made of sugar-candy.

Look at the Londoners, the Cockneys, look at what they have stood up to, grim and gay with their cry "We can take it" and their war-time mood of "What is good enough for anybody is good enough for us". We have not asked that the rules of the game should be modified. We shall never descend to the German and Japanese level. But if anybody likes to play rough, we can play rough too. Hitler and his Nazi gang have sown the wind. Let them reap the whirlwind. Neither the length of the struggle nor any form of severity which it may assume shall make us weary, or shall make us quit.

But it was what he said about the fall of France and Britain's dangerous situation in the wake of that disaster that went round the world, ensuring that this speech would become one of the most famous of the war. He stated that when, at that uncertain and difficult time, he informed the French Government "that Britain would fight on alone whatever they did, their Generals told their Prime Minister and his divided cabinet: 'In three weeks England will have her neck wrung like a chicken.'"

There was a pause. His Canadian listeners sensed there was more to come. It came with the brilliant timing of a seasoned orator, or of a comedian producing the perfect pay-off line, and it sent his audience into raptures of laughter and applause:

"Some chicken! Some neck!"

It was as good a verdict as there could be on the Spitfire Summer, when Britain stood alone.

Operation "Sicklecut": The German 'Blitzkrieg' Attack of May–June 1940

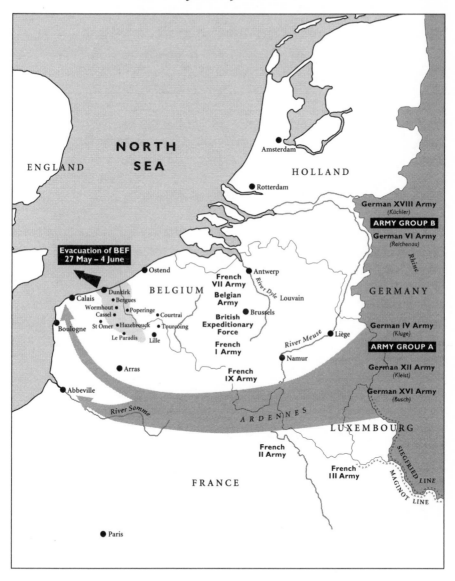

Fortress Britain 1940:
Air Defences during the Battle of Britain

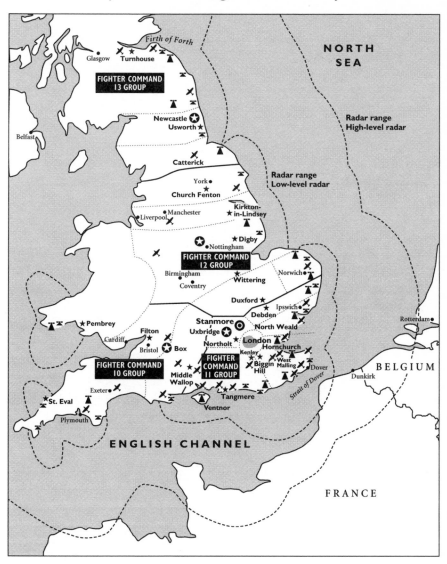

◎ Fighter Command headquarters	⋯⋯ Sector Boundary
✪ Group headquarters	✗ Fighter base
— Group Boundary	🜊 High-level radar station
★ Sector HQ	🗲 Low-level radar station

ABBREVIATIONS AND CODE-NAMES

AA	Anti-Aircraft
A/C	Aircraft
ARP	Air-Raid Precautions
BBC	British Broadcasting Corporation
BEF	British Expeditionary Force
CO	Commanding Officer
CORB	Children's Overseas Reception Board
"Cromwell"	Code-Name to alert British Home Forces to the possibility of invasion
DV	Deo volente (Latin), i.e. God Willing
Do	Dornier (German Bomber)
"Dynamo"	Code-name for the evacuation of British and French Forces from Dunkirk
E/A or E/a	Enemy aircraft
Gruppe	Unit of German aircraft, equivalent to RAF wing
HMS	His Majesty's Ship
He	Heinkel (German Bomber)
Ju	Junkers (German Bomber)
Kampfgeschwader	German Bomber Group
LDV	Local Defence Volunteers – later Home Guard
Me	Messerschmitt (German Fighter)
NCO	Non-Commissioned Officer
OOW	Officer of the Watch (Naval term)
Panzer	German for armour, or tank; hence Panzer Division = Armoured Division
RA	Royal Artillery
RAOC	Royal Army Ordanance Corps
RASC	Royal Army Service Corps
RDF	Radio Direction Finding – British name for Radar until 1943
RHA	Royal Horse Artillery
R/T	Radio telephony
"Sealion"	Code-name for projected German invasion of Great Britain
"Sichelschnitt"	Code-name for German operation against Low Countries and France
Stuka	Dive-bomber (Ju 87)
Vector	Compass bearing
Vic	V formation
WAAF	Women's Auxiliary Air Force
WLA	Women's Land Army
WVS	Women's Voluntary Service

CHRONOLOGY

May–October 1940

MAY

10 Germany invades the Low Countries. Churchill becomes Prime Minister.

12 German Army Group B smash through the Ardennes.

13 German Forces cross the River Meuse.

14 Rotterdam bombed. Holland surrenders. Queen Wilhelmina flees to Britain. Anthony Eden announces formation of the Local Defence Volunteers.

17 Brussels falls.

18 Germans sweep across the Somme reaching Albert and Amiens.

20 German Panzers reach English Channel at Abbeville.

21 Allied counter-attack south of Arras.

23 Boulogne, Amiens and Arras fall.

24 Hitler halts German armoured divisions before Dunkirk at Gravelines.

27 Fall of Calais. Belgium surrenders. Dunkirk evacuation begins.

29 Germans occupy Lille, Ypres and Ostend.

JUNE

4 Final evacuation from Dunkirk. Germans capture Dunkirk taking 40,000 French prisoners.

10 Italy declares war on Britain and France.

14 Fall of Paris. British Government order prescribing church bells to be rung only in the event of invasion.

17 Sinking of SS *Lancastria* at St Nazaire.

18 Churchill's "Finest Hour" speech. De Gaulle's broadcast from London

22 French sign armistice at Compiègne.

30 German forces occupy Channel Islands.

JULY

2 SS *Arandora Star*, en route for Canada with over 1000 internees, sunk by German U-boat.

3 British attack French naval squadron at Mers-el-Kebir, Algeria.

10 Opening of Battle of Britain. Lord Beaverbrook's "Appeal for Aluminium".

16 Issue of Hitler's War Directive 16, ordering preparations for Operation "Sealion":

19 Hitler's Reichstag speech: "A Last Chance for Britain".

AUGUST

13 Mass air attacks on British airfields, factories and docks.

24 "Unintentional" German bombs fall on London.

25 First reprisal raid on Berlin

SEPTEMBER

7 Major raid on London: start of Blitz. Fear of possible invasion leads to issue of Code-name "Cromwell"; premature mobilization of some Home Guard forces.

15 RAF claim 185 aircraft shot down; actual number 60 but an undisputed victory by Fighter Command. Subsequently named "Battle of Britain Day".

17 Hitler postpones "Sealion" indefinitely, but orders preparations to continue. Sinking of SS *City of Benares*.

OCTOBER

1 New phase of bombing campaign, with night raids on London throughout the month on every night except one.

31 End of intensive night bombing phase. Generally accepted date for "closedown" of Battle of Britain.

ACKNOWLEDGEMENTS

My gratitude goes first to Piers Murray Hill of Carlton Books Ltd for approaching the Imperial War Museum with the idea of commissioning a book on the "Spitfire Summer" of 1940 and to Dr Christopher Dowling, Keeper of Museum Services, for suggesting that I should be invited to write it. For someone who has specialized in books on the First World War this has represented a major leap forward, but not into the unknown, in that I have been dealing with a period I lived through and saw something of myself, if only through the eyes of a child. The task has proved a challenging but fascinating one and I am delighted at having been given the opportunity to attempt it.

I must also offer my warm thanks to those many talented members of the Museum staff who created the outstanding exhibition from which this book took its name, and also, to no small extent, its inspiration. Though a book necessarily must take its own route and create its own terms of reference, I have constantly returned to the exhibition to inhale the atmosphere of 1940 which it has so expertly captured, and I am pleased to record that there are numerous echoes of it in these pages. While thanking the Museum for its support, I should also like to thank its literary agent, Barbara Levy, for the professional skill and speed with which she negotiated the contract, thus allowing me to concentrate entirely on the work of research and writing from the moment the idea of the book was conceived.

I have been a freelance historian at the Museum for eleven years, but before that I was a member of the BBC and so have taken an especial satisfaction in writing about a time when that organisation had one of its finest hours. I am thus pleased to offer my gratitude to the BBC in general and in particular to Jacquie Kavanagh and Michael Websell of the BBC Written Archives, Caversham, Reading, who have given me much valuable help and guidance.

The book has greatly benefited from a constructive reading of the text by a number of Museum colleagues. Terry Charman of the Research and Information Department, whose knowledge of 1940 is very considerable, read the whole manuscript, offering numerous improvements, as also did Roderick Suddaby, Keeper of the Department of Documents. Julie Robertshaw of the Department of Printed Books read the book at speed to assess its readability and narrative stride, while several others read selected chapters in which they had a special interest; these included Angela Wootton of Printed Books and Stephen Walton, Anthony Richards and Amanda Mason of the Department of Documents. Also greatly assisting with their knowledge and wise advice were Roger Smither of the Film and Video Archive and Conrad Wood of the Sound Archive (to whose outstanding work on the project entitled "Air Operations, Battle of Britain, 1940" I would like to pay special tribute), while expert help in the matter of illustrations was given by Michael Moody and Pauline Allwright of the Department of Art and Bridget Kinally and the visitors' room staff of the Photograph Archive. Sarah Paterson fulfilled her usual function of correcting to strict, professional standards my Source Notes and Bibliography.

Jan Mihell, formerly of the Museum staff, gave me much valued help at the research stage by combing the files of certain contemporary newspapers, the most important being *The Times*, finding rare and fascinating treasure much of which has found its way into the narrative. I am also much indebted to Oliver Hoare of the Public Record Office, who offered me some excellent contemporary material much of which I have been pleased to include.

Most importantly my thanks go to my wife Betty, who played a vital role throughout, transcribing, reading, commenting, correcting, proof-reading and generally offering moral and literary support; and to the production staff at Carlton, particularly the executive editor Sarah Larter and the picture editor Lorna Ainger, for their expert help, advice and encouragement.

As in all the books I have written in association with the IWM, an honoured place must be reserved in any acknowledgements for those, whether private individuals or publishers, who have kindly allowed me to use extracts from material in which they hold copyright. With the exception of letters to the press, the provenance of which is made clear in the narrative, all sources so quoted are referred to either in the Notes and Sources section or the Index of Contributors, while published works quoted or mentioned are also listed in the Bibliography, their presence there being intended as an acknowledgement as well as a matter of information.

Strenuous efforts have been made at some speed to approach for the necessary permissions all individuals or institutions concerned; I offer my apologies for any errors, omissions or oversights in this area. Any such error will be amended in future editions of this book.

Of one "contributor" much quoted, who is in many ways the hero of this tale, special mention must be made: I refer to the then Prime Minister and am pleased to record that all quotations from his war speeches are republished by courtesy of Curtis Brown on behalf of the estate of Winston S. Churchill.

NOTES AND SOURCES

For full details of books mentioned, see Bibliography (p.197)

CHAPTER 1: The Hour, the Man, the Weapon (pp.13–16)

Norway campaign; Mark Arnold-Forster, *The World at War*, pp. 39, 42; VC of Captain Warburton-Lee, *Daily Telegraph*, July 6; Chamberlain comment to Montgomery, David Fraser, *And We Shall Shock Them*, p.30; Richard Hillary's admiration of the Spitfire, *The Last Enemy*, p.58.

CHAPTER 2: Operation "Sicklecut": Defeat in France (pp.17–36)

Alistair Horne comment on "*Sichelschnitt*", *To Lose a Battle*, p.141; Liddell Hart quotation, *Macmillan Dictionary of the Second World War*, p.501; attacks by Colonel de Gaulle's armoured division, Jean Lacouture, *De Gaulle, The Rebel*, 1880–1944, p.181ff; Lord Gort authorized to withdraw to Dunkirk, Arnold-Forster, op.cit., p.52; RAF role in French campaign, John Terraine, *The Right of the Line*, p.162ff.

CHAPTER 3: Operation "Dynamo": Escape from Dunkirk (pp.37-58)

Role of Vice-Admiral Bertram Ramsay, Mark Arnold-Forster, op.cit., p.52; Captain R.C.V. Ross as a "salt-horse", *Daily Telegraph* obituary, 5 February 2000; numbers of troops taken off by various ships, Russell Plummer, *The Ships that Saved an Army*, passim; BBC "Postscript" on Dunkirk by J.B. Priestley, reprinted by permission of PFD on behalf of the Estate of JB Priestley; comment on a Dunkirk survivor by Irene Thomas, *The Bandsman's Daughter*, p.32; Churchill on Dunkirk evacuation, speech of June 4, *Into Battle*, p.219.   .

CHAPTER 4: "If Necessary, Alone" (pp.59–82)

Further extracts from Churchill June 4 speech, op.cit., pp.222-3; comment by the King on Britain being alone, John W. Wheeler Bennet, *King George VI, His Life and Reign*, 1958, p.460; reference to Britain being "in the final", ibid, p.461; cartoon by David Low, London *Evening Standard*, June 18; RAF flight-sergeant's reaction to Churchill's offer of British union with France, Robert Kee, *We'll Meet Again*, p.10; Napoleon's alleged visit to Lulworth Cove, Thomas Hardy, *A Tradition of 1804* (short story); LDVs firing on RAF pilots, S.P. Mackenzie, *The Home Guard*, pp.59-60; imprisonment and transportation of aliens, Peter and Leni Gillman, "Collar the Lot!", p.153 and passim; T.E. Lawrence letter quoted by F. Sittner, David Garnett, *The Letters of T.E. Lawrence*, Jonathan Cape, 1938, p.871; nightmare voyage of SS *Dunera*, Peter and Leni Gillman, op.cit., p.245; founding of Amadeus Quartet, details from Muriel Nissel, *Married to the Amadeus*, Giles de la Mare, 1998.

CHAPTER 5: "Go To It!" (pp. 83–101)

Churchill "finest hour" speech, June 18, op.cit., p.234; material on BBC "Go To It" series, *Radio Times*, editions of June14 and 21, Robert Reid article, edition of August 16, courtesy BBC Written Archives, Caversham, Reading (BBC WAC); "If the Invader Comes", IWM Battle of Britain Document Pack; Harold Nicolson quotations, *Diaries and Letters* 1930–1964, pp.185–6; Richard Hillary quotation, op.cit., pp.54–5; information about film *Britain at Bay*, Clive Coultass, *Images for*

Battle, p.46; poem "Salvage Song", from *Poems of the Second World War: The Oasis Selection*, p.145, also published in the Penguin anthology *The Voice of War*; David Low cartoon, from dust-jacket of Gordon Beckles, *Birth of a Spitfire*; John Betjeman quotation, *The Listener*, BBC WAC, also courtesy Desmond Elliott; Charles Gardner broadcast, transcription from BBC tape; *Radio Times* letters, BBC WAC; information on BBC announcers and Lord Haw Haw, BBC WAC and Tom Hickman, *What did you do in the War, Auntie?*, pp.39-40; reference to Women's Land Army, Angus Calder, *The People's War*, p.428.

CHAPTER 6: Waiting for the Enemy (pp.102–119)

Quotation from Vera Brittain, *England's Hour*, p.34; founding of Children's Overseas Reception Board (CORB), Michael Fethney, *The Absurd and the Brave*, passim; Vera Brittain quotation, op.cit., p.55ff; text of radio feature "Spitfires over Britain", BBC WAC; quotations from *The Listener*, ibid; cash for planes and Spitfire funds etc, Angus Calder, op.cit, p.149, also Gordon Beckles, *Birth of a Spitfire*, p.57ff; British naval attack on French naval ships, Ivor Matanle, *History of World War II*, p.30; Hitler Speech to Reichstag, Alan Bullock, *Hitler and Stalin*, p.752; Alistair Horne quotation on "*Sichelschnitt*", op.cit., p.512; War Directive No.16 and comparison of cross-Channel invasion to river crossing, Chester Wilmot, *The Struggle for Europe*, pp.26; Len Deighton comment, from his *The Battle of Britain*, p.78; Irene Thomas on Battle of Britain pilots, op.cit., p.32; Stephen Spender, *World Within World*, p.226; "myths" of the battle, Richard Hough and Denis Richards, *The Battle of Britain: The Jubilee History*, pp.325-8; Churchill speech of 20 August, op.cit., p.259; Angus Calder quotation, op.cit., pp.145-6.

CHAPTER 7: Battle in the Skies (pp.120–136)

Air Chief Marshal Dowding's Battle of Britain Despatch, PRO ADM 199/110; first and last days of the Battle of Britain, Hough and Richards, op.cit., pp.357 and 370; Richard Hillary quotation, op.cit., p.96; reaction of golf club members to shot-down fighter pilot, Hough and Richards, op.cit., p.211; attack on RAF Tangmere, ibid, pp.188, 194; description by "Sandy" Johnstone, from his *Enemy in the Sky*, quoted Len Deighton op.cit., p.140, but see also Bibliography; "The Flight Engineer Who Jumped To It Too Quickly", PRO AIR 20/9482; Pilot Officer David Crook's log book, PRO AIR 4/21; Richard Hillary quotation, op.cit., pp.97-8; the mess bills joke is also quoted in Angus Calder, op.cit., p.145.

CHAPTER 8: When the Bomber Got Through (pp.137–149)

H.G. Wells's *The Shape of Things to Come*, was published in 1933, the film *Things to Come* was made in 1935 and distributed in 1936; details of weather and activity on August 24, Hough and Richards, op.cit., p.361; Home Security Intelligence Summary for September 7, PRO Document HO 203/4; reaction of Home Guard to code-word "Cromwell", including Conway Home Guard story and *Daily Herald* quotation, S.P. Mackenzie, op.cit., pp.60–62.

CHAPTER 9: "In Peril on the Sea" (pp.150–160

Chapter title, from the famous "naval" hymn "Eternal Father, strong to save"; Churchill quotation on the U-boat peril, Churchill, *The Second World War*, Vol II, p.529; Doenitz and the "grey wolves", John Terraine, *Business in Great Waters*, p.264; U-boat captain Gunther Prien and the *Arandora Star*,

Peter and Leni Gillman, "Collar the Lot!", p.201; fate of SS *Severn Leigh* and her crew, G.H. and R. Bennett, *Survivors: British Merchant Seamen in the Second World War*, pp. 105, 160–1; CORB and the fate of the SS *Volendam* and the SS *City of Benares*, Michael Fethney, op.cit., passim; newspaper accounts of arrival in South Africa of SS *Llanstephan Castle*, papers of Miss Freda Troup, later Mrs Levson, IWM Department of Documents (see also Index of Contributors).

CHAPTER 10: Blitz and Closedown (pp.161–183)

Details of Blitz between September 1940–May 1941, Elizabeth-Anne Wheal and Stephen Pope, *The Macmillan Dictionary of the Second World War*; for "Baby Blitz", see Basil Collier, *The Defence of the United Kingdom*, Appendix XLII; letter re ending of Promenade Concerts, *From Parry to Britten*, p.236; Myra Hess and the National Gallery Concerts, *Myra Hess: By Her Friends*, pp.57, 95; Stephen Spender quotation, op.cit., p.248; London's cinemas during the Blitz, Guy Morgan, *Red Roses Every Night*, p.31; Battle of Britain statistics, *The Macmillan Dictionary of the Second World War*, p.71.

POSTSCRIPT: Ottawa, Winter, 1941 (pp.184–5)

Churchill's visit to Washington and Ottawa, Martin Gilbert, *Road to Victory: Winston S. Churchill*, Vol,VII, pp.30–1; text of Ottawa speech, *The Unrelenting Struggle*, pp.343–5

BIBLIOGRAPHY

All books published in London unless otherwise stated

Mark Arnold-Forster, *The World at War*, William Collins, 1974

Ronald Atkin, *Pillar of Fire: Dunkirk 1940*, Sidgwick and Jackson, 1990

Tony Bartley, *Smoke Trails in the Sky*, William Kimber, 1984, Wilmslow, Crécy Publishing Ltd, 1997

The Battle of Britain, August–October 1940, HMSO, 1941

Gordon Beckles, *Birth of a Spitfire*, William Collins, 1941

G.H. and R. Bennett, *Survivors: British Merchant Seamen in the Second World War*,
    The Hambledon Press, 1999

Vera Brittain, *England's Hour*, Macmillan, 1941, Futura, 1981

Alan Bullock, *Hitler and Stalin: Parallel Lives*, Harper-Collins, 1991

Angus Calder, *The People's War: Britain 1939-1945*, Jonathan Cape, 1969, Pimlico, 1969

Basil Collier, *The Defence of the United Kingdom*, HMSO, 1957, IWM facsimile reprint, 1995

Richard Collier, *1940: The World in Flames*, Hamish Hamilton, 1979

Winston S. Churchill, *The History of the Second World War, Volume II: Their Finest Hour*,
    Cassell, 1949; *Into Battle: War Speeches by the Rt. Hon. Winston S. Churchill CH MP*,
    Cassell, 1941; *The Unrelenting Struggle: War Speeches by the Rt. Hon. Winston S. Churchill CH MP*,
    Cassell, 1942.

Clive Coultass, *Images for Battle*, London and Toronto, Ontario Film Institute, 1989

Len Deighton, *The Battle of Britain*, Jonathan Cape, 1980

Michael Fethney, The Absurd and the Brave, Lewes, The Book Guild, 1990

Lewis Foreman (ed.), *From Parry to Britten: British Music in Letters 1900–1945*, B.T. Batsford, 1987

Sir David Fraser, *And We Shall Shock Them*, Hodder and Stoughton, 1983

Martin Gilbert, *Road to Victory: Winston S. Churchill, Vol VII*, Heinemann, 1986

Peter and Leni Gillman, *"Collar the Lot!"*, Quartet Books, 1980

Tom Hickman, *What did you do in the War, Auntie?: The BBC at War 1939–45*, BBC Books 1995

Richard Hillary, *The Last Enemy*, Macmillan, 1942, Pimlico, 1997

Richard Hough and Denis Richards, *The Battle of Britain: The Jubilee History*, Hodder and
    Stoughton, 1989

Alistair Horne, *To Lose a Battle: France 1940*, Macmillan, 1969

Robert Kee, *We'll Meet Again*, J.M. Dent 1984

Jean Lacouture, *De Gaulle, The Rebel, 1880-1944*, Collins Harvill, 1990

Denise Lassimonne and Howard Ferguson (editors), *Myra Hess: By Her Friends*,
    Hamish Hamilton, c 1966

S.P. Mackenzie, *The Home Guard*, Oxford, Oxford University Press, 1995

John Masefield, *The Nine Days Wonder (The Operation Dynamo)*, Heinemann, 1941

Ivor Matanle, *History of World War II*, Tiger Books International, 1994

Guy Morgan, *Red Roses Every Night*, Quality Press, 1948

Harold Nicolson, *Diaries and Letters 1930–1964*, William Collins, 1980, Penguin, 1984

Muriel Nissel, *Married to the Amadeus*, Giles de la Mare, 1998

Poems of the Second World War: The Oasis Selection, J.M. Dent, 1985;

Russell Plummer, *The Ships that Saved an Army*, Wellingborough, Patrick Stephens, 1990

Stephen Spender, *World Within World*, Hamish Hamilton, 1953

Peter Stahl, translated Alex Vanags-Beginskis, *The Diving Eagle*, William Kimber, 1984

Ulrich Steinhilper and Peter Osborne, *Spitfire On My Tail*, Bromley, Independent Books, 1989

The Story of the Mary Datchelor School, 1877–1977, Hodder and Stoughton, 1977

John Terraine, *Business in Great Waters: The U-Boat Wars* 1916–1945, Leo Cooper, 1989,
    Mandarin, 1990; *The Right of the Line: The Royal Air Force in the European War 1939–45*,
    Hodder and Stoughton, 1985, Sceptre, 1988

Mrs Irene Thomas, *The Bandsman's Daughter*, Macmillan, 1979, Futura, 1980

Laurence Thompson, *1940: Year of Legend, Year of History*, William Collins, 1966

Elizabeth-Anne Wheal and Stephen Pope, *The Macmillan Dictionary of the Second World War*,
    Macmillan, 1997

John W. Wheeler-Bennett, *King George VI: His Life and Reign*, Macmillan, 1958

Chester Wilmot, *The Struggle for Europe*, William Collins, 1952

Philip Ziegler, *London at War, 1939-45*, Sinclair-Stevenson, 1995, Mandarin, 1997

INDEX OF CONTRIBUTORS

The formula "IWM Docs" indicates the source is the Imperial War Museum's Department of Documents, "IWM Sound" that the source is the Museum's Sound Archive. Names of copyright holders, where known, appear in brackets after the name of the contributor; the author and publishers would like to express their sincere gratitude to all those who have allowed material in which they hold copyright to be published. For abbreviations, see List of Abbreviations, p.190 The titles of books quoted are given in italics; for full details see Bibliography (p.199). The formula "private correspondence" indicates material contributed at author's request.

INDEX